Baedeker Bangkok

Baedeker
BANGKOK

Imprint

77 colour photographs; 5 maps and plans; 1 large city map

Conception and editorial work:
Redaktionsbüro Harenberg, Schwerte

Original German text: Hanna Tichy

General direction: Dr Peter Baumgarten, Baedeker, Stuttgart

Editorial work, English language edition: Alec Court

Cartography: Ingenieurbüro für Kartographie Huber & Oberländer, Munich

English translation: Babel, Norwich
Revised and additional text: Wendy Ball, Julie Waller, David Cocking

Source of illustrations: Dietrich (49), dppa (3), Kaufmann (2), Mauritius (1), Prenzel (3), Tourist Authority of Thailand (11), Uthoff (12)

Following the tradition established by Karl Baedeker in 1844, sights of particular interest are distinguished by either one or two stars. Hotels and restaurants of particular quality are also distinguished by stars.

Only a selection of hotels and restaurants can be given: no reflection is implied, therefore, on establishments not included.

In a time of rapid change it is difficult to ensure that all the information given is entirely accurate and up to date, and the possibility of error can never be completely eliminated. Although the publishers can accept no responsibility for inaccuracies and omissions, they are always grateful for corrections and suggestions for improvement.

4th English edition

© Baedeker Stuttgart
Original German edition

© 1992 The Automobile Association
United Kingdom and Ireland

© 1992 Jarrold and Sons Ltd
English language edition worldwide

US and Canadian Edition Prentice Hall Press

Distributed in the United Kingdom by the Publishing Division of The Automobile Association, Fanum House, Basingstoke, Hampshire, RG21 2EA.

The name *Baedeker* is a registered trademark
A CIP catalogue record for this book is available from the British Library.

Licensed user:
Mairs Geographischer Verlag GmbH & Co., Ostfildern-Kemnat bei Stuttgart

Printed in Italy by G. Canale & C. S.p.A. – Borgaro T.se – Turin

ISBN 0–13–063553–7 US and Canada
    0 7495 0407 2 UK

Contents

Note: The transcribing of Thai names is not easy, for there is no
accepted system of rendering the Thai language in English. A sys-
tematic standardisation would come up against the difficult that
even in factually reliable Thai sources different versions of the same
words can quite often be found.

The Principal Sights at a Glance

Preface

This pocket guide to Bangkok is one of the new generation of Baedeker guides.

Baedeker pocket guides, illustrated throughout in colour, are designed to meet the needs of the modern traveller. They are quick and easy to consult, with the principal features of interest described in alphabetical order and practical details about location, opening times, etc., shown in the margin.

Each city guide is divided into three parts. The first part gives a general account of the city, its history, administration and so on; in the second part the principal places of interest are described; the third part contains a variety of practical information designed to help visitors to find their way about and to make the most of their stay.

Baedeker pocket guides, which are regularly updated, are noted for their concentration on essentials and their convenience of use. They contain many coloured illustrations and specially drawn plans, and at the back of the book will be found a large plan of the city. Each main entry in the A to Z section gives the co-ordinates of the square on the plan in which the particular feature can be located. Users of this guide, therefore, should have no difficultly in finding what they want to see.

Facts and Figures

Krungthep (Bangkok)

General

Geographical situation

Bangkok (officially Krung Thep), the capital of the Kingdom of Thailand, lies on about latitude 13° 7' north and longitude 100° 5' east at the junction of Thailand's four main regions, the North-West (Pak Nya), the North-East (Isaan), the South-East (Pak Dai Towan Org) and the South-West (Pak Dai) in the fertile delta of the Chao Phraya, the Menam Plain, known as the "rice bowl".

Bangkok is situated at the southern end of the central region of Thailand which stretches about 270km/168 miles north. The dominant feature of this region is the Menam Basin and the delta of the River Menam Chao Phraya which flows from the east southwards through Thailand entering the Gulf of Thailand in a wide spreading delta (about 20,000 sq.km/7,722 sq. miles). The river is the main artery of the entire country which explains its name "Menam" ("Mother of Rivers"). The Menam arises from the tributaries Ping, Yom and Nan which unite at Nakhon Sawan but soon disperse into a multitude of subsidaries forming a many-fingered delta in the middle of the Central Basin. In addition there is a man-made system of channels which at one time provided irrigation for the rice fields and was important as often it was the only means of transport. It is obvious that the Menam Chao Phraya has not been used by ships travelling to the interior from the Gulf of Thailand for some time. The heavy build-up of sediment has caused the estuary in the Gulf to become silted up making passage impossible. This has led to new deep sea harbours being built in Sattahip and Laem Chabang to replace Bangkok harbour.

In the south the basin borders the sea with the mountains surrounding it on its remaining sides; in the west the Central Cordillera runs from the upland area of Northern Thailand south to the Malayan peninsula; in the north is the mountainous upland and in the south the outer edges of the Khorat Plateau.

The Menam Basin is divided into two geomorphological zones: whereas an upland area with hills over 500m/1640ft rises to meet the mountains in the north of Thailand the main part of the basin is an alluvial plain with the occasional steep limestone peak towering above it, such as at Lopburi. The central plain is geologically young, being formed predominantly by the transport of sediment carried by the Menam. Geological bore holes indicate the sediment reaches depths of 400m/1312ft in Bangkok. These alluvial deposits cause a continual silting-up of the river delta, which is expanding into the Gulf of Thailand at the rate of five to six metres a year.

The landscape of the wide valley is characterised by hillsides and terraces with fertile alluvial soils which have been intensively cultivated for generations. Typical of this countryside are

◀ *The Grand Palace, with Sanaam Luang in the foreground*

the many villages with wooden houses built on stilts owing to the constant threat of flooding.

The low-lying situation of the Menam Basin means that the tides reach far inland (Bangkok is only 2 metres/6 feet above sea-level). This results in severe flooding during the annual monsoon rains of October and November with the entire plain and even large areas of the capital Bangkok being under water.

In the north-west and west Thailand borders on Myanmar (formerly Burma), in the north and north-east on Laos, in the south-east on Kampuchea and in the south on Malaysia and the Straits of Malacca. It covers an area of 513,115 sq.km/200,000 sq.m.

The climate of Thailand is determined by the monsoon which effects tropical weather conditions throughout the year. The average temperatures lie between 24°C/75°F and 30°C/86°F with maximum temperatures of 40°C/104°F being recorded between February and June. The "coldest" months are December and January with average daily temperatures of 25°C/77°F, this being the most pleasant time for Europeans to visit. Yet the mercury level can fall below 10°C/50°F in the early mornings. From May to October the south-west monsoon brings the most rainfall. Often during this period the only means of transport in Bangkok is by boat. Thailand is occasionally hit by the Bengal cyclones and typhoons which are dreaded by the rural population.

Area and population

5.5 million people are crammed into the inner city area of 6500 sq.km./2510 sq.m. with the entire conurbation of Bangkok encompassing a population of over 8 million. The number of slum dwellers remains unknown as they are not registered. Around one seventh of the total population of Thailand lives in the capital city. With 3,511 inhabitants to every square kilometre Bangkok ranges among the most densely populated cities in the world. In contrast, Chiang Mai, the second largest town in the country has only about 116,000 inhabitants. Since it was joined with Thonburi (on the west bank of the Menam Chao Phraya) Bangkok is literally bursting at the seams. Originally it only covered an area of 13 square kilometres, the boundaries of which can still be seen between the loop of the Chao Phraya, west of the Royal Palace and the Krung Kasem Canal. The widespread suburbs which were bustling with agricultural activity right up until the late 19th century no longer exist. They have been swallowed up into a gigantic conurbation by urban development. The old centre of Bangkok is the least densely inhabited owing to the continual threat of flooding. In April 1987 the population suffered from especially devastating floods. Government resettlement plans mean that the number of city centre dwellers will fall still further.

Capital city

Since 1782 Bangkok has been the capital of Thailand, seat of the Royal Family, the Government and Parliament. Up until then and since the fall of Ayutthana in 1767 Thonburi on the opposite bank of the Chao Phraya was the capital. Nowadays Thonburi and Bangkok are united in one city. The Thais gave their city the official name "Krung Thep" (City of Angels) or "Pra Nakhorn" (Heavenly Capital). It is not widely known that Bangkok has the longest name for a town in the world. In full it is Krung Thep

Mahanakom Amorn Rattanakosin Mahintara Mahadirok Pop-
noparat Ratchathani Burirom Udommahasthan Amompiman
Awathansathit. The name "Bangkok" is not usual in Thai and
probably was a corruption of "Ban Makok", which stands for
"village of olives".

Population

The origin of the Thai people has not been explained beyond all
doubt. However, research has shown that they originated from
the valley of Yang Tse in Southern China. They are said to have
founded the first independent kingdom called Nan Chao
around 650 A.D. The conquest of this kingdom by the Mongol
Kublai Chan in 1253 led to an exodus in which Thais mixed with
those races that originated from China from 800 A.D. moving to
the Mekong delta and settling there. In 1257 the first sovereign
kingdom of Siam was founded with Sukhothai as its capital.

General

Nowadays the population of Bangkok and Thailand is an ethnic
mixture with Chinese, Indians, Malay, Burmese and even Europeans, 85% can, however, be described as Siamese. Among
the Thai people are the Chan on the Burmese border, the Lao
and Meo in the north and north-east along with the Malays in
the south. The culture of the Indian and Chinese communities is
most apparent in Bangkok whereas the rural population has
retained its Thai origins.

Europeans, Americans and Australians employed by multinational concerns contribute to the cosmopolitan character and
lifestyle of Bangkok which is not typical of Thailand. They have
created their own world in Bangkok with symphony concerts,
grandiose parties in the gardens of luxury hotels and ballet
companies which until recently were unheard of in the Thai
capital. A certain degree of Westernisation began with the
regents of the Chakri dynasty who were educated in Europe.
Rama VIII, for example, was born in Heidelberg, the present
king Rama IX grew up in Switzerland with his brothers and
sisters.

One in three of Bangkok's population was born outside of the
city. At the bus station the visitor can witness the arrival every
morning of hundreds of new citizens predominantly from the
rural areas. Like their predecessors they hope to find work and
bread in the "Heavenly Capital". A large number of immigrants
come from the north-east and the neighbouring country of
Laos where an almost common language along with a "little
border trade" facilitate living in Thailand.

Immigration

The influx of immigrants is responsible for the population
explosion in Bangkok in contrast to the Thai villages where a
small family of two children is rare. Between 1960 and 1981 the
population rocketed from 1.7 million to 5.4 million. In comparison the population of Bangkok in 1860 was 300,000 and only
460,000 by 1900. Part of the reason for this steep rise was no
doubt the integration of Thonburi with Bangkok in the 1970s.

Population growth

Today about 63% of Thailand's population are below 30 and
only 3.9% over 65. The birth rate has even dropped in the last 15
years. At the beginning of the 1970s it was around 33 births per

Population structure

Faces of an Asian metropolis

1000 inhabitants but recently it has dropped to 22.3 per 1000. It is expected to fall further as a result of a government programme making contraceptives available for a small charge. Improved medical care has increased life expectancy since 1960 from 50 years (women 55) to 63 (women 67). According to world predictions for world population in 2025 the population of Thailand is expected to rise by more than 60% to more than 88 million.

Living conditions

Two-thirds of Bangkok's people live in two, three or four-storey street blocks with the ground floor and even the pavement being used for transacting business (shops, hairdressers, repairers, printers, etc.). The staff, mostly relatives, live on the first floor, the boss and his family on the second, while the older members of the family are installed on the floor above. If it is a prosperous family the old people's flats will have trellised roof gardens where shadow boxing takes place in the morning and people socialise in the evening.

About two-thirds of Bangkok's inhabitants live in the districts of Thonburi, Bangkapi, Dusit, Chinatown, Petchaburi and Suk-humvit. Thonburi, criss-crossed by canals, has mostly one-family homes set in luxuriant wild gardens. Apartment houses, with their own swimming pools, are almost exclusively the homes of the transitory Westerners, since for Thais these modern dwellings are not only incredibly expensive but their inward-looking anonymity is also thought to be extremely uncomfortable. The family homes which belong to Thais or Chinese are mostly wooden, two-storey at the most, and have fans instead of air-conditioning. They are the homes not solely of the rich but also the professional middle classes. The servants seldom if ever live under the same roof as their masters but mostly have a small annexe in the garden, with its own Thai-style wood-stove and bathroom (bathtub and dipper). A wooden house like this surrounded by water and lush tropical greenery, even if not part of a private garden, in, for instance, Thonburi, is well within the means of the low-earner, provided that the size of the family means that servants are not needed, or that the members of the family have a sufficient total income.

In the Thai family right from infancy the young Thai experiences this sense of togetherness. A mere whimper is enough for the child to be scooped up, soothed and rocked back and forth. As soon as it can crawl and toddle it is carried everywhere, usually naked, perched on an older sister's hip, in the crook of her arm, a position in which the little one can sleep, play and even eat whenever it wants. There does not seem to be a rigid daily routine with set sleeping times. It seems strange to the visitor to Thailand that even the smallest children are still awake at midnight and only go to bed when they are really tired. The little ones already possess perfect manners when they first start school and go on to show respect through school and college not only to teachers but also towards their parents and teachers and all grown-ups. No pregnant woman is given baby-clothes or other gifts for the baby before the birth, since she might well be scared by evil spirits, mostly the spirits of women who had died childless and unmarried and for at least three days up to a month after the birth the baby is still their "spirit child". It is the custom to avoid the attentions of the evil spirits by referring to the newly-born as frog, dog, toad, etc., and it will be a month before relatives and near-neighbours, are invited to a little party – and sometimes the monks, too, are given a token gift. Now mother and child may receive presents and amid much merriment an attempt is made to choose a "baby-talk" name (such as diddums, birdie, mousikins), although only the "school-name" will be registered on the birth certificate. Baby birthdays are not celebrated.

Asian children are hardly ever scolded or smacked nor is rejection a form of punishment. Gentle methods of conditioning are

Family and children

13

No Thai baby is every lonely

preferred; a Thai mother would never say "If you do that you will be punished!" but instead appeals to the child's sense of shame and says "If you do that the others will laugh at you!" There is an essential difference in the way Asian and Western societies bring up their children. Whereas Western parents try to encourage the child to be independent from an early age Asian parents protect their children from worries and conflict and keep them in the bosom of the family for as long as possible. The result, to a certain extent, is a collectivisation which manifests itself in later life as indecisiveness or shying away from conflict.

Hierarchies

In Thailand the concept of rank is all-pervasive, every Thai is always aware of his rank in society. It is expressed even in terms of address, e.g. Khun preceding the name indicates someone of higher or occasionally similar status, never someone who is of a lower social position. It is, however, not comparable with the Indian caste system. The Thai is only concerned with his own role in life which he carries out to the letter. Yet he lives in hope of a better existence in some future life. Despite the difference in rank the relationship between the master or mistress and their servants is a close one. Colleagues often refer to each other as "nongchai" (younger brother) or "pi-ssau (older sister) and a boss may refer to his staff as "pinong" (older and younger brothers and sisters). Many employees, even in large American and European companies hand in their notice when their superiors leave. For it is the personal relationship that determines one's enthusiasm for the job, self-confidence and image. This applies equally from the youngest office messenger to the boy who works in the garden of a private house and hardly gets a wage.

Respect for the elders by the younger generation is very important in Asian societies. Grandparents command the greatest respect followed by the parents, relatives and older sisters. Total obedience is second nature to the Asian child. This later finds expression in almost unconscious suppression of one's own self so that the contradiction of a superior is unthinkable. Yet to the foreigner the family relationships appear somewhat casual. For example, it is rare for all members of the family to sit down to meals together, preferring instead to avail themselves, when they feel like it, of the services of one of the many street-vendors, itinerant cooks or cheap noodle shops. If members of a large family are seen having a meal together, then they are invariably Chinese. Never being alone accounts to a large extent for the sense of security within the family. People never sleep alone, even in houses with plenty of rooms, unless they insist on it. Neither is anyone left on his or her own in house or flat. Consequently hardly anyone objects to the vast dormitories in the lodgings provided by factories or the accommodation in high schools, colleges and even universities. To the academics who have studied in the west even the dormitories divided by a glass screen or curtains are no longer acceptable.

Way of life

In order to understand the Thai way of life some basic explanation is necessary. In Asian societies it is the collective community rather than the individual which is of major importance. The consequence of this view is a continual struggle for compromise and to involve as many people as possible. Putting one's own interests before those of others is unusual, the Asian always considers the aim of the whole community. Personality scarcely comes into play, much more important is the subordination to existing social order. On the other hand the striving for harmony as a basic philosophy is peculiar to Asian society. The origins of this pattern of behaviour can be found in the teachings of Confucius which sees people not as individuals but as a total being. This "being" is ideally at one with the "three harmonies": the harmony with the human world, harmony with nature and harmony with the spiritual world.

Role of women

The role of women in Thai society also has its roots in tradition but in recent years it has changed. Girls and boys are brought up in the same way until they are six years old when preparation for their separate roles begins. For girls this consists of motherliness, shyness, selflessness and modesty. At the same time the woman is portrayed in legends as a heroine but symbolically dressed in men's clothes. Often cited are the two sisters, Chan and Muk, who disguised themselves and all the other women as men during the siege of Phuket in order to trick the enemy into believing it faced a large army.

True emancipation, however, in spite of the Western influences referred to, is limited to certain areas of employment. According to the latest figures for 1988 out of 27.5 million Thai women 11.5 million are engaged in employment! It is unusual to find women in positions of commercial responsibility although educational and career opportunities are open to all in theory. King Chulalongkom (Rama V) opened up access to all schools but equality for boys and girls was not realised until a law was passed by King Rama VII. It was 1930 before women could study law and they were barred from political office until the beginning of the Thirties. Not until 1949 did a woman enter

Parliament from the province of Ubon Ratchathani, 27 years later Loesak became the first female minister of the Kingdom, as Minister for Transport. However, in the last parliamentary elections in 1988 it was obvious that Thai women, often metaphorically described as the rear legs of an elephant (without which it would fall down) still had to fight to establish themselves in public life: of the 3612 candidates only 366 were women.

Government

Government

Never in the course of its history has Thailand been ruled by a foreign power or nation. This is reflected in the name of the country Thailand (in Thai: "Prathet Thai"), literally "land of the free". The fact that Thailand was never colonised, despite various half-hearted attempts, (especially by Great Britain and Portugal) was due to skilful chessboard diplomacy in particularly troubled times worldwide.

From its origin until 1932 the Kingdom of Siam took the form of an absolute monarchy. Following a coup in December 1932 Thailand has been a constitutional monarchy with a constitution for the first time based on democratic principles. But even today the king is sacrosanct. Though much has changed since Rama I took the throne in 1782, the first member of the Chakri dynasty. The Holy Kingdom, in which even up until the reign of King Taksin physical contact with the Royal Family was punishable by death, has had its day along with the belief in the infallibility of the monarch. Nevertheless, King Bhumibol (Rama IX) is held in great esteem by the people, who in a referendum in 1987 awarded him the title "the great one". There is little criticism of the monarchy; even Thais living abroad hold the monarch in deep respect. The visitor is therefore well advised not to make any disrespectful or insulting remarks about the Royal Family.

Head of State

Bhumibol succeeded his elder brother Ananda, who was found dead in his Bangkok palace in mysterious circumstances in 1946. Although Bhumibol assumed regal office immediately following his brother's death the official coronation did not take place until 1950 after he had completed his studies in Switzerland and married Sirikit, the daughter of a diplomat. Rama IX is the longest reigning monarch in Thai history. The 42nd jubilee in June 1988 was celebrated in style. The King is the head of state, in the final instance he determines the acceptance or rejection of a new law. However this has not been the case for years. In Thailand the "royal decree" is a special legislative power which the monarch can employ without the consent of parliament. Even after the most recent military coup, on the 26 February 1991, which temporarily put a military junta in power, this decree which affirms the King as the head of state was left untouched.

Parliament

The Thai Parliament consists of two chambers, the Senate and the National Assembly, composed of 267 Senators appointed by the King for a period of six years and 357 elected Deputies who hold office for four years. It ressembles the British system of government (monarch, Upper and Lower House). Following the military coup in February 1991 the constitution was temporarily withdrawn, being the eleventh since the change from an absolute to a constitutional monarchy in 1932. A new constitution still has to be formulated and passed by a Parliament which has yet to be elected. The first democratic constitution was preceded by massive student protests which were triggered by the secret homecoming of the ex-Prime Minister Thanom Kittikachorn. It resulted in a bloodbath with the Thai army attacking the demonstrators causing innumerable deaths.

Thailand is divided into 71 provinces (changwat) which are generally named after the main town. The administration is headed by a Provincial Governor who is also the Government Deputy for Bangkok and Leader of the Provincial Administration. The provinces are subdivided into 537 districts (amphoe) which in turn subdivide into communes (tamban) with the smallest unit being the villages (mu ban) which have at their head a "mayor" appointed by the provincial government. The provincial government is, subject to certain restrictions, responsible for the budget and is itself accountable to the central government in Bangkok. The Bangkok government has drawn up Five Year plans which should guarantee economic growth and direct state investments. The King has allowed himself a say in these investments which are intended to benefit agriculture in the underdeveloped regions of Thailand. Bangkok is the country's newest province and also the only city state. Like all the other provinces (changwat) Bangkok is divided into districts (amphers) and has a Governor appointed by Central Government.

Province and city-state

The military has always played an important part in the selection of ministers and senators. The predecessor of the Prime Minister, Anand Panyachuran, who has been in office since the coup in February 1991, Chatichai Choonhavan, came, indeed, from a military background but despite this was the first elected representative to hold office to be awarded the task of forming a government. Experts on Thailand believe that even if the present Prime Minister is a trained diplomat the military will have an important role to play in the future. Should it feel insufficiently involved in the country's political affairs then there will be the threat of another coup d'état.

Role of the military

Such a coup (the 16th incidentally since 1932) took place on the morning of the 26 February 1991; there was no bloodshed and it was successful. After the rebels led by General Sunthorn Kongsompong had occupied the most important public buildings, ministeries, radio and television stations they placed Prime Minister Choonhavan under house arrest. During the days which followed he was advised to leave the country otherwise he would face charges of corruption and misuse of office. Officially he was advised "to take a holiday abroad".

Coup of 26 February 1991

Prime Minister Anand Panyachuran (born 1932) has been at the head of the interim government since 1 March 1991, chairman of the "Committee of National Salvation". The youngest son of a former headmaster his career reads like a Thai storybook. Having studied in London and Cambridge he went into the diplomatic service as the youngest Thai ambassador to represent his country at the United Nations in New York and then as ambassador to the United States and from 1977 to 1978 to West Germany. After returning from West Germany the reform-seeking Panyachuran left the diplomatic service to enter the market

Prime Ministers

place and from then on exerted political influence on the economy of his country. He became involved in numerous sub-organisations of the ASEAN League and was President of the Thai Employers Association when the military asked him to take over.

Panyachuran took over from Chatichai Choonhavan (born 1922) who was suspected of corruption. The son of a Chinese immigrant and of a well-to-do family he became Major General of the army at the age of 32 (the youngest in Thai military history) and from 1973 served in Thai governments as Minister for Foreign Affairs and Industry among others. Under his predecessor Prem Tinsulanonda he served as one of five deputy heads of government. He was member of the Chart Thai Party (TNP) and headed a coalition government made up of socialists, commoners, democrats and national democrats which gained 58% of the vote in the 1988 election.

Party system

The party system (in reality a loose association of parties) is diverse, no one group can claim to have a monopoly of opinion. In the past governments were only formed through co-operation of several parties; it is almost tradition that after the election not one of the various parties receives a majority large enough to form a government. Even the Prime Minister presently in office leads a three party coalition which has been appointed by the military as an interim government. Communist parties are banned but are active underground among students. There is no overall political consciousness of social class in Thailand; the voter elects a representative who is, even if only by limited means, able to assist him in the event of dire need. This is based on a pronounced respect for authority and strict traditional hierarchical order. This is not the case among intellectuals with whom, after initial problems of identification, democratic ideas have taken root.

Foreign policy

Thailand has always been influenced by the United States in its foreign policy which has brought considerable investment for improvements in the infrastructure of the north-east of the country, particularly on the Kampuchean border. This was responsible for the American construction of the "Road of Friendship", today one of the most important national roads from the south to the north-east. After its completion its primary function was as a supply-line for the American forces. In return for economic aid this south-east Asian state allowed American troops to be stationed on its territory during the Vietnam war. In the course of a mood of independence towards the end of the Seventies the American forces were asked to leave. Thailand has since followed a relatively independent foreign policy but, in accordance with a UN resolution, can always depend on American support in the event of military conflict on the border with Kampuchea.

International membership

Thailand has been a member of the United Nations (UNO) since 1946 and also of organisations affiliated to the UN. It was a founder member of the Association of Southeast Asian Nations (ASEAN), founded in Bangkok in 1967, and was involved in the Colombo Plan developed in 1950, its aim was "to raise the living standards in member countries" after the model of the "Marshall Plan".

Language

Thai belongs to the Sino-Tibetan family of languages, but in the narrower sense is only related to Chinese (it is still spoken in China today as a southern dialect). The influence of Buddhism and Khmer kingdom (Angkor) has meant the incorporation into the language of many words from Pali and Sanskrit, recognisable by their multisyllabic character, but these seldom occur in popular speech. Hardly ever heard by the tourist, they linger on only in the vocabulary of the Court, the monastery, in classical literature and in the "nobler" surnames and modes of address. In 1283 Rama Khamheng "the Great" King of Sukkothai (as Thailand was named before it became to be called first Ayutthaya, then, by the Europeans, Siam), created a phonetic Thai alphabet in which he also drafted his "government declaration" engraved on stone (see A–Z National Museum).

The signs are patterned on Sanskrit but supplemented by signs for tones which, like vowels, can stand before, above, below or next to "their" consonants. This alphabet, with slight variations, was also adopted by Burma, Laos and Kampuchea, and is still used today, which is why most Thais (the illiteracy rate is only about 15%) can actually decipher and understand writings which may be hundreds of years old.

Thai, also called Siamese, consists mostly of monosyllabic invariable words. These are written from left to right, without being separated, and spaces only mark the end of sentences or clauses, or denote proper nouns. Because the language is monosyllabic it is only possible to have about 420 phonetically

The Thai alphabet, created by Rama Khamheng in 1283

different words, so the meanings of words are determined by which of the five tones is used in pronouncing them. Auxiliaries replace grammatical forms such as tense, gender, active, passive, etc. The number of different consonants and vowels ranges between 50 and 82, according to Western sources, especially as there is a tendency for many signs to change according to their position in a word, hence, "l" and "r" at the end of a word are pronounced "n", at the beginning of a word both are spoken by Thais as "l", two "r"'s in the middle of a word become the vowel "a" and, finally, "r" is silent after an "s", which is frequently found in religious and royal names, e.g. "Sri Ayutthaya".

Thai phraseology

Visitors will always be coming up against the phrases "mai pen arai" (that's alright or OK) and "sanuk" (fun). "Sanuk" is like food and drink to the Thais, and they try to get some fun out of every occasion. A new inexhaustible source of fun is the "farangs", the Western visitors, as they rush around looking for something to photograph, or recoil at the sight of a bat, which Thais look upon fondly as playmates. The best fun of all, however, is to hear farangs speaking Thai, since a word can have a completely different meaning if given the wrong intonation, and thus provoke gales of mirth. Just the word "mai" can mean widow, silk, wood, burning, new or stand for a question mark, depending on the tone it's uttered in. A farang may innocently ask whether the widow is wooden or silk, new or burnt, and if a farang actually says he has "por" (enough) to eat, and by way of emphasis, pronounces it "por", it is his own father that he has eaten. A Thai heart can stumble (be surprised), fall (take fright), but if it becomes damp (dschaichyyn), i.e. cool, then it feels good and if it is full up with water (naamdschai) then it is a merit-making, compassionate heart. The Thai language is also flowery and eloquent in banter between the sexes. Girls, both big and small, are fondly described as "muu" (pig) since "muu" is not only a favourite food of the Thais, it is also rounded and rosy. Anyone who whispers sweet nothings to his muu is "eating joy from another" (rabuskgan), and anyone who asks a girl for sweet-smelling roots (kor horm) could expect a kiss on the cheek in return. As for swimming or playing in your birthday suit, that is not nude but "dressed in sky and wind".

Economy

Agriculture

Thailand has remained an agricultural state despite all efforts at industrialisation. Over one third (18,300 sq.km./7065 sq.m.) of its total land area is taken up with agricultural production which comprises one fifth of the gross national product.
Rice is the mainstay of agricultural production in this region which is known as the "rice bowl of Southeast Asia". Thailand is the world's fifth biggest producer of rice. 9.4 million hectares/3.8 million acres yields about 20 million tonnes, 5.3 million tonnes of which were exported in 1989 with proceeds of 23.3 billion baht. Only white rice is suitable for export, brown rice is produced chiefly in the north and north-east for domestic consumption. Greater yields per hectare have resulted in increased harvests and a drop in price so the Thai government has guaranteed farmers a minimum income. Rice production in

Thailand is lower than that of neighbouring countries; in Myanmar, for example, yields per hectare are up to one third higher.

Besides rice agricultural crops make up Thailand's major exports and production of these is being expanded to reduce dependency on world market prices. Manioch (a tropical plant), sugar beet and maize are also intensively farmed. In 1989 Thailand exported 5.5 million tonnes of tapioca (grain extracted from manioch) to the European Community.

Fishing remains vital to the economy, with Thailand being the world's largest exporter of tuna fish. Although quotas have stagnated since 1972 the number of fishing boats more than doubled between 1976 and 1985. In 1989 the Thai fisherman landed 1.7 million tonnes of fish for processing in the modern fish-processing plants along the coast, most of which was for export. Rice farmers inland who supplement their income with private fishing receive financial support from the Thai government.

Fishing

Textile production (1989: 48 billion baht) and the export of jewellery (1989: 13 billion baht) are other important sources of income. After Italy Thailand is the second major exporter of jewellery in the world. The Bangkok School of Jewellery is of world renown.

Jewellery

In 1989 the gross national product amounted to 58 billion US $, representing 5.5% annual growth in real terms since 1980. Industry and trade made up 32% with 48% falling to the services sector. The major increase was in tourism which since 1982 has topped rice exports as the biggest earner of foreign currency with returns of 96.4 billion baht. In 1988 Thailand imported goods to a value of 18.5 billion US dollars, whereas exports amounted to 15.3 billion baht. Only once, in 1986, has there been a trade surplus in the Thai economy. A trade deficit is considered normal. Over the last five years inflation has been 3.2 %. However, an increase in living costs of 8% is anticipated for 1991. Income pro capita stands at 828 US dollars.

Gross national product

Bangkok is the industrial and commercial centre of Thailand. All Thailand's international and national concerns have their headquarters in Bangkok. The office blocks of multinational companies and service industries dominate the city of Bangkok. Over the last ten years numerous foreign companies have chosen the Thai capital as their base. It is easy to overlook the fact that Bangkok's indigenous industries have also expanded. Even today there is a myriad of wharves, rice-mills, wood, metal and textile workshops with the workers living along the riverside almost hidden away from view. Modern industries are located on the outskirts of the city manufacturing and processing chemicals and foodstuffs. Automobile production is planned as part of a "joint venture project" but until then cars will continue to be assembled from parts manufactured in Japan. The vehicles will be shipped from the deep-sea harbour at Laem Chabang, which lies midway to Pattaya.

Traditional and modern industries

Thailand has reserves of important minerals such as tin. As the price of tin has dropped dramatically in recent years on world markets being the fourth largest producer in the world Thailand has not escaped unscathed. 324 tin mines (around half) were closed down and exports fell by 40%.

Minerals

21

Economy

Energy production

There are no nuclear power stations in Thailand. Oil, gas and in the north brown coal provide for the country's energy needs. Supplies of brown coal are estimated at 1.8 billion tonnes. In future gas will become increasingly more important as a source of power in Thailand when the reserves below the Gulf of Thailand are developed. Two power stations in Bangkok have already been connected to a 400km/250 mile long pipeline, part of which is the longest undersea pipeline in the world. Consumption and export of this natural gas will bring savings and revenue worth billions to relieve the Thai balance of payments. Following the exploitation of oil reserves in the Gulf of Thailand at the beginning of the 1980s Thailand was able to reduce its oil imports. In future about one third of Thailand's total energy requirements should be met by domestic sources of power.

Tourism

Alongside agriculture and fishing tourism has, over the last ten years, developed into one of the major sources of income and the number of tourists is increasing annually. The main non-Asian visitors are Americans, Germans and British: in 1990 4.8 million Europeans visited Thailand. In its recent Five Year Plan of 1990 the Thai government seeks to expand tourism further by offering state aid to service industries and foreign investors. In 1960 tourism netted 195 million baht compared with 100 billion baht in 1989. It long since overtook rice exports (1989: 23 billion baht) as the main source of income from abroad. This serves to underline the importance of tourism which employs over 700,000 people according to most recent information.

Employment

According to estimates from 1986, when the last Five Year Plan was drawn up, there were 27 million employed in Thailand (49.8% of the population). It is forecast that by 1995 32.5 million will be working and by 2000 over 38 million. Southeast Asia has a high proportion of children who also form part of the working population. In 1980 1.3 million children between the ages of 11 and 15 were engaged in paid employment. The bulk of the workforce are aged between 20 and 35 which reflects the structure of the population as a whole. It is interesting to note that as many women as men work. The reasons for this are traditional rather than because of state incentives or social legislation. The largest percentage is employed in agriculture and foresty, followed as in other Asian countries by manufacturing and services. The unemployment figures are not published regularly and only refer to those who are officially registered as looking for work as well as the sick registered with the authorities. They do not include the high number of casual workers. This resulted in a low official figure of 1% for 1989, compared with 5.4% quoted by the Bank of Bangkok. Unemployment is expected to rise in the future, especially in textiles and agriculture. In Bangkok there is a state employment exchange which offers its services free of charge to those looking for work.

Trade unions

Free trade unions were permitted for the first time in the history of the country during the period of great social upheaval between 1973 and 1976. Trade unions had existed since the end of the Second World War and had successes such as a legal minimum wage but they were under state control. Not until 1975 was there labour legislation to protect workers' rights such as maternity leave. Today there are 23 trade unions under one umbrella organisation. Farming co-operatives are particularly active in the Government's new settlement zones. Bangkok is prone to strikes and demonstrations. 1975 was a record year with 241 strikes. The most recent available statistics relate to 1981 when there were 54 strikes with 22,000 people involved.

The trade unions have been unable to take much action against the continual flouting of the employment laws to protect children under 14. Strictly speaking they are only allowed to help out occasionally with their parents' business. It is well known that boys and girls of a very young age have to contribute to the family income and work in small firms such as printers and match factories or sell newspapers and flowers for a pittance, but it is tolerated.

Child labour

Transport

Thailand has a well developed communications network which links all parts of the country. The roads and railways in and around Bangkok are of a good standard even though the increasing volume of traffic has been an insoluble problem for many years. The visitor needs to have the patience of the locals and business travellers should realise that arrival times cannot be calculated in advance and should make appointments accordingly.

General

Don Muang international airport, opened in 1987, is the turntable for almost all continental and intercontinental flights between Europe and Asia. It is the base for Thai Airways International.
A few years after this new airport came into service it was dealing with ever-increasing numbers of passengers, modern terminal buildings having replaced the old airport nearby. And yet it is already too small to cater for the expected numbers of passengers in the coming decade; a new airport at the other end of the city is being considered.

Airports

56 international airlines fly to Don Muang as well as many charter companies which carry a large proportion of the visitors. In 1990 it handled 15.6 million passengers (including stopovers) compared with 1.2 million in 1975, a twelvefold increase in 15 years.

Numbers of passengers

The new cargo terminal, situated near the passenger terminals, handled 440,000 tonnes of cargo.

Air cargo

The railway network of the State Railway of Thailand (SRT) is well developed, even by European standards, although there has been little investment in new lines since 1977. Altogether 3728km/2316 miles of track link the towns of the kingdom. The main routes are between Bangkok and Chiang Mai and other major towns with connections to Malaysia and Singapore. Long-distance express and overnight trains are comfortably furnished with couchettes and sleeping compartments. Modern diesel engines have replaced the steam locomotives which are common elsewhere in Asia.

Railways

Only a seventh of the total population of Thailand lives in Bangkok yet more than half of all vehicles are registered here. In 1990 2.3 million vehicles were registered compared with

Roads

608,000 ten years earlier. Many of the picturesque klongs have long been the victim of traffic with new roads being built on them. Hardly any other city in Thailand is more threatened by air pollution from traffic which has reached harmful levels.

Traffic in the Thai capital is subject to rules which are not apparent to the European. Three things are essential to drive in Bangkok: an over-sized rear-view mirror, a very loud horn and trust in Buddha. Driving on the left, in the British fashion, only adds to the difficulty facing the visitor from mainland Europe or America combined with the chaotic traffic conditions. Tourists are well-advised not to venture into this turmoil in a hired car as even experienced drivers end up going in the wrong direction. Despite the increase in traffic the accident rate and number of deaths on the roads has fallen after fatal car accidents doubled between 1970 and 1981.

The construction of new roads has brought no relief, instead more cars are being purchased and registered. The only answer seems to be a government imposed import tax of up to 400% of the purchase price.

In 1984 the government gave the green light for the extension of the existing motorway (partly toll road) which was to form a 19km/12 mile long north–south axis and a further 9km/6 mile long east–west axis. It is approaching completion. On 5 December 1987 the King Bhumibol bridge over the Menam Chao Phraya was opened opening up South Bangkok to traffic.

Buses and Taxis

Buses and taxis, including the typical Asian "tuk-tuks" and "samlors", are an important means of transport. They will take the visitor quickly and cheaply to his destination but a lungful of exhaust fumes is an added extra in these three-wheeled open scooters. Bangkok has over 15,000 registered taxis along with an unspecified number of unofficial taxi drivers who ply for trade after work and at weekends and are unlikely to be adequately insured. Official taxis have a yellow sign on the roof and display their registration number.

Motorcycle taxis are fast and rather dangerous.

Boats and ferries

Boats and ferries are not so important nowadays as when Bangkok was criss-crossed by canals. The ferry is still the fastest way of crossing the Menam Chao Phraya. Regular boat and ship services operate up and downstream and although they are relatively cheap the number of passengers is steadily decreasing. It is not long ago that hundreds of thousands of people travelled to work, school, university or market by boat.

Future plans

The swampy ground has always caused problems for Bangkok and caused it to be called the "Venice of Southeast Asia". This makes an underground system impossible. However, ways are being considered to combat the ever-increasing traffic which according to experts, threatens to suffocate the city before long. Plans to build an overhead railway were rejected on grounds of cost. In the meantime roads have been made one-way at certain times of day in an attempt to alleviate congestion at rush-hour.

Culture

General

Since its foundation in 1782 Bangkok, succeeding the earlier royal cities of Sukhothai and Ayutthaya, was the only centre for culture and science until well into the second half of the present century. Traditionally the "chao krung", the big-city dweller, is more highly esteemed than the provincial, and "chao krung" also applies, for example, to eminent academics and politicians who, although they may be living and working in the provinces, nevertheless through their extended family ties still have a place to stay in Bangkok, and spend their week-ends and holidays there.

The National Theatre, the only permanent theatre company, and the National Museum (see A to Z), Thailand's only real showplace for its art and culture, together with almost all the country's radio and TV stations, and Press, are all located in Bangkok.

The Ministry of Education and the Ministry for National Development have, with the Royal Family, been in the forefront in promoting and carrying out "cultural decentralisation", and since 1975 the Tourism Authority of Thailand (TAT) has also pursued the same aim. As a consequence young intellectuals, who like travelling around their country just as much as Western visitors, have discovered that the provinces also possess a wealth of cultural and natural treasures.

Education

The Ministry of education is responsible for all schools, whether private or State.

Schools

Children can go to nursery school from the age of two, and this is generally the practice with Bangkok's middle and upper classes. Currently there is compulsory (primary) education for six years. Efforts in the 1960s and 1970s to raise this to seven years, as well as enormous strides in teacher training all over the country and the building of schools even in the smallest villages have meant that the illiteracy rate among adults up to 40 years of age is thought to have fallen to about ten percent already. This figure is understandably higher among the older age-groups, however; the last census was in 1980, admittedly, but this indicated that only about a half of Thailand's older population could read and write. Children who get very little or no schooling are mostly from immigrant families which have not been officially registered and live in illegal slums. Even there, however, some make the effort to teach themselves, and Buddhist monks have always been ready to offer extra-curricular schooling and accommodation to young men.

Education in State schools is free, but school uniform has to be worn, although this rule is not always strictly observed. Grants for school uniforms, as well as for further education and teaching seminars, are among the most frequent gifts bestowed by the Royal Family and private welfare groups.

Technical colleges and, for some years now, training colleges in Bangkok and the larger provincial cities have become increasingly overcrowded. Entrance exams to further education are compulsory, but there still exists the opportunity for young people to enrol free of charge at Chulalongkorn University in Bangkok for a course of general studies which carries no graduation certificate at the end of it. Students at university and teacher training colleges are forbidden to marry until they have obtained their degree. Colleges and universities are usually boarding establishments with large dormitories attached. Normally, female boarders have to be in by 8pm.

Technical colleges, universities

Preservation of historical monuments

Trends

For many years tomorrow was always regarded by the Thai government as being much more important than yesterday. It was not until the 1970s that there were real signs of any scientifically-based research into the past; even then it was mainly foreign institutions which made the first move, an indication of the lack of any real sense of history among the Thai people. Until that time, for example, the curators of the Bangkok National Museum had concentrated solely on preserving important religious memorials, temples and statues of the Buddha. Little attention was paid to chance finds, such as those made by the Dutchman van Heekeren when he was a prisoner of war working on the "Death Railway" from Burma to Thailand. In caves near where they were building the "Bridge over the River Kwai" in Kanchanaburi van Heekeren found stone implements from the Paleolithic period, and later published an article on them in England. Even though this article aroused some interest and surprise among a small group of experts it was still not enough to lead to any organised research or properly planned archaeological digs. This may well arise from the fact that – after the fall of the old capitals of Sukhothai and Ayutthaya and the resultant loss of an inconceivably vast collection of important treasures – Bangkok alone was regarded as the centre of culture and learning.

Historical research

Since the 1950s, however, there has been a change of thinking which has had a considerable influence on research; the Thailand Council of National Culture recognised the importance of giving more thought to the country's ancient history and with international, especially American, aid it embarked on a programme of intensive research. Since then things have progressed in leaps and bounds; every year numerous new discoveries are made which prove that Thailand is a country with a fine historical past. Thai art historians have made every effort to keep as many finds as possible in the regions in which they were discovered, and a large number of new national museums have been founded for that purpose.

Finds at Ban Chiang

Much still remains buried, however; spectacular finds continue to be more a matter of luck than the result of planned excavations. The little village of Ban Chiang, 50km/30 miles from Udon Thani in north-eastern Thailand, is an interesting example of that. Until 1967 hardly anybody had even heard of Ban Chiang and its few hundred inhabitants – within the course of a day or two it was literally invaded by an army of archaeologists from all over the world. The reason was the truly sensational finds made there. which proved that – contrary to all previous ideas – this region had been inhabited during the Bronze Age, at least 3,800 years before the birth of Christ. Until 1967 it had been assumed that the first settlers had been Laotian immigrants a mere 170 years ago. Pottery fragments, iron and bronze tools and even bones had in fact been unearthed over a period of years by farmers working in the fields, but scant attention had been paid to them.

It was scientists from distant Bangkok, alerted by an American named Steve Young, who first decided to examine the reddish-painted pieces of pottery more closely. Thermoluminescent tests showed that they were up to 5,800 years old, contemporary with the Bronze Age in Mesopotamia, between the rivers Euphrates and Tigris, which had begun earlier than the Bronze

Age in Northern Europe. That caused quite a sensation, because until then it had been assumed that it had been the inhabitants of Mesopotamia who had produced the very first bronze articles. If the results of the tests are verified – and there is no reason to think they will not be – then the bronze tools found in Ban Chiang are the oldest so far uncovered anywhere in the world!

Examinations of the ceramic items produced surprising results: the vessels, painted with spiral and ribbon ornamentation and probably grave-goods rather than items made to be used, were of an artistic quality not yet found anywhere else in south-east Asia. Stylised plants and animals, painted probably with the finger, initially on simply-formed, round-bellied vases and later on pottery vessels of more elegant shape, are evidence of a people enjoying a very high cultural standard.

The pottery containers were made during three separate and well-defined periods. In the earliest period (c. 3600–2500 B.C.) they were in black and had decorative bands with ornamentation between the lines. During the second phase (c. 2500–2000 B.C.) the vessels were painted with a coarse pattern, and in the third the painted decorative bands were complemented by others cut into the surface. The final phase of the First Ban Chiang Period saw the addition of stylised drawings of people and animals. The keynote of the Middle Period (c. 1000–300 B.C.) was the simplicity of the pots and other containers, with scarcely any painted decoration, the potter having concentrated almost solely on the shape.

The highest artistic quality was attained during the Later Period (c. 300 B.C. to A.D. 200), when most of the ceramic items displayed in the museum were made: clay, left in its natural state and burnt, was painted red; the designs indicate a wide range of ideas and an extraordinary feel for unity of form, design and colour. Shortly after (about A.D. 400) its inhabitants appear to have left Ban Chiang; at any rate, no later finds have been made.

Art periods

While the styles typifying the various periods can be seen in all the artistic spheres, it is in the fine arts that the country's cultural history is best exemplified. It was not until the end of the 1970s that archaeological finds were fully evaluated in such a way as to indicate that in certain regions – those close to rivers and where there are caves – a very high level of art and craft skills was attained during the Stone and Bronze Ages. **General**

How culture spread from the probable country of origin of the Thai peoples, now southern China, one cannot say. What is certain, however, is that there must have been a distinctive culture, with strong Indian influence, which the Thais adopted and moulded to conform with their own – especially religious – ideals. That seems to be their nature, because right up to the present day Thais have always added their own highly developed and artistic refinements to the cultures of other peoples, but have never demonstrably created any new ones of their own. **Nan Chao epoch (c. A.D. 650)**

The cultures of the time of the Dvararati or Mon Dynasty – between the end of the 6th and the 11th/12th c. and when the capital during the dynasty's heyday was probably Nakhon **Dvararati or Mon style (6th–13th c.)**

27

Pathom – can best be seen in the Thailand central plain (Nakhon Pathom, Prachinburi, Lopburi) and in the north (Sukhotai and Lamphun). Although only a few buildings from this period still remain, those that do bear witness to a developing Thai cultural identity of its own. Stupas or chedis of burnt brick, square or octagonal in plan, are already being richly decorated with pillars and window-ledges; the central section already shows the typical bell-shape, and the conical spires consist of numerous rings laid one on the top of the other. Ornamentation is of stucco and terracotta. A particularly fine example of a chedi from the Dvarati period is Wat Kukut in Lamphun. The Buddhist influence is already evident in these early examples of Thai culture; examples remain of the "Wheel of Law", based on the first sermon by the Enlightened Buddha in Benares.

Srivijaya style
(7th–end 13th c.)

Buddha sculptures, at least those from the first two Dvaravati periods, appear quite clearly to be based on Indian models. While Thai art as we know it today was enjoying its first great flowering in the Dvaravati period another style was also developing, indicating that art was in fact living a "double life" at the time. In the early years at least two cultures were evolving quite separately: the Dvaravati style was devoted unmistakably to the teachings of Buddha, while the Srivijaya style – which originated in the kingdom of Srivijaya in the Indonesian archipelago – was initially dedicated to Hinduism. Vishnu, the multi-armed god far from his own doctrinal home, is depicted as is Linga, the phallic symbol of Shiva. Influences emanating from the island of Java can be seen in, for example, the figures of Buddha at Songkhla. Towards the end of the Srivijaya period some of the Khmer style art-forms were also incorporated, numerous examples of which have been preserved to this day.

Khmer style
(7th–13th c.)

Parallel with the styles just described unfolded the very important Khmer style, examples of which still show unmistakably that it had a very profound effect on the cultures of the kingdoms of Dvaravati and Srivijaya. Outstanding examples are the buildings in what is known as the Angkor style of the late 9th c., named after the city of Angkor where markedly differing versions have appeared over the years. In the Khmer kingdom, which reached from present-day Cambodia as far as Thai country at times. Hinduism and Mahayana Buddhism ruled supreme. Lopburi ranked as the most important cultural centre of Mon.
Not many buildings from this era have survived; the few that have will be found, mainly in ruins, in the places mentioned.

Angkor Wat style
(late 12th c.)

Especially typical of the Angkor Wat style is the Crowned Buddha seated on a wounded serpent with his head protected by a splayed-out shield in the shape of a seven-headed serpent. This form can be traced back to an old legend, which says that, on the 42nd day after Buddha received Enlightenment, Muchalinda (Naga), the King of the Serpents, spread out his many heads to protect him from the heavy rains which poured down on him all day long as he sat under a tree. As well as religious and historical themes the everyday life of the Thai is now also beginning to be depicted.

Chiang Mai style
(11th–mid 16th c.)

The main centres of this cultural form are the cities of Chiang Mai, Chiang Saen and Lamphun; it is the style of the Lan Na kingdom. A distinction should be made between statues influenced by the early Chiang Saen style, which probably prevailed at the end of the 12th c. when Thai princes resided in this region, and those in the Chiang Mai style, which developed in the middle of the 14th c. some 50 years after the founding of the city from which it took its name. Some examples of the latter still remain, while hardly any of the Chiang Saen style have in fact survived.

Figures of Buddha from this period have stern, almost arrogant features, with plumpish bodies and barrel chests. Normally he is found seated on a double row of lotus leaves complete with stamens. Important examples have survived, such as the famous Jade Buddha in Wat Phra Kaeo (see entry) in Bangkok and many others in Thailand presumed to be from the Chiang Mai epoch.

Named after King U Thong, who also built a city of the same name in central Thailand, the title U Thong style embraces sculptures of certain forms which clearly differ from the contemporary Sukhotai style which at the time was considered to be the "Golden Dawn" of pure Thai culture. There were three distinct forms of U Thong, those which show an unmistakable Mon or Khmer influence and those clearly leaning towards the Ayutthaya style. Some art experts think they can detect signs of the U Thong style in architecture as well, although it is in fact very difficult to differentiate between this and the Lopburi Khmer style.

The Sukhotai style (mid 13th–early 15th c.) is usually regarded as the most beautiful even if not the purest of Thai architectural styles. It was influenced by no fewer than nine Kings, in particular perhaps by the third of them, the aesthetically-minded Ramkhamhaeng, who reigned from 1279 to 1299. Surviving examples can be found today not only in Sukhotai itself but all over Thailand as well. A particularly fine example is the Buddha figure in the northern wiharn of the Phra Pathom chedi in Nakhon Pathom (see entry). Although the body is more recent, a close inspection reveals that the head, hands and feet are from a statue of the Sukhotai period.

The first great culture of the Thailand of more recent times blossomed during the time of the magnificent Ayutthaya style, in which the search for new forms led to a surge of artistic creation such as had not been seen before. Although at the outset the influences of past styles could be clearly seen it was not long before some almost entirely unique building fashions came to the fore, concentrating on fine structuring, lofty edifices and lively decoration.

Ayutthaya style (c. 1350–1767)

Now, too, the manner in which Buddha is depicted sets the pattern for a whole era: the very massiveness of the figures shows the importance of this realm and the self-portrayal of the ruler.

After the Burmese attacks in 1767 little remained of Ayutthaya except a vast area of ruins, giving only a faint idea of the city's former glory. There are said to have been 400 temples in the city alone; visitors described it as "the most beautiful they had ever seen".

It took some time for the Thais to recover from the total destruction of their culture in Ayutthaya and the development of new art forms – themselves largely based on old traditions – during the reign of King Taksin was a slow process indeed.

Thonburi style (c. 1767–80)

Painting alone displayed new ideas; architecture, on the other hand, showed little change from what had gone before (see, for example, Wat Arun).

**Rattanakosin or
Bangkok style
(*c.* 1780–1930)**

Magnificent buildings, betraying Western influences, sprang up in the new capital of Bangkok. The rulers of the Chakri dynasty in particular made their mark as architects in the city where they resided, although their buildings are largely lacking in spiritual expression. Rich decoration and lively ornamentation are evidence that they are based to a large degree on earlier styles.

In order to document historical continuity some famous statues from all eras and from all over the country were assembled here. Only in painting were there signs of a progressive influence, as can be clearly seen in a number of Bangkok temples.

**Transitional period
(after 1930)**

Since the 1930s attempts have been made to emulate modern Western artists, especially in the field of painting. Since about 1960 an increasing amount of original Thai art has been uncovered in the outlying provinces, and since 1975 such finds and the areas where they were discovered have systemically been made available to the new generation of art students as well as to tourists. There is a general feeling of nostalgia and a return to traditional Thai styles, with some additions, such as introducing perspective in paintings.

Literature

General

Until well into this century Thailand literature was restricted almost entirely to Court circles, something created by the aristocracy, by kings in particular, for the aristocracy. Subjects covered, too, were those favoured by the Court: academic verse, tales of journeys and voyages ("Nirat"), rowing ballads, epic poems and books teaching language and literature. All early writings were in rhyming verse; it was not until the Bangkok period that prose works and translations from English and Chinese – novels, short stories, essays – began to appear. Much of ancient Thai literature was lost for ever as a result of the destruction of Ayutthaya by the Burmese in 1767; most of the little that was saved is now hidden in archives awaiting research.

In 1283 King Ramakhamhaeng created a Thai alphabet, which is still in use today and has proved to be the most significant milestone in the history of original Thai literature. The king used it to draft his own declaration of accession to the throne, engraved in stone and now housed in the National Museum in Bangkok (see entry); it was also probably he who compiled a poem on the modes of moral behaviour to be followed in the different situations one meets in life. The description of the Buddhist cosmography ("Traiphum") is attributed to his successor, Liu Thai (1347–68), and the definition of life at the Sukhothai Court is probably by one of the ladies-in-waiting.

Court literature

Typical subjects covered in Court literature – many of which also found their way into the country's music (see entry) – include love stories filled with romance, plotting and intrigue and always with a hero who survives daredevil adventures. Many of the stories are enriched with settings based on fantasy, religion or myth, and some were based on ancient folklore and subsequently enriched and changed as the result of later events in Thailand's own history.

Religious traditions, stemming mainly from Indian literature, have always played an important role. Mahabharata and Ramayana both form part of world literature, as do the Old Javanese poem of Inao and numerous legends from the Jataka, the 500 lives of Buddha.

Mahabharata probably has its roots in history, namely, the struggle between the Pandava and the Kaurava for supremacy in the region around what is now Delhi. This particular event has, however, become intermixed with numerous other poems, myths about gods and heroes, love stories and religious and philosophical discourses which have little to do with its true roots. The whole work consists of 110,000 verses dating from somewhere between the 4th c. B.C. and the 4th c. A.D.

Mahabharata
(Indian poetry)

The Javanese dramatic poem Inao describes the adventures of the Prince with the Glass Dagger who finally succeeded in winning the hand of the beautiful Princess Busba.

Inao
(Javanese poetry)

The epic poem Ramakien is the Thai version of the Indian Ramayana ("To the Glory of Rama"), which had probably been written in the 3rd c. B.C. Its central theme is the struggle between gods and demons, a sort of knightly epic of 24,000 lines. In two books added later the hero becomes an incarnation of the god Vishnu who, in the form of the Rama, comes down to earth for the seventh time in order to destroy the demon-king Ravana. He becomes born one of the three sons of the King of Ayodhaya (a city on the River Sarayu in northern India) and falls in love with the king's daughter Sita who is abducted by a demon-king who forces her to live with him. After all kinds of adventures Rama succeeds, with the help of the King of the Apes, in freeing Princess Sita. However, the people are against their union even though Sita, as a sign of her innocence and virginity, arises from a burning funeral pyre. Fifteen years after Rama had disowned her he takes her back when he recognises twins which have been born to Sita as his own sons. Again Sita protests her innocence, saying that the Earth will open up if she is lying. The Earth does open up and swallows Sita. The final outcome varies; the Indian version says that Rama and Sita are re-united in Heaven, whereas in the Ramakien this happens on Earth. In the eyes of the Thais the Ramakien is a timeless tale which, made into a theatrical play by several kings, is today performed on Buddhist Holy Days.

Ramakien
(Poetry of Indian origin)

Literary accomplishment blossomed during the Ayutthaya period, with Formalism being the focal point. In "Yuon Phai" King Boroma Trailokanat (1448–88) describes the victory over Chiang Mai, and in "Mahachat", also in verse form, the last of Buddha's previous existences. The epic poem "Phra Lao" by an unknown poet (possibly King Boroma Trailokanat or even King Narai) tells of the love of Prince Lao for two princesses in a hostile country, ending with the deaths of all three. The sentimental descriptions go into great detail and give a deep insight into the lives of the characters.

Literature in the
Ayutthaya period

One of the great patrons of Thai literature was King Narai, who invited many artists and writers to his Court in Lopburi, including the poet Sri Phrat. The latter also wrote the love stories "Anirut" and "Kamsuon Sri Phrat". The theme of such stories is always the same: obstacles are put in the way of the lovers, they are separated but find one another again after numerous adventures. The rule of Narai also saw the writing of "Cinda-mani", a manual of language and literature, as well as the travel poem "Thawathosamat", describing what the traveller saw in his year-long wanderings through the country. After the fall of Ayutthaya Thai literature also faded away for a time, even though King Taksin worked on four episodes of the Ramakien for the Lakon Theatre.

Later writings

A new literary surge took place under the rulers of the Chakri dynasty. Rama I, for example, produced the only complete version of the Ramakien epic in the Thai language. One of his sons, Poromanuchit Chianrot, made a name for himself as a prolific writer, including a biography of Buddha and the novel "Naresuan" which describes the duel between King Naresuan and the Crown Prince of Burma.

A high point in the more recent history of Thai literature was reached during the rule of King Rama II when he made Sun-thorn Phu from south Thailand the Court Poet. Sunthorn is the country's foremost writer, famous for his vivid imagination and for his poetic language. His masterpiece is "Phra Aphaimani", comprising 24,500 verses and telling of the loves, struggles and adventures of a prince. The theme is traditional, it is true, but the language breaks free from rigid forms and adopts a more folksy style. Sunthorn also wrote a travel poem, several tales written in prose, as well as academic poems for ladies and princes. In conjunction with King Rama I he produced a revised edition of the romantic novel "Khun Chang, Khun Phaen" which had been first written during the Ayutthaya period, and the King himself compiled several episodes of the Ramakien and of the Inao for the Lakon Theatre, and wrote five plays for the Folk Theatre. Under King Rama III Sunthorn Phu fell into disfavour and spent eighteen years as an itinerant preacher, alchemist and monk; later, however, Rama IV bestowed on him the honorary title of "Phra Sunthorn Woham", the equivalent of "Lord Sunthorn, the Enlightened One".

Later kings also made names for themselves as poets. Rama IV wrote "London", describing his impressions on a trip to Lon-don; Chulalongkorn (Rama V) reports on his second journey to Europe in "Klai Ban" (Far from Home), actually a collection of letters to his daughter. Considerable linguistic skill was dis-played in translating some of the stories from "A Thousand and One Nights".

However, it was Rama VI who proved to be Thailand's most prolific author. He wrote 54 plays for the theatre, including the very popular "Mathana Patha" (The Killing of the Rose), epic and lyrical works as well as political treatises. He also made a name for himself as a translator of a number of Shakespeare's dramas and sonnets.

Contemporary literature

Contemporary Thai literature is linked to reality and deals with present-day problems. It is based on European patterns. 1932 was the year when Thailand published its first constitution and the absolute monarchy was changed into a constitutional one; many of the stories written after that date deal with the lot of the peasants and criticise social conditions. In addition a unique lyric form has evolved, represented by such names as the teacher and writer Magut Araridi (b. 1950), Nimit Bhumitha-vorn (1935–81) and the housewife who writes as a hobby, Man-Nan Ja.

For his outstanding services to the literature of Thailand the author Naowarat Pongpaibool (b. 1940) was awarded the ASEAN Prize for Literature in 1980.

Music

The teaching of music in Thailand is as old as the alphabet devised by King Ramkhamhaeng in 1283. Research has shown that music played at that time was little more than a means of transposing language into sounds. As there had been no alphabet before Ramkhamhaeng's time, sounds were used to convey human communications.

Thailand music has always been characterised by the three elements of song, instrumental music and dance. Indian, Khmer, Laotian and Chinese influences played an important part; for many centuries music entered their cultures only as a means of portraying and conveying ancient legends and stories.

Seven full notes make up the Thai scale, there being no semitones such as, for example, the harmony we know in Western music with mathematically computable sequences of notes. Even the layman will immediately recognise the relationship with musical compositions in the fields of both Court and popular music from China, Laos, Cambodia, Burma, India and Indonesia (Bali), but while xylophones, flutes, oboes, gongs, metallophones, string instruments, drums and cymbals are also widely used in the above countries, the parts they play and the rhythms employed in Thailand are quite different.

In spite of the introduction of Western musical notation by Peter Feit (see Famous People) musicians in Thailand still like to improvise and carry music in their heads, without putting it down on paper. Compared with Chinese opera that of Thailand is more rhythmic and less monotonous.

The conventional Thai orchestra, the "Phipat", consists of a minimum of five and a maximum of fifteen musicians playing an equivalent number of different instruments. It accompanies practically everything that can be described as festive, attractive to watch or even sensational, ranging from temple and Court ceremonies by way of classical dance and drama to the popular "Lykay" at annual markets, shadow-theatres or sporting competitions. As in any dance tempo, the main melody is established and played by only one instrument, the round "Wong Yai", similar to a xylophone, while the remaining instruments repeat it or play variations on it. School children and beggars are the main exponents of the "Ang Dalung", a triple-reeded bamboo flute, which can play both the melody and the accompaniment as required. To the Western ear Thai popular music appears somewhat sentimental; the register of the male voice is usually very high. On the other hand, native folk-music – often combined with ambiguous humour and always with dancing – is lively and full of rhythm. The tourist will find a higher standard of music in the nightclubs, for example, where the bands are usually composed of local musicians.

Visits from European bands and orchestras playing classical music arouse considerable interest in Thailand; the Goethe Institute boasts a fine chamber and symphony orchestra composed, rather unusually, of amateur Thai musicians.

Theatre

General

In contrast to Western cultures, if we exclude dance and music it has to be said that true theatre as such has not really taken off in Thailand, even though there exist some excellent translations of plays by Molière, Shakespeare and Goethe, among others. Thai theatre is an amalgam of dance, pantomime, music and song, and this is what the Thailander craves every time he goes. This means that the problem areas which form part of any Western tragedy hold no interest for the Thai Buddhist; in fact he would be against such a thing, because for him it is almost a religious taboo to present personal sorrows and differences to the public gaze. The same goes for music; anything in the form of an aesthetic entity – such as Mozart or the "Nutcracker" ballet suite – always attracts a full house, but the reverse is true of Richard Strauss, Wagner or even modern free dancing.

In his book "In the Kingdom of the White Elephant" written in 1885 the German writer Carl Bock describes the Thai theatre (see Quotations).

Lakon Nai, Kon

The Thai word for theatre is "lakon". There are four main categories, the most important of which is the lakon nai, or indoor theatre, commonly known as "kon". Originally restricted to royal palaces, it now forms the main repertoire of the Bangkok National Theatre. Actors and actresses train for a year as dancers and musicians in a school attached to the theatre which ranks as a college. The pupils are chosen when aged between eleven and fourteen, from schools all over the country, after strict tests of talent and application.

All male roles depicting rank, such as princes or kings, have always been and continue to be filled by young actresses, while demons and animals – especially monkeys – are acted by acrobatically-trained male graduates of the college. The main theme of this classical dance drama is based on episodes from the "Ramakien" (see Literature). Every Thai child grows up familiar with the colours and designs of the costumes and headgear worn by the actors and knows that the masks hide only demons and animals; the "goodies" no longer wear them, and briefly inform the audience who they are. Sixty-eight gestures – mainly movements of hands and head – hint at words unspoken, especially those linked with sorrow or eroticism.

Nang Yai,
Shadow-theatre

The second category of Thai theatre is shadow-theatre. Until the end of the absolute monarchy these Nag Yai pictures artistically impressed on buffalo-hide measuring at least three feet square performed both a festive and popular function: when a royal cremation ceremony took place on the Sanamm Luang, the royal meadow in front of the Grand Palace in Bangkok, these pictures would be raised on 20m/66ft tall bamboo poles in front of the fire to illustrate dramatic scenes from the Ramakien. Today this theatrical form has been almost completely superseded by the cinema. When, from time to time, it is wished to honour a deceased teacher from the National Theatre College, they no longer use Nang Yai pictures painted on buffalo hide; instead, the graduates themselves are the actors and "entertain" the mourners.

Puppet shadow-theatres

Puppet shadow-theatres, on the other hand, have continued to flourish, especially in southern Thailand, but also at local festivals and in temple gardens in Bangkok itself. Just as artistically

Young Thais playing takraw

Shadow-puppetry during a performance

stamped out in leather, but measuring only 20 to 50cm/8 to 20 in. high, these figures are manipulated in front of a cotton screen illuminated from the rear. The people involved, usually members of the same family, consist of a reciter, who explains what is going on, a musician and one or two who manipulate the puppets. They position as many as 100 figures on the stage and move them in turn as required. There is no question that this form of puppetry originated in Indonesia and Malaysia, but restricting it to black and white figures and silhouettes and a few epic themes is genuine Thai, which above all keeps to the Thai style of script, verse combined with prose.

Lykay

Probably the most popular form of theatre, however, is Lykay, a mixture of operetta, cabaret and circus effects conjured up by the effective use of colour and light. Scarcely comprehensible to anyone not fluent in the language and familiar with local politics, however, at first glance the Westerner may see little in it to interest him, but the fact that it attracts large audiences of all ages and classes of people shows that it has a fascination all of its own.

Puppet shows

The fourth form of Thai theatre, puppet shows, will be available to the brief visitor to Bangkok only if he is well acquainted with somebody locally, because they are usually put on only at private parties and the like, which would not normally be advertised or open to foreigners and strangers.

Traditional sports

Kaeng Wau
(Kite-flying
competitions)

From the middle of February the Sanaam Luang area in front of the royal palace is used as a practice-ground for the annual "Kaeng Wau" kite-flying contest. In the afternoons, when the wind is blowing at its strongest, competitions are held for the coveted Royal Cup donated by the King. The contests, which are held in conjunction with chess tournaments, reach their climax in the second half of April. Then huge crowds of onlookers, some seated but mostly standing, place their bets, eat, drink and follow the events with expert enthusiasm. In contrast to the highly colourful kites flown by their Chinese and Islamic neighbours, the Thai kiteifight represents a "celestial" version of the battle of the sexes. The male kite is called "Chula", and shaped not unlike a fighter pilot, man-sized and with a wing span of more than three feet, an artistic masterpiece with a price to match. The rules state that the framework has to be of bamboo poles, if possible three years old, and artistically overlaid.

Takraw
(Ball-game)

In Takraw the player has to propel a ball, 12cm/5in. in diameter and made of basketwork, through the air using any part of his body except his hands and get it either into his opponent's net suspended from a loop 2·75m/9ft high or – another variation of the game – over a 2.5m/8¼ft high net into the opponent's court. This latter "net-Takraw" form of the game is the one agreed upon by all the Asiatic countries taking part in the annual "ASEAN Games". In Thailand, however, the more popular form is "circle-Takraw", with six or eight players and either with or without a net suspended in the middle of the circle. When played in this way the players stand in a circle an equal distance away from each other. The longer the ball remains in the air the

Thai theatre, a combination of music, dancing, singing and mime

Preparing for a kite-fight on Sanaam Luang

more involved become the contortions of the players, and the higher the ball is headed and the more varied the leaps and parts of the body used to propel the ball the higher the points scored. A particularly high score is obtained with a "catch-throw", with the foot kicking the ball through a loop formed by the player's own arms, either when jumping up in the air or with the loop being formed behind his back. The ball is "dead" when it lands on the floor. The game lasts forty minutes and there is no rest period. For a small payment you can obtain a ball and try it for yourself. The minimum required is nine different ball exercises, including throwing the ball round the body or rolling it over various parts of the body. If, playing solo, you can keep the ball off the ground for ten to twelve minutes you are up to performing in a European circus and pretty good even by Thai standards.

Another form of the game requires a playing strip measuring 50 by 3m/165 by 10ft along which you race with the ball, again remembering that it must not be touched with the hand. The inventors of this wonderful ball-game were two brothers named Däng and Dii who – with true Chinese business acumen – made a prosperous business out of it, exporting it and giving demonstrations throughout the USA. Däng is said to have been able to keep the ball in the air, using all parts of his body except his hands, while interchanging between lying, sitting, standing and walking. That was about the year 1900; before that a similar game had been played but using a ball made of feathers or bamboo strips and varying in size. In King Naresuan's time (c. 1579) the balls must have been extremely big, because elephants used to play "football" with them, with criminals condemned to die rolling about inside.

Nowadays there is nothing so macabre about Takraw. The Ministry of Education, numerous clubs and the King himself all patronise the game which, at minimal cost, provides maximum fitness, team spirit and great spectator-appeal. Net-Takraw can be watched every week from February to May in front of the City Hall, near Wat Suthat. At the same time "circle-Takraw" has rapidly become an annual super-tournament held on the Sanaam Luang, where a member of the royal family awards the top trophy, the Royal Cup, to the winning team.

Krabee-Krabong
(Sword-fighting)

The origins of the Thai version of sword-fighting go back many hundreds of years to duels between men – often royal personages – riding on the backs of elephants. Although modern fire-arms superseded this form of battle it was nevertheless jealously preserved as late as the beginning of this century, when King Chulalongkorn ensured that all the princes received instruction in this form of self-defence. King Chulalongkorn himself often practised the "Sword Dance" on elephant-back, not in a duelling sense but as a royal mark of respect to Buddha. Today the swords are blunt or made of wood, but injuries still occur nevertheless. The triple "Wai" during the opening ceremony is intended as a request for a royal pardon should injury be caused.

"Krabee" means "small weapons", which can be fixed to the elbow or held in one hand, such as knives, sabres, cudgels, short-swords and shield, or two swords, one in each hand. In "Krabong" lances, spears, longstaffs or pikes are used, all of which require two hands to hold and wield them. The rules vary according to the equipment used.

Usually the tourist will have the chance of watching a performance such as used to held in the palace as a "Royal Command
Performance". Both opponents will each have two swords,
starting in the "on guard" position, when the two swords are
held out in front at an acute angle, both feet placed so as to be
prepared for attack from left or right. This type of duel is traditionally accompanied by music, from the initial "adagio" to the
"crescendo fortissimo" as the fight nears its climax.
This duelling sport obliges the participants to defend themselves by means of technical skill and lightning reactions and
attacking moves. Women participate almost as much as men
and are quite often the winners.

Thai boxing is more a fighting art than a sport. Legend has it
that King Naresuan was able to escape from captivity by the
Burmese in 1560 only because he was the best wrestler. This
event is still recalled in Thai boxing, which has now become a
national sport. Originally it was a form of self-defence which
was even taught by the monks in the monasteries.
The rules of Thai boxing can scarcely be compared with those
of the noble art of self-defence as we know it in the West,
although "kick-boxing" is in fact now rapidly becoming established here too. The boxer punches and kicks any area of the
body which his opponent may offer to him. Stomach and kid-
ney regions are the main targets. Only in recent years have
scratching, strangling, biting and spitting been prohibited.
When an important contest is being staged in the Bangkok
National Boxing Stadium on a Saturday night the whole nation
is glued to television sets, and tickets are usually sold out well
in advance.

Muay Thai
(Thai boxing)

Religion

More than ninety-two per cent of the population of Thailand,
equivalent to 51 million people, is Buddhist, most of them
believing in the doctrine of the "small vehicle", while some
twelve per cent adhere to Mahayana Buddhism, whose teachings are described as the "large vehicle", or sometimes Ther-
awada Buddhism. The founder himself, the Buddha, is
worshipped rather than prayed to.

General

While Buddhism is the state religion in Thailand others are
officially recognised. These include Hindus (mainly Indian),
Islamites (chiefly Malays from southern Thailand) and of
course Christians. Only 0·4 per cent of the population is of no
religious persuasion.

Buddha – the name comes from the Sanskrit and, roughly
translated, means "The Enlightened One" – was born about
563 B.C. in Nepal at the foot of the Himalayas, the son of a rich
landowner, and given the name Siddharta Gautama. His father
also took the title of King so that his offspring grew up as
members of a noble line with the name Sakya.
Although he spent his childhood in the lap of luxury, on his
three travels Siddharta became acquainted with human sorrow, when he first encountered an extremely old man, then a
sick person and finally experienced a bereavement. The way he
was to lead the remainder of his life was decided for him when,
on his fourth journey, he met a hermit who persuaded the

Buddhism

thirty-year old to give up the life he had been leading and to become a travelling ascetic seeking answers to questions about the reasons for man's existence on Earth. Legend sets out to prove how serious a decision this must have been for him by explaining that, on the very day he set out, a son was born to him.

After seven years wandering in the wilderness, meditating profoundly and seeking a middle path between abundance and ascesis, it was in his thirty-fifth year that finally, having passed through the Four Stages of Contemplation, he reached the State of Enlightenment under a pipal tree by the River Nerajara in India. He preached his first sermon in the Indian town of Benares, using as his text the principles of the Four Holy Truths, "This is Suffering", "This is the Cause of Suffering", "This is the Solution to Suffering" and "The Way to Abolish Suffering". Three months after delivering this sermon the number of his disciples had grown to sixty, and he sent them out into the land with the words "Spread the joyful message to everyone you meet; no two of you are to take the same road!" During the fourty-five years that followed he travelled throughout India spreading his teachings of the "Wheel of Law" (dharmacak-rapravartana). Through the strength of his merciful love he was able to avoid attempts by his cousin Devadatta to murder him, for instance by inciting elephants to charge at him. Although Buddhist tradition has it that in the year 543 B.C., in his 80th year, Buddha died and passed into Nirvana, a stage in which all earthly desires dissolve into a state of Beatitude and Eternal Rebirth, historians have in fact established the date of his death as 480 or 470 B.C.

However, the year 543 B.C. as the date of his death remains still one of the most important dates in the Buddhist calendar. The visitor to Thailand will often come across a date arrived at by adding together the year in which Buddha died and the normal Western "anno domini" date: for example, 1992 becomes 2535 (1992 + 543) in countries practising the Buddhist religion.

Principles

The principles stem from the Hindu religion, from which it derived the concept of Karma, the invincible Law of the Cosmos. Karma means that the sum of a person's actions in one of his successive states of existence must be paid for in the next. Good deeds will be rewarded by a better existence in the next life. This constant cycle of lives is inevitable; Buudha himself reported that he had to complete more than 500 life cycles in varying forms. In simple terms, however, an individual can be influenced by each of these separate existences while basing his own life more or less on the principles laid down by Buddha. Those normally nearest to Nirvana, however, are the monks residing in the monasteries, who devote their whole lives to the study of Buddha's teachings. This explains why monks in Thailand are held in such high esteem.

The difference between Mahayana and Hinayana Buddhism lies in the possibilities of breaking out from the Birth–Death–Rebirth cycle. While Hinayana Buddhism maintains that every Believer must attain this state without any assistance, Mahayana Buddhism which evolved in the 1st and 2nd c. A.D. included some Bodhisattvas, men who had already reached the State of Enlightenment but remained unrecognised on Earth to show others the "Eightfold Path of Knowledge" and the true road to Nirvana. Even Buddha himself, after completing his 500 life-cycles of Birth, Death and Rebirth, became a Bodhisattva before finally entering Nirvana.

It was in the 3rd c B.C. that the first Buddhist monks, sent out by the Indian ruler Ashoke, arrived in the Nakon Pathom region, and it was here that the doctrine taught today evolved. The laws laid down by the Enlightened One became intermixed with elements of Hinduism, such as the Indian image of the world. One of the many versions of this image of the world stems from King Loei Thai (1299–1347). according to him the world exists within an infinite space, and is itself broken up into a material world, another pure in form and yet a third composed of intangible things. In the material world are the cold and hot Hells, and above it a flat world, with Mount Meru as its centre, inhabited by men, animals and spirits. The uppermost of the worlds is that of the Deities, who are in a state of meditation lasting thousands of years and have laid aside all physically recognisable forms. Above these three worlds lies Nirvana, which man is incapable of describing because it is totally beyond his powers of imagination. While pure Buddhist teaching made no reference to gods as such, over the centuries doctrines evolved which served gods of related religions, such as Hinduism.

As a result parts of Hindu mythology became absorbed, such as the trinity of Brahma, the Founder of the Universe, Shiva, the god with the third eye threatening disaster, or Vishnu, the Benefactor, Guardian and Redeemer. These also appear in the Buddhist religion in various different incarnations, for example Vishnu as Rama, the main hero of the epic poem "Ramayana".

Actually a feature of Animism, spirits play an important part in Thai religious life. The individual is divided into three parts, the material body (Kai), an own and a free spirit (Winyan and Khwan). If the person succeeds in tying the Khwan down inside the body this will result in good health, well-being and a successful career. This is the reason why small children have a piece of wool tied round their wrist, in order to attach the Khwan to the body. After illness or death the Khwan is able to leave the body, but will sometimes wander restlessly around seeking a living being in which to make its home. At every Buddhist funeral a lavish rite is performed in order to prevent the Khwan returning to earth. The mountain peoples of northern Thailand attach even more importance to spirits and perform special animistic rites.

Belief in spirits

The visitor will be sure to see some little buildings said to house spirits, built rather like a temple (Wat) and of animistic origin. Thais are normally extremely mistrustful of anything concerning Heaven and Earth. Buddhism is however a sufficiently tolerant religion to allow widespread Animism, or belief in spirits. The rites practised are mainly quite unfathomable to the lay visitor. Nevertheless, a visit for instance to the Erawan Shrine or Lak Muang, both in Bangkok, could be worthwhile. Here – paying due respect and keeping a suitable distance – the visitor can observe Thais practising their religion. At the rear of the little spirit house will be found a wooden or clay figure representing Phra Phum. The houses are often brightly lit at night, and during the day Thais can be seen bringing rice, tea, orchids or other gifts, seeking the blessing of the good spirits. The Erawan Shrine (see entry) on Rama I Road in Bangkok, which is visited daily by many hundreds of Thais, is actually only a

Houses for spirits

Miniature portal of the wiharn, the outer sanctum

spirit-house, but enjoys special deference. It is in these little spirit-houses, known in Thai as Saan Phra Phum, that the power of the spirits in deciding one's animistic future is revealed.

Phra Phum is everyone's true everyday comforter, since he actually lives with people – not under their roof, it is true, or in the shadow of a house, but very close by, usually on the northern side, so that he is never overshadowed. As guardian spirit of the household his dwelling is an artistically-fashioned wooden or papier-mâché shrine set on a post at eye-level with a narrow platform round it to hold the virtually daily offerings he receives. On special occasions – at times of illness, birth, debt or the hope of winning first prize in the lottery – he finds his share of serviceable or entertaining tributes enriched by delicately fashioned paper or wooden horses and elephants, slaves and dancing girls.

Phra Phum himself, leaning against the back wall of his little house, fly-swatter in one hand and a big book in the other, can observe and watch over all that goes on through his open front portal; he enters family events in his register and punishes lack of respect with nightmares and sometimes even burglaries or fires.

There are, of course, both evil spirits and good ones, earth spirits (Phra Phum) as well as house spirits (Phi Ruan). In and around the house alone live nine spirits. If recognised as such, good spirits are accepted into the family, while evil spirits find their home in Saan Phra Phum, where they are pacified every day by means of suitable offerings. Evil spirits are thought to be mainly dead people who have been denied rebirth and a further step towards entry into Nirvana.

The astrologer alone can tell where a spirit house should be and the time it and everyone else should move in; it may well be just before work begins on a new house, road or other building, so that the spirits have time to get accustomed to their new abode. On streets spirit-houses are usually positioned at dangerous spots where accidents often occur. As these are, of course, caused by evil spirits it goes without saying that a Saan Phra Phum is needed . . .

Almost every Thai believer enters a monastery at some time in his life. Until 1945 this was for a minimum period of three months, but now the – normally young – Thai needs to spend only a few weeks there to enhance his knowledge of the teachings of Buddha. Previously one had to be at least 20 years of age; now even boys can be seen in the temple, beginning their education there and being accepted as novices when they reach the age of fifteen. The estimated number of monks (Bikkhu) for the whole of Thailand is about 200,000.

Monks

Even as novices the boys have to keep the three most important rules applied to monks: they must give up all earthly possessions and beg for their living, inflict no sorrow or suffering on any fellow creature, and deny themselves any sexual pleasures. The novice is allowed to bring in only the eight utensils of an ascetic – the monk's staff made in three sections, a needle, a razor to shave his head, a strainer for water, an alms-dish and a string of 108 beads which he allows to run through his fingers during meditation.

In the early mornings in particular the streets of Bangkok are studded with groups of monks in their saffron-yellow robes (Kasaya) and shaven heads. They collect their food for the day

Buddhist monks in the monastery

which they place in cotton bags, but it is not really true to call this begging, because the Buddhist faithful are happy to contribute their share of the food the monks need, as by so doing they are helping to save their own souls, and they give thanks for it by making a "Wai", placing the hands together in a respectful sign of greeting.

The monks are not allowed to take anything which has previously been touched by a woman's hand, but this rule was not actually imposed by Buddha himself, as a matter of fact it was some time after his death when people tried to accuse him of having said that women have only a very small part to play in the world's affairs. Nevertheless, even today a monk will decline food or money proffered by a woman. Nuns, or Maetschis, also live in the monasteries. They are not subject to the same rules as the monks, and are allowed to carry money and manage the running of the monastery.

Islam

There are about 1·7 million Muslims in Thailand, 99 per cent Sunnites and one per cent Shiites, mainly of Malay-Arab origin and living mostly in southern Thailand. In the whole of the country there are over 2000 mosques, 100 of them in Bangkok, and 200 Koranic schools. King Bhumibol has been personally responsible for having the Koran translated into Thai, and he or his representative takes part in the annual birthday celebrations of the Prophet Mahomet. The King also appoints a high-ranking Muslim dignitary to the Senate to be responsible for all matters pertaining to the Muslim community. Muslim officials have a half-day off on Fridays to attend the religious service known as Djum'a, and also get a one-off four months' paid holiday to make the pilgrimage to Mecca. To avoid conflicts with the Muslim community the Thai government has prohibited publication of Salmon Rushdie's "Satanic Verses".

Christianity

Christianity was introduced in the 16th and 17th c. by Portuguese, Spanish and French Jesuits. Thailand has a total of about 220,000 Christians, who are highly regarded for their charitable and social work and the way in which they run, with the blessing of the State, orphanages and old-people's homes, hospitals and deaf-and-dumb schools and the like. One of the oldest Catholic churches is the "Kalawa", built in Neo-Gothic style and one of Bangkok's 50 or so churches, half of them Protestant and half Catholic, which have been built since the 1950s in the Thai style. Also of interest is the Cathedral of Notre Dame, built by French Christians in Chanthaburi and the largest Christian church in the country. The German-speaking community in Bangkok runs a boarding-school for youngsters from socially deprived backgrounds and gives them a proper education. Other reformist faiths are also active in Thailand and run a number of charitable organisations.

Hinduism and
allied doctrines

Believers in Hinduism and allied doctrines total 22,000. The cosmopolitan thinking present within the Thai government and set out in the 1978 Constitution is illustrated by the great measure of freedom they enjoy. Hindi, Sanskrit and English are taught in Hindu schools alongside the obligatory Thai curriculum, and the beturbanned Sikhs maintain an undenominational school for all castes of the socially underprivileged, and run caring services for the elderly and the sick.

Religious Practices

For a man his greatest event – mostly before marriage – is his entry into the Buddhist Order of a temple. It is as much a feast for family and neighbours (especially the eve of the temple ceremony) as it is a religious celebration. Long before the event the young man makes the rounds of all relatives and neighbours, asking them to forgive his "misdeeds". On the eve of the ordination the whole neighbourhood (in Bangkok the congregation of the temple in question) will assemble en masse, bringing at least one and often two orchestras along with them. One orchestra will consist largely of mature players, but the other will be made up of the guest of honour's friends and contemporaries, and may include jazz and pop in its repertoire. While the young people and their families stroll in the lamplight along the street or by the water's edge, feasting on rice and sweetmeats from gigantic cooking-pots, the older relatives and neighbours assemble in the home of the "Siddharta's" parents where he, in princely garb, stretches out on the floor, with just his head or elbow resting on a silk cushion, in front of a white-clad Brahmin (always an Indian), who reminds the young man once more of all the good things his parents have done for him. The Brahmin has previously been given the details by neighbours and relations and, for a fee, has made them up into celebratory poems. Now they all sit and listen on the hard floor around him and the young man, breaking off from their betel-chewing, cigarette-smoking and tea-drinking on hearing of some particularly meritorious deed (Tambun) to utter an approving "Huuii", with the young man more often than not emmitting a grateful and penitent sob. This ceremony lasts

Buddhist ordination

The family circle on the eve of a Buddhist ordination

several hours until midnight. The room contains only a triple-decked altar and a plaited-paper "Naga" or "Naag", the seven-headed snake which once shielded the meditating Buddha from the rain and asked to be admitted to his Order (Sangha). Although this was refused, the "Naag" still has the consolation of knowing that everyone on the eve of ordination is called by its name.

The celebration is resumed at an early hour the following morning, with all the friends and relations colourfully processing to the temple, singing and dancing to the sound of drums. If there is no princely steed available the "Naag" is carried on the shoulders of his peers. The others bear gifts which are piled up in transparent golden paper on silver trays, and include a number of small but useful items which the young man needs for his future monastic life. The ceremonial head-shaving then takes place in the temple itself. On the third day there the young man will receive his saffron-yellow robe from his fellow monks. This occasion is excuse enough for the family to continue the celebrations without the presence of the novice himself.

Funerals

Again, as with the ordination, this is another family occasion demanding the presence of monks. The next-of-kin, dressed in mourning black or white, gather for a full seven days around the body to hear the sutras of the monks sitting in a row on raised padded seats or on a podium. On the day of the cremation – which can be as much as a year later, depending on how high a person's rank is – the mourners assemble in the temple precincts and receive little straw stars which, in a symbolic act, they throw to form a funeral pyre piled up with wood under a magnificent paste pagoda, which is then ignited by the most exalted guest. Only the next-of-kin attend the actual cremation,

Pra Puûm, God of Gods

Mae Toranii, Mother Earth

which is often only a few metres distant from the burning pyramid.

With Buddha's express toleration, providing there is no harm to either his teaching or a living creature, the countless gods, while in fact ranked below the great teacher, are not deprived of their consoling power for people's lesser everyday concerns. Whereas a Brahmin will be called in for major family events, for blessing the harvest and on the eve of a monk's ordination, everyday hope and consolation is normally sought from the stone and marble Hindu gods. For them more modest offerings will suffice, such as a few scented candles, a garland of flowers (Pyan Malai) and, naturally, a humble show of respect.
Tao Maha Prom, the many-armed god (on the corner of the Erawan Hotel) is especially venerated; however, Erawan, the triple-headed elephant (in front of the Academy of Arts, next to the National Theatre) and Phra Mae Torani, the Earth Mother (in the shrine opposite the Royal Hotel Klong) are also very popular. Blessings flow with the water flowing through her hair during the Loy Kratong Festival in November, the high point of her worship (see Practical Information, Events)

In the evening at every red traffic-light there are children trying to sell motorists Pyan Malai, the beautifully woven garlands of sweet-smelling jasmine, orchids or roses. They are hung around the necks of people who have passed their exams or who have been given an honorary title, to bring them luck, but are also, as a token of respect, laid at the feet of statues of Buddha or that most earthly of all the animist spirits, Phra Phum.

Animism

Garlands of flowers

Temples

Although the country's religious architecture clearly bears the stamp of the various Kings of Thailand as reflected in the religious views held at the time, almost all the temple complexes show the influence of foreign cultures as well. Missionaries or merchants trading with Thailand have left Indian and Singalese designs in their wake. For centuries the Khmer dictated the style of temple architecture along their trade routes which led them through Thailand, although over the years those in the north-east were largely abandoned and allowed to fall into decay. In the north it is the magnificently embellished buildings left by the Burmese and Laotians which are still copied today. Finally, in the 19th c., European styles were introduced, a particularly fine example being Wat Benchamabophit (see entry) in Bangkok.
In temple-building, however, the same thing happened as in other forms of cultural expression – the Thais often copied from neighbouring countries, only to show themselves to be masters of the art of complementing and refining the styles of others. This explains why many temple complexes show a number of features from various eras.

India during the Gupta Period (A.D. 310–500) saw the development of the free-standing temple with a tower, which replaced those in caves or rocks. The "tower-temple" consists of a cube-shaped building on a square terrace. Above the main internal structure, the Cella, rises a tower, pyramidal in design

General

Bases of construction

and usually stepped, with relief decoration on the outside. On each of the four sides a staircase leads down to the terrace, while only one side is accesible from the Cella. The oldest remaining examples of Indian tower-temples are the Shiva Temple at Geogarh, built in about the 5th c. A.D., with a tower about 13m/43ft high, the brick-built temple of Bhitargao near Khanpur, also 5th c., and the Buddhist Mahabodhi temple – c. A.D. 562, tower 51m/168ft high – in Bodhgaya, where Buddha received Enlightenment. The Wiharn in Wat Chet Yot in Chiang Mai is a smaller copy of the latter.

Hindu temples

Later an assembly hall, called a mandapa, was added to the cella, and then a covered walk (antarala) was created between the cella and the mandapa. The cella porches (gopuras) were richly decorated. This established the basic form of a Hindu temple which was further developed into an architectural style of its own and its external features were altered. Some elements of this style of temple building are still to be found in the Thai wat.

Khmer temples

The influence of the Khmer, who imported their art and building styles into Thailand from neighbouring Cambodia, can still be seen today, especially in the north of the country. Along their trade routes, which passed through Thailand to Burma and Laos, buildings of high architectural quality sprung up, such as the temple at Phimai. From this city in north-eastern Thailand a road 240km/150 miles long led to Angkor, the capital of the kingdom of Khmer, with its holy sanctum Angkor Wat, which is still woven in legend today.

Phimai was built at a time when Mahayana Buddhism was at its height. Based on Hindu temples, the most important religious buildings were arranged around a central sanctum, called the Prasat by the Khmer. Also taken from the Hindu designs were the perambulatories, library and fortifications and the separation of the individual areas by walls.

The basic features of construction used in Hindu and Khmer temples can be seen in many temple complexes in Thailand, but there are clear differences to be found in the way the craftsmen decorated the interiors of the holy buildings. For example, the Khmer restricted themselves to working – albeit displaying superb artistic skills – in sandstone, whereas the Thais used a great variety of materials, such as wood, glass, porcelain and stone.

The word "wat" is often translated as monastery, and this is largely correct. Like medieval monasteries, the wats of Thailand provide refuge and accommodation, as well as being schools, hospitals or orphanages. In addition, however, a town's wat is often the place where festivals are celebrated. The complex is divided into the sacral area and the monks' living quarters, normally separated from one another by a wall, known as the Kampeng Kheo, or "wall of jewels". The monks' quarters (khana), the large assembly hall (wiharn), a courtyard with chapels around it, the actual temple (bot), usually standing on a terrace and surrounded by a wall, and the working areas all combine to form the temple complex. In addition, depending on the size, there may be a library, known as the Ho Trai, or triple basket, in which the Sutra (writings of the teachings of Buddha) are kept, as well as one or more cloisters where the monks can stroll and meditate.

Again depending on the size of the temple precincts there may be more than one wiharn, each named after the Buddha statue it contains.

The holiest building in the temple is the bot, or ubosot. This is where the monks' ordination is celebrated and only they are allowed to worship here; lay people must use the wiharn. Eight boundary-stones (semas) surround the holy precinct and separate it from the unconsecrated ground around it; they are usually pointed in shape and decorated with reliefs, mainly scenes from the life of Buddha. The bot itself is a long, rectangular building, with windows on the longer sides and the entrance always at the east end. Larger bots will have several entrances, one always larger than the others, as well as a covered walk which often contains statues of Buddha. The front of a bot is normally decorated with magnificent, gilded carvings, the finest examples being found in northern Thailand. It is a feature of these that the stout walls and columns usually taper towards the top.

Bot (Ubosot)

In the larger buildings the interior is divided into three naves, whereas the smaller have only one. On the west side, opposite the entrance, will be found the Buddha figure held in the most reverence, often surrounded by a number of other statues, garlands of flowers, offerings and a vessel full of sand in which the faithful place their joss-sticks. The atmosphere of the room is determined by the harmonious colour schemes in red, gold, blue and black as much as by the fine proportions and the fan-like timberwork, often complemented by a superbly ornate coffered ceiling. The wall-paintings normally depict scenes from the life of Buddha or from one of his earlier lives (Jataka). Particularly fine are the portals to temples in northern Thailand which are usually modelled on Burmese examples. Bodies of Naga serpents form a balustrade, their heads covered in numerous tiny glass mosaics.

Similar to the bot is the wiharn, where lay people come to offer their devotions. It, too, houses one or more statues of Buddha and is often tastefully decorated. Larger temples often have more than one wiharn.

Wiharn

Salas are small, open halls built in the Thai style, with their roofs supported on columns. They are found at various places in the temple precincts, and provide resting-places for visitors.

Sala

The Ho Trai is the library containing holy scriptures and cult objects. It has a high, square substructure which protects the books from vermin and damp, and which is partly surrounded by a peristyle. A temple may have one or several Ho Trais, depending on its importance.

Ho Trai

The roofs of temple buildings are in the shape of stepped pyramids and inlaid with small, multicoloured mosaics; the spire symbolises a stylised naga serpent winding its way up to heaven. The internal walls are often broken up by rich sculpture, e.g. in Wat Phra Kheo in Bangkok (see entry). Small bells suspended from the roof-ledges tinkle softly in every breeze; the noise is produced not by clappers but by little metal discs cut like the heart-shaped leaves of the holy Bodhi tree.

Roofs

The prasat, mostly a tall building with a peristyle, is like a Greek cross in plan and is normally surrounded by prangs on all four sides. It is the classical building form of the Khmer (Mon), much

Prasat

of which has been preserved, especially in north-eastern Thailand. Particularly fine examples are to be found in Phimai as well as Wat Prasat Phanom Rung in Prakhon Chai. A tower rises from where the four multi-stepped roofs converge. If the building is used for religious cult or memorial purposes, like the Pantheon in Wat Phra Kheo, it becomes a prang; if it serves as, say, an audience chamber for the King or a chapel of rest, like the Dusit Maha Prasat in the Grand Palace in Bangkok (see entry), the tower ends in a spire, as on a Mondhop.

Particularly important temples are also labelled (wat) Phra Mahathat, or "Temple of the Great Holy Relic". Every royal city has or had at least one such Wat Phra Mahathat which housed in its chedi or prang a relic of Buddha, such as hair, bone or tooth. These relics are walled-up and not open to inspection by anybody.

Chedi and Prang

The building which stands out and towers above the others is the chedi or prang, a typical feature of the Thai Wat. The chedi (Chaitya in Sanskrit) is a variation on the Indian stupa and the Singalese dagoba, the shapes of which are as laid down in one of the last requests made by Buddha. When during his last hours, some of his disciples asked him what visible memorials should be erected to him he replied "Small hills of sand or rice, something which everybody needs".

The Indian stupa and thus also the Thai chedi developed from a burial mound covering the remains of holy monks. The oldest Stupas are said to have been built by King Ashoke (273–231 B.C.), for example, the four in Pattan in Nepal. The oldest include those in Anarudhapura in Sri Lanka (3rd c. B.C.), where they were called Dagobas.

Stupas, prangs and chedis are not churches but cult-buildings not open to the layman, which contain the relics of Buddha and are designated as clearly defined memorials to Buddhism. In Burma, Nepal, Java or Bali the stupa is known as pagoda, in Laos as "that". Basically it is shaped like a semi-circle or bell and made of brick (anda), then rendered or stuccoed, with a square superstructure surmounted by a multi-stepped "parasol" roof, the symbol of holiness (chattra). The largest chedis of particularly holy temples are crowned by a gilded spire, sometimes even one of pure gold.

In order to show due deference to Buddha it is customary to walk round stupas and chedis in a clockwise direction, using a terrace surrounded by a stone balustrade. There are four large gateways in all four sides of the balustrade, and the building itself is decorated with rich sculptures.

The chedi provides the best example of how the original Indian design became changed. Whereas the classical stupa is bulbous and almost plump in shape, the Thai chedi is like a bell, with the upper part – with the central section often in the form of rings – coming to a point which, originally shaped like a lotus-flower, became even more slender as the years went by, and gave the original stupa that degree of elegance normally associated with Thailand.

Basically, a chedi can be divided into three sections, the substructure (maluva), the anda or garbha (where the central section is round) or harmika (where it is square), and the spire made up of "parasols" laid one on top of the other, sometimes gilded. The terraced substructure has niches containing statues of the Buddha. Whereas the Sukhotai style of chedi often has elephant figures at each of the four corners the Burmese model more often has lions. The anda, mostly round or bell-shaped, and faithful to the Indian or Singalese model, may serve to symbolise the firmament of Heaven or the all-embracing principle of Enlightenment, the Harmika portrays the sanctum above the world and beyond death and reincarnation, while the stylised "parasol" roof is a sign of holiness. Sometimes the individual sections melt so subtly one into the other that it is difficult to distinguish them.

The interior of a chedi often houses Buddha relics and sometimes also those of kings or particularly holy monks, for example, their ashes.

The prang was also evolved from the Indian model, during the long period in which the Khmer ruled Thailand. The silhouette above the base is slender and tapers only very slightly towards its peak. Other prangs, on the other hand, are very stocky in design. Usually the prang also contains a reliquary chamber with a roofed porch situated in the centre of the building, with a flight of steps leading up to it. Prangs are mostly tastefully decorated and adorned with sculptures; the most impressive example is that of Wat Arun in Bangkok.

Before entering a shrine shoes must be removed; it is considered highly improper to wear them when facing a statue of the Buddha (see Practical Information, Thai society and the visitor).	Tip
In the cambaria, one of the most important but plainest of the buildings in a wat, the monks preach sermons from a pulpit between noon and 1pm.	Cambaria
In the khana, where the monks actually live, their quiet, reserved and strictly regulated daily life can be observed. Visitors are usually welcome here and will often become engaged in conversations with English-speaking monks on the origin, calling, age and reasons behind their stay in Thailand. However, visitors should respect the silence and reserve observed by the monks and not disturb it by unruly behaviour of any kind.	Khana (monks' living quarters)
Suan literally means "garden", and is open not just to people but also to poultry, ownerless dogs and grazing cattle: good examples of this in Bangkok are seen at Wat Chai, on the road from Sanaam Luang Royal Square leading between Chakraphong and Phra Athit Road. Such temple gardens, usually containing bodhi trees decorated in yellow or saffron-coloured ribbons, are treated with special reverence. According to legend, it was under one such tree that Buddha received Enlightenment. The Bodhi trees found in Thailand are said to be saplings from the parent tree in northern India. Some temple gardens tend to resemble a market, offering for sale souvenirs as well as food and drink. The faithful followers of Buddha are keen to buy little birds in wooden cages which are thought to help them to attain spiritual salvation. In rural areas the suan is also the place where community festivals are keenly celebrated and public meetings held.	Suan (Garden)
A wat will also have a bell-tower, the ho rakang, with a swinging drum or gong hanging in the lower floor.	Ho rakang
Frequently you will see – either at the entrances to the temple complex or at the approach to the wiharn or bot – dschaks (temple guards of Chinese origin) kinnari (bird-maidens), garudas (Vishnu's steeds) and other figures, almost all from Hindu mythology.	Temple figures

Famous People

Peter Veit
Musician
(1883–1968)

Peter Veit, the son of a Thai mother and a German from Trier who taught music at the court, was appointed Royal Music Expert (Phra Chen Duriyang) as a young man by King Chulalongkorn (Rama V). He was the first to transpose Thai music into notation, thus preserving a valuable national and cultural asset, and he also composed the royal hymn in 1932, the national anthem of the Thais (literally, the Free).

Alma Link
Benefactress
(1898–1964)

After being educated and trained as a nurse in Russia, Germany and England, with stops in London, Manila, Bangkok and Baghdad, in 1939 she married Herbert Link, a German industrialist based in Bangkok. It was here that she embarked on her life's work, and founded Thailand's Cheshire Home. Group Captain Leonard Cheshire was an RAF officer who witnessed the raid on Hiroshima. Subsequent stays in a military hospital convinced him that the terminally ill without sufficient income and caring relatives needed a "home", a familiar place to turn to. Alma Link was responsible for the establishment in 1965 of Thailand's first Cheshire Home, which transformed these ideas into a practical programme. Alma Link is the first, and so far the only, foreign woman to have had the honorary title of "Khunying" bestowed upon her.

Naowarat Pongpaibool
Poet
(b. 26.3.1940)

In 1980 the ASEAN (Association of Southeast Asian Nations) annual prize for literature was bestowed by Queen Sirikit on the 40-year old Thai poet Naowarat Pongpaibool. A law graduate in 1963 from Bangkok University, he was at Prince Soongkla University in southern Thailand 1971 – 72, and today is Director of Bangkok's Bank Museum. His main interests, after many months as a monk, are Buddhism, traditional Thai music and social problems. It is difficult to translate his finest works into European tongues. Connoisseurs of Far Eastern culture may well follow the alliteration, tone music, rich symbolism – the moon as the face of the beloved, cold and wind as kindness, etc. – but these are virtually untranslatable.

The Princess Mother
(b. 21.10.1900)

The mother of Rama VIII and Rama IX, the present King, is highly revered throughout Thailand. Still very active at over 90, she was not born into a noble family but at the age of 18, because of her outstanding performance in her nursing exams, she was sent on a royal scholarship to continue her studies, especially in preventive medicine, in the USA, where in Boston, Massachusetts, she met the doctor who later became her husband, Prince Mahidol. She is known as the "Royal Mother from the Sky" (Mae Fa Luang) in many of the remote villages of the northern mountain tribes, which is not a religious phrase but one meant literally, for on her first visit in 1964 (and many subsequent ones) she swooped down in a hitherto unknown "Bird from the Sky", i.e. a helicopter. It was the start of her campaign to bring medical care to even the remotest parts of the country. In this way the Princess Mother is said to have helped at least 700,000 sick peasants (90% of Thailand's doctors are in Bangkok), and over 22,000 are proud to number themselves among her voluntary helpers. Once a year she

Alma Link (left), Dr Pierra Vajabul (right), both honorary "Khunying"

allows herself a holiday in Switzerland to collect flower and vegetable seeds, which are then sown in Thailand's northern mountains to replace the opium poppies that grew there.

Rama I, or Phra Phuttayodfa Chulalok as he was also called, reigned from 1782 to 1809, and saw himself as creating anew the self-confidence and unity of the Ayutthaya kingdom and continuing its expansion as well as preserving its cultural and spiritual legacy. A punitive expedition against Burma succeeded in winning him back Sukkothai and Chiangmai, and extended his realm as far as Trengganu in what is now Malaysia. In founding the new capital he wished to fashion Bangkok in the style of Ayutthaya, its predecessor, and in order to create the former "Venice of the East" he ordered the digging of countless canals (including Krung Kasem Klong). He ordered Wat Suthat to be built to house the guilded Buddha carried off from Sukkothai, modelling it on Wat Phanam Choeng in Ayutthaya. His own palace complex, which had suffered a fire, was rebuilt with the niche high in the wall for the audience throne – Dusit Maha in the Grand Palace. As preserver of the spiritual legacy, Rama I reassembled the holy scriptures of Buddhism and produced a new edition of the "Ramakien" (or the Indian "Ramayana"), enlarging upon the religious and Court ceremonial of the Ayutthaya period. He was also responsible for the recodification of the laws into the Law of the Three Seals.

Rama I
(1737–1809)

When Rama I died in 1809 he was succeeded on the Throne of Siam by his son Phra Phuttaloetla (Rama II) who, while continuing his father's temple building programme also started the building of the present Wat Arun, commencing with the founding of the monastery complex. His particular interest, however,

Rama II
(1768–1824)

53

The Princess Mother, the "Royal Mother from the Sky"

was literature and he wrote a shortened version of his father's "Ramakien", brought the poet Sunthorn Phu to his Court, and together with him produced the romance "Inao" and the opera "Kung Chan – Khun Phaen". In 1818 it was Rama II who for the first time in 130 years resumed official relations with Europeans.

Rama III
(1788–1851)

Rama III succeeded his father at the age of 36 and ruled his kingdom, then known as Siam, from 1824 to 1851. While trade and economic co-operation with China blossomed to its fullest extent during his reign (Chinese were granted concessions for sugar plantations and tin mines in southern Thailand), politically he was increasingly under threat from European and American attempts at colonisation.

Rama IV
(1804–68)

Rama IV was 47 when, as Prince Mongkut, he succeeded to the throne on the death of his half-brother, having spent the previous 27 years as a monk both wandering about Siam and as Abbot of Wat Bovornives, where he founded the Dhammayuttika Order which, in its dark-brown robes, can still be seen today. Unlike his predecessors who had grown up in the palace and been surrounded all their lives by courtiers, he was familiar with the cares and needs of every level of society. He has gone down in history as renewing the Buddhist faith by having the Pali source texts translated and taking the faithful back to the original teachings. His country's greatest debt to him, however, was that because of his astute and speedy diplomacy, the colonial threat to Thailand was averted. The King was able to react in this way because not only did he have knowledge of the West, he had also studied Western languages, having learnt

Rama IV

Rama V

Peter Veit

English from American missionaries and Latin from a Catholic bishop. And anyone familiar with the "King and I" will know he employed an English governess to teach his children.

The King's hobby was astrology, which indirectly was also the cause of his death. In 1868 he predicted a full eclipse of the sun and while observing this in swampland he caught malaria and died.

Rama V, also known as Chulalongkorn (the Great), succeeded his father at the age of 16. Favourably disposed to Western ways, one of his first official acts was to declare all his subjects "Thais", i.e. freemen and dispensing with their customary obligation to prostrate themselves before their King as an act of homage, though, in fact many Thais continue this practice.

Rama V
(Chulalongkorn;
1853–1910)

In 1905, the King, considered Thailand's greatest reformer, abolished all forms of slavery. He was, however, also aware of the difficulties of emancipation, for earlier in 1874, when he had freed the children of slaves, he had said, "what is most needed today for the slaves is food and a roof over their heads; they have never been able to learn how to look after themselves", so now he ordered that every personal service had to be paid for, since the slave masters had to change their way of thinking, too.

Particularly close to Rama V's heart as King was the economic development of his country: he established a national communications network, introducing the country's first postal service and the first railways, sent young Thais to study in Europe and America, while bringing in hundreds of scientists and engineers from abroad (preferably from countries with no colonial interests, including Germany, Switzerland, Austria, Italy and Scandinavia). He adopted the law of the French and the commercial law of the English, but his consultative council held a number of Thai, Japanese and Dutch advisers.

The King's political strategy secured his country peace, freedom and independence. Through diplomatic channels he ceded to France and England a large area of his country (Laos, Cambodia and four – now Malay – provinces), that had been conquered over a period of 650 years by his forefathers. Although the ceded area was twice the size of Austria he sacrificed not a single soldier for its defence, and in return France and England accepted that Siam should be left untouched and act as a buffer State between their Asian colonies.

Rama VI
(Vajiravudh;
1881–1925)

Rama VI, an Oxford graduate, succeeded his father as King at the age of 19 in 1918, and ruled until 1925, carrying on his father's modernisation programme (work on the rail network, electrification and water supply), and forming a Western-trained staff of advisers, while having Thais study and train in Europe. He continued the Europeanisation of Thailand with the founding of an English-style Boys' College and Boy Scouts. He also changed the national flag from a white elephant on a red ground to a copy of the French tricolour (blue, white and red). The young King, with his Western education, translated the plays of Shakespeare and Molière into Thai, wrote several dramas about his own country's heroes and heroines, and founded 20 newspapers, of which two were published in Chinese, two in English and the rest in Thai. He himself made critical and thought-provoking contributions to these papers under a variety of pseudonyms.

In domestic policy he earned a name for himself by introducing compulsory education for four years and in his foreign policy he demonstrated his support for the French-English Entente by dispatching to them his own personally trained 2000-strong Tiger Corps. This political ploy proved a shrewd move since it gained him Thailand's membership of the League of Nations.

Rama VII
(Prajadibok;
1893–1941)

Rama VI's relatively early death at the age of 46 brought his younger brother Prajadibok to the Throne as Rama VII (1925 –1935). Wholly unprepared when he assumed the monarchy, this King had little zest for reform. He appointed five older princes to be his Supreme Council, and this was to relieve him of most of the burden of government and to see that there was plenty of "blue blood" in high office.

His reign was marked by financial difficulties sparked off by the world economic situation, which impacted in full on the Thai economy. Britain left the Gold Standard, world recession set in and Thailand's rice exports, its main source of income, became too dear for the Sterling Area. Although the King twice cut back his Court's budget (by about 65% altogether), this brought many dismissals with it, besides salary reductions for civil servants and the Armed Forces. The young intellectuals and officers who had been encouraged by his predecessor to train in Europe found there was no work for them and thus also no opportunity to implement the governmental, economic and social reforms they wanted. Those who had returned from being educated in France and Germany proved particularly turbulent and with the bloodless revolution of 1932 Rama VII became the country's last absolute monarch, his sarcastic reaction to their ultimatum earning him positive fame: "in order to maintain national order, to prevent bloodshed and revolution I hereby declare myself prepared to become a puppet king and thus to make forming a new government easier". He died childless in 1941, having abdicated in 1935. He was succeeded by his nephew Ananda Mahidol, a nephew of Bhumibol, chosen by the government.

Famous People

Although he had been crowned King in 1935 at the age of 10, most of Rama VIII's royal functions were performed by a Regent, so that the young King could continue his education in Switzerland. At the end of the Second World War, however, the government asked him, now 20, to return home, as they put it, "for the sake of unity". Once back the young monarch spent several months travelling around his country getting to know his people, mostly accompanied by his younger brother, Bhumibol, (the present King).

Only four days before he was due to return to Europe to continue his studies, Rama VIII died in unexplained circumstances in his palace bedroom in Bangkok.

Rama VIII
(Ananda Mahidol;
1925–1946)

His Majesty ws born in Cambridge, USA, the youngest child of Prince Mahidol of Songka, the son of Rama V (Chulalongkorn). His mother, the Princess Mother, is highly esteemed in Thailand. After the early death of his father in 1929 his mother settled in Switzerland with the children, where they were given an international but entirely bourgeois upbringing in a democratic setting. The possibility of succeeding to the throne was wholly unlikely for the two boys, since Rama VII, the ruling monarch, was only in his mid-forties. His abdication in 1935, however, unexpectedly put 10-year-old Ananda (Rama VIII) on the throne, and after his sudden death Bhumibol found himself his successor. He changed his course of study from law and political science to natural sciences, and in 1950 returned to Thailand from Switzerland.

His official coronation was in Bangkok on 5 May 1950 and in 1951 he finally assumed the reins of government.

In what is now a reign of over 40 years, the King has become to be called by his subjects, with affection as much as respect, "Father of the People", and the greater part of his rule is taken up with visiting by rail, road and air, as well as on foot, all parts of his country, but especially those suffering natural disasters or in need of social aid.

His many development projects, which he also oversees personally, have made him the absolute embodiment of Thai integration, holding the country together and at peace.

His people demonstrated their gratitude to him by awarding him the title "the Great" in a referendum in May 1987. In honour of his 60th birthday (5.12.1987) crowds of 3 million attended a celebration in Bangkok.

Rama IX
(Bhumibol;
b. 5.12.1927)

The present Queen, daughter of a diplomat, was 15 when in Fontainebleau she made the acquaintance of an attractive fellow countryman called Bhumibol whose passions, apart from his study of natural sciences, were fast sports cars and jazz.

The sports car led to an accident which caused a severe eye injury but also, at his request, brought him a frequent visitor, Sirikit, to his bedside in Lausanne. After their engagement and marriage before returning to Bangkok in 1951 they were able to spend their last student year together. Like the rest of the Royal Family the Queen is also active in the social and charitable sphere. She is President of Thailand's Red Cross, as well as about 150 other private and public welfare organisations. She even combines her travel and holidays (in Hua Hin) with the introduction of socially necessary measures. She has been primarily responsible for promoting the cause of educationally and socially disadvantaged women and children, as well as to

Queen Sirikit
Somdech Phraborom
Rajininath
(b. 12.8.1932)

King Bhumibol with Queen Sirikit (left) and their daughters (right)

the new direction given to traditional craftsmenship (e.g. weaving skills). It is to her personal credit that the home products she promotes also find a market in other countries of the world.

Royal children

Ubol Ratana, the eldest daughter, has long since been married and lives abroad, having renounced all her rights and duties. The other three children are Prince Vajiralongkorn (b. 1952), Princess Sirindhorn (b. 1955) and Princess Chulabhorn (b. 1957).

Prince Vajiralongkorn, who has always had a military bent, has graduated from a military academy in Australia. His sister Sirindhorn was awarded the title "Maha Chakri" for her social, cultural and diplomatic commitment during her mother's illness, giving her equal status to the Prince. She is studying in Australia for a doctorate in archaeology. The youngest Princess Chulabhorn is studying agriculture and forestry at Chiang Mai and Bangkok.

In 1979 an amendment to the constitution broke with the 700-year-old tradition whereby only men of a certain age could ascend to the throne. With the consent of Parliament and the Crown Counsel any of the King's children may accede.

Chin Sophonpanich
Entrepreneur
(b. June 1910)

The 32-storey high Bayoke Tower, the second highest building in Bangkok, is the headquarters of the Bangkok Bank Ltd. and was consecrated in 1982 by the bank's founder Chin Sophonpanich on the occasion of his 72nd birthday, which was attended by over 4,000 guests from all over the world.

Born the son of Thai and Chinese parents in Bangkok, he was sent to study in Canton by his father. However, he returned home at 17 having run out of money with no other alternative than to do the same as thousands before him: carrying sacks of rice and cooking noodles in the Chinese quarter.

Four years later he had taken the first step up the ladder: he was manager of a small company selling building wood, tools and tinned food. During the Second World War he exported rice to Indonesia, opened up saw-mills and in 1944 founded the Bangkok Bank. Willing to take risks and trust an honest face, even if it belonged to someone in dirty shorts and sandals, he was prepared to give credit to people who had been turned down by "respectable" banks.

Today Chin is one of the wealthiest businessmen in southeast Asia with 140 firms and companies covering the whole range of commercial activity. Chin has business interests in Hong Kong and Singapore, his bank finances 40% of all Thailand's exports and controls a third of the banking business in Thailand. He still calculates exchange rates in his head – faster than a computer. And when others have just decided it is the right moment to make a profit on the commodity market his ships have long since set sail for their destination. His six sons attended the best universities in America, Britain and Australia and have taken over the day-to-day running of his businesses.

The Thai poet Sunthorn Phu is thought to have been born in Thonburi, his mother soon parting from his father to become a nanny at Court. Young Phu grew up in Wang Lang, a princely palace, where he learnt to read and write, and the basic art of poetry.

Sunthorn Phu
Poet
(1786–1855)

Sunthorn Phu had a definite inclination to "wine, women and song" – Thai verse is closely related to song in any case. This tendency led him to assume a wandering existence, constantly moving between monastery and the Court at Bangkok. He particularly frequented a monastery on the island of Klaeng, near Ravong, where his father had been abbot. Whereas Rama II had very much favoured Sunthorn Phu and had also involved him in reworking the "Ramakien" and other literary projects, with Rama III he fell out of favour. Then followed a wandering life when for 18 years he worked as a stage narrator, jobbing poet, alchemist and monk. His finest "Nirat" works date from this period. Honour and esteem were only his again under Rama IV, when he had even more exalted titles bestowed upon him (Phra Sunhorn Woharn).

The American architect James ("Jim") Thompson came to Bangkok after the Second World War as an officer in the secret service but soon resigned. He decided to settle in Bangkok and following a spell as the manager of the Oriental Hotel discovered the Thai art of silk-weaving. Thompson is responsible for the world-wide reputation enjoyed by Thai silk today. His modern methods of production combined the established techniques. Himself a gifted designer, he made an enormous contribution to the development of the Thai silk industry. After visiting his factories and spending an evening having dinner at his home the famous writer Somerset Maugham wrote in the visitor's book: "Not only have you created beautiful things but you have also exercised exquisite taste in building your unusual collection of art".

James ("Jim") Thompson
Architect
(1906–1974?)

Thompson travelled widely throughout Thailand bringing beautiful things back to Bangkok and rescuing them from decay. One of the finest examples of his passion for collecting are the traditional Thai houses which he had dismantled on their original site and rebuilt in the capital. Only now can his far-sightedness be appreciated as such well preserved wooden houses are found hardly anywhere else in the country.

At the height of his creativity Jim Thompson disappeared at the age of 61 in unexplained circumstances. During a short holiday in the Cameron Highlands of Malaysia he disappeared without trace in the afternoon of Easter Sunday 1967. Seven years later (1974) he was officially declared dead. His life's work is open to visitors and administered by a charitable trust.

Prateeg Ungsongtham
Educator
(b. 1951)

Definitely the youngest and by far the least academic person to receive the Far Eastern equivalent of the Nobel Prize, Prateep Ungsongtham was in 1978 awarded this distinction in Tokyo at the age of 27 "for personal effort in schooling slum-dwellers and their children".

Born herself into the "third biggest slum in the world", by Klong Toey waterfront, she managed to learn to read and write and at the age of 16 began giving lessons to children in her neighbourhood. When "illegal" schools were condemned to be driven off the sites where Prateep had set them up, the city fathers intervened and in 1974 requested her to carry on. Since "Miss" Prateep immediately put her prize-money, valued at about 10,000 US dollars, into a foundation, all Bangkok's civil servants think the world of her, and back her projects, as do many private benefactors.

There are now nearly 2000 schoolchildren and over a dozen properly qualified teachers sitting down to lessons in buildings of stone, something unheard of in a slum. "Kru" (Miss) Prateep has made Duang (gleam of light) Foundation with its "penny" school (at 1 baht a day) into a model for all the developing countries in Southeast Asia. Nowadays the curriculum also includes adult education, family planning, occupational training and lessons in health and hygiene. International and national donations help to provide scholarships, terms of monastic study, sports and leisure programmes, as well as measures to help prevent juvenile delinquency and cope with unemployment.

Pierra Vejabul
Doctor
(b. c. 1900)

Pierra Vejabul, Thailand's first woman doctor, had to leave home to achieve her professional ambition. She went to Paris where she paid for her studies by working as a cleaner. After graduation she spent some months in Berlin before returning to Bangkok in the early 1930s, where she was put in charge of the department for female venereal diseases. In those days the health authorities "tattooed" these women and girls, even when they were children of 14. This slight but forceful woman doctor put a stop to this practice and then took on all her patients' rejected babies as adopted children, for which her family name and honour were taken away from her (her present name means "good patient doctor" and was given her by the Royal House, as well as the honorary title of "Khunying").

Her orphanage, with its day nursery and infant school, has since seen about 3000 children grow up to adulthood, many of them entering the professions. She is still very active in the running of this orphanage, has her own practice, and also operates an occupational retraining centre on the edge of the city where prostitutes who are pregnant or want to change their way of life can go for education and training.

History

Origins of Ban Chiang culture in northern Thailand, of which little is known.	Around 7000 B.C.
Monks sent by Kong Ashoke to region around Nakhon Pathom to spread the word of Buddha.	Around 250 B.C.
Probable founding of first Thai empire in Yunnan (South China).	Around A.D. 600
The area that is modern Thailand is inhabited mainly by the Khmer. Some smaller areas in the north-east are occupied by people from Burma and what is now Kampuchea. These can be regarded as the earliest inhabitants of Thailand. Over the next centuries (until the 11th) they spread into Laos where they farm the fertile Mekong delta. A permanent state is not yet recognisable. Burmese Mon people develop a vibrant culture dominated by Buddhist elements (Theravada Buddhism).	A.D. 800 to 1100
Reinforcements move in from southern China, provoked by the bellicose behaviour of Ghengis Khan's successor, Kublai Khan.	Around A.D. 1200
Thai people found the first sovereign Kingdom of Siam.	1257
Reign of King Ramkhamhaeng in which Thai culture flourishes. He introduces the Thai alphabet, still used today, with elements of Indian Dewanagari script. Sukothai becomes the first capital of the new Kingdom of Siam.	1279–98
Mengrai conquers the Kingdom of Haripunchai. Further Thai principalities (Chiang Rai and Chiang Saen) are formed.	1281
The Thai Prince Mengrai founds Chiang Mai (New Town), on the River Mae Ping, as capital of the Kingdom of Lan-Na Thai (Kingdom of 100,000 rice fields).	1290
Following the death of Ramkhamhaeng the Kingdom is divided into principalities and Sukothai ceases to be capital; Ayutthaya is the new capital.	Around 1300
Liu Thai succeeds his father Lo Thai to become Mahadharmaraya I. He displeases the rulers of Ayutthaya by preferring the religious orders to the military and is forced to recognise their supremacy.	
King Rama Thibodi I (U Thong) becomes King and Ayutthaya the capital, thereby laying the foundations for Thailand's development into the most powerful state in south-east Asia until the fall of Ayutthaya in 1767.	1350
During several acts of aggression against neighbouring states the Thais succeed in 1430 in conquering and plundering Angkor Wat, situated in modern-day Kampuchea. In so doing they destroy the most valued culture in south-east Asia.	14/15th c.

History

1512	The first Europeans – Portuguese, trading under the orders of their Viceroy, Alfonso d'Albuquerque – sail from Malacca (now Malaysia) up the Chao Phraya to Bangkok. Their mission becomes a diplomatic ploy. The Portuguese had conquered Malacca in 1511, then learnt that the country actually belonged to the King of Sayam in Ayutthaya. They were now offering him firearms and gunpowder for his war with the Burmese in return for the trading rights in Ayutthaya and being allowed to practise their religion. This enables the King to abandon retaliation against the Portuguese in far-off Malacca without losing face, and to sally forth well armed against the enemy much closer to hand in Burma.
1556	The Burmese conquer Chiang Mai which remains under their control until the 18th c.
1569	After numerous unsuccessful attempts the Burmese occupy Ayutthaya but this time do not destroy it as is the case almost 300 years hence.
1584	King Naresuan, who was able to escape Burmese imprisonment by winning numerous duels unarmed, regains Ayutthaya. Thailand regains its former territory after Naresuan succeeds in driving out the Burmese.
1592	Sir James Lancaster, an Englishman, gives the country the name "Siam" which is what Europe is to call it for the next 350 years.
1593–1684	Ayutthaya's population reaches a million, and Europeans describe the city as the "Venice of the East" and "abounding in gold and diamonds". They pass Bangkok by, terming it, "a place with two fortresses" and build trading-posts on both banks of its river, ignoring the fact that the "village of olives" has monasteries and pagodas and is a hive of Chinese trading, full of bustling craftsmen.
1605	King Ekatotsarot accedes to the throne. He puts an end to the aggressive policies of his predecessors and his brother Naresuen and instead promotes economic development. He imposes a business tax which earns him the name "the greedy one" with European traders.
1656–88	King Narai of Ayutthaya's reign. He is the first to realise that the great merchants who had been so warmly welcomed are not just trading in ivory, rice and skins but are also bringing in gunboats and setting up garrisons. In 1664, with Dutch gunboats menacingly close to Bangkok's forts, King Narai is forced into an unfavourable trade treaty. In this situation the French missionaries who had returned in 1656 are welcomed as his saviours and in 1681 the King makes first ambassadorial overtures to King Louis XIV of France. The royal fleet carrying the envoys disappears in mysterious circumstances near Mauritius, but a fresh diplomatic mission in 1684 reaches Versailles, meeting with "gracious" reciprocation.
1685–86	Louis XIV sends his embassy to Siam in March 1685, headed by the Chevalier de Chaumont and backed up by a considerable number of Jesuit missionaries.

The first French ambassadorial fleet leaves Siam, carrying on board precious porcelain from China and a few "small slaves for conversion" as parting gifts. Versailles' second envoys, Cébéret and de la Loubière, arrive in Siam, with 1400 French troops as reinforcements. They and Narai's Greek Prime Minister, Phoulkon, are regarded with deep distrust by a group of anti-Western courtiers who, led by Phra Phetraja, Commander of the King's Elephant Batallion, take advantage of the King being gravely ill to accuse Phoulkon of high treason. He is taken prisoner and beheaded. On Narai's death his adopted son, a Catholic convert whom he had made his heir, is also killed and Phetraja assumes the throne (1688). All Europeans, including the "Farangs" as the French were called, are expelled from the country which remains sealed off from the West for the next 130 years. — 1687–88

The Siamese are constantly having to defend themselves against the Burmese and the only peaceful interlude is King Boromokot's reign from 1733 to 1758. There is a fresh flourishing of Ayutthaya Buddhism, art and literature. Ayutthaya is destroyed by the Burmese after a 15-month long siege and out of its population of a million only 10,000 survive, including 500 soldiers commanded by Phya Taksin, who manage to escape, through Bangkok, to Chiangmai. The Burmese are finally driven out of the country. — 1689–1767

Phya Taksin makes himself King, declaring Thonburi to be the capital but never finds time to organise it as he is involved in military expeditions fighting rebels inland and in pushing the borders as far as Laos and Cambodia. — 1768

King Taksin is condemned to death on the grounds of insanity, sewn into a silk sack and beaten to death. After his execution his friend and chief general, Chao Phya Mahakasatsuck, is offered the Crown, and ascends the throne at the age of 45 as Rama I (Phra Phuttayodfa Chulalok). He is the first Regent of the Chakri dynasty and transfers the royal residence to Bangkok on the left bank of the river. — 1782

Death of Rama I, who is succeeded by his son, Phra Phuttaloetla (Rama II). — 1809

Rama II resumes official relations with Europeans. A Portuguese, Carlos Manuel Silveira, is granted permission to trade and build ships in Bangkok. — 1818

An official English mission appears at Court under Dr John Crawford who asks for trading concessions. The reasons for their refusal are given as the Thai demands for arms supplies, sugar sales and the difficulty in understanding one another's language. — 1822

Rama III ascends the throne at the age of 36 following his father's death. His regency lasts until 1851 and is remembered for his patronage of the arts and science. Rama III founds the first public university at Wat Pho; attendance is free. Britain embarks on its first campaign to conquer Burma, thus freeing Thailand from constantly having to defend its western flank. — 1824

Captain Henry Burney arrives in Bangkok with a fresh request for an English trading concession. A friendship and trade treaty — 1826

	– in Thai, English, Portuguese and Malay – is signed but only trading privileges are allowed.
1828	Captain Low develops Thai typeface and publishes (in Singapore) the first book for European visitors to Bangkok, "A Grammar of Siamese Language".
1833	US President Jackson dispatches Edmund Roberts, together with missionaries and merchants, as American Envoy to Bangkok where he is allowed to remain, subject to the same conditions as the British.
1839	A Royal Decree – printed on 9000 handbills – outlaws smoking and dealing in opium.
1851	Death of Rama III at 63; succeeded by his son Rama IV (also called Mongkut), a wandering monk from the age of 20. Rama IV promotes the educational and medical activities of the Christians in his country, but without becoming a convert himself. He reorganises the police and army along European lines. During his reign he passes 500 new laws including laws prescribing equality irrespective of rank or status, better conditions for slaves, a ban on abduction and the right to religious expression. He founds the first official mint. Sir John Bowring, Queen Victoria's Governor of Hong Kong, concludes a friendship and trade treaty with Rama IV which guarantees British trade more freedom.
1860–61	The Prussian envoy Fritz Graf journeys around Siam and records his travels.
1869	An 8km/5 mile stretch of paved road, "Charoen Krung" (may the city thrive), also known as the New Road is opened.
1870	Dr Bradley's Mission Press in Singapore publishes Bangkok's first printed map. It shows four Christian churches, two cemeteries, several mosques and over 80 Buddhist temples.
1882	Passengers are allowed to travel on their first stretch or railway line, covering the 70km/39 miles from Ayutthaya to Bangkok.
1883	A single-track electric tramline runs for 10km/6½ miles through Bangkok to the King's Palace.
1892	Rama V establishes 12 Ministeries on modern Western lines and centralises the administration of provinces ("Changvat") and districts ("Amphoe") under the ministeries as part of his complete reform of government and administration.
1910	A railway line is built by an engineer sent by Emperor Wilhelm II from Bangkok to Surat Thani.
1913	"Gambling houses" are banned.
1916	Rama IV makes surnames compulsory.
1917	Education is made compulsory for a minimum of four years between the ages of 7 and 14.
10.1.1920	Founding of the League of Nations. Siam is a member.

Prince Paripatra, representing Rama VII in his absence, is taken hostage and an ultimatum is sent to the King holidaying in his palace at Glai Gangwon.	24.7.1932
Announcement of a provisional constitution, turning the Kingdom into a constitutional monarchy.	27.7.1932
The "permanent" constitution is proclaimed.	10.12.1932
The leading reformers of the previous year divide into civilian and military camps.	1933
Successful military coup, Prime Minister Phya is deposed.	20.6.1933
Out of the many new laws, the people of Bangkok are particularly incensed by the decree on monogamy.	1934
Rama VII abdicates. A regency council takes over the job of ruling on behalf of the new young King, Rama VIII, who is at school in Switzerland.	1935
Thailand signs a friendship treaty with Germany.	1937
The name of the country, Siam, is changed to Thailand, locally Prathet Thai.	14.6.1939
The Japanese march into Bangkok establishing their headquarters at the Oriental Hotel.	1941
Rama VII dies mysteriously and his younger brother Bhumipol, is appointed his successor (Rama IX).	9.6.1941
The Japanese introduce Thailand's first banknotes.	1943
Thailand applies to become a member of the United Nations but comes up against opposition from France and the Soviet Union in the Security Council. Having ceded Laos and Cambodia to France and accredited a Russian Ambassador to Bangkok, Thailand is unanimously accepted as a full member of the UN.	15.12.1946
Another military coup puts a junta temporarily in power.	8.5.1947
King Bhumibol marries Queen Sirikit, and their coronation follows a week later.	28.4.1950
Korean War. Thailand contributes 4000 troops, including air force and naval personnel, to the UN force.	1950–53
A defence pact between Thailand, Australia, Great Britain, France, New Zealand, Pakistan, the Philippines and the USA is concluded in Manila.	8.9.1954
The defence pact signed the previous year comes into force on 19.2.1955 in the form of SEATO (Southeast Asian Treaty Organisation).	1955
Bangkok becomes the headquarters of SEATO.	1956
Pibul is overthrown by General Sarit Thanarat who, until his death in 1963, is the "strong man" ruler of the country. The	16.9.1957

	result is all too speedy death sentences and an iron-willed enforcement of law and order against the Thai's yearning for individualism and freedom.
28.10.1958	Sarit's Revolution Party puts the country under martial law and from now on certain offences, especially those involving Communist activity, are tried by military tribunal.
1960	The King and Queen pay a State visit to the USA and 15 European countries.
1961	Association of Southeast Asian Nations (ASEAN) is founded, its members being Thailand, Malaysia and the Philippines.
1963	Marshal Thanom Kittachorn becomes Prime Minister on Sarit's death.
1965	The military value of the American "development aid" aimed, since the early 1950s, at enlarging the infrastructure in the north-east, becomes apparent. During the Vietnam War Thailand allowed American airbases on its soil, from which attacks on Vietnam were carried out.
1967	ASEAN becomes more important with the end of SEATO, being joined by Singapore and Indonesia. Prehistoric finds at Ban Chiang, probably the earliest bronze tools ever made, throws the archaeological world into a frenzy.
1968	Thanom proclaims a new constitution.
1969	Introduction of universal suffrage.
17.11.71	The National Executive Council (NEC) makes Thanom its Chairman, suspends the constitution and dissolves Parliament, banning political parties and bringing in martial law.
15.12.1972	The King proclaims an interim constitution. The NEC is replaced by a Government with a cabinet of 28 and Thanom as Prime Minister. The King appoints the 299 members of the National Assembly, which has legislative powers.
14.10.1973	Young Thais, mostly students and youngsters still at school, assemble at the Democracy Monument. Their demonstration is ruthlessly put down, leaving over 70 dead. The King is responsible for stopping the tanks from pursuing the 400,000 young demonstrators. Thanom, Narong and Prapass flee into exile and the King installs a provisional civil government.
7.10.1974	Proclamation of a new democratic constitution and reintroduction of universal suffrage.
1976	Thanom returns from exile, dressed as a monk. Student demonstrations on the Thammasad Campus, and 50 students are killed.
6.10.1976	The army assumes power. The constitution is suspended and a state of emergency announced. A 12-year plan for consolidation and a gradual return to democracy is announced.
November 1977	General Kriangsak Chomanan becomes the new Prime Minister.

First conference between ASEAN and the European Community with the aim of dismantling trade barriers.	1978
Thailand is hit by wave of refugees fleeing from Vietnam and Cambodia to camps in the south-east and north-east of the country. Thailand feels unable to cope and requests help from other countries.	1979
General election, General Kriangsak remains Prime Minister with the Democratic Party suffering heavy losses.	22.4.1979
Kriangsak steps down, to be succeeded by General Prem Tinsulanonda.	3.3.1980
Thailand joins in the boycott of the Moscow Olympic Games.	1980
Bicentenary of Bangkok and also of the Chakri dynasty. Rama I is posthumously awarded the title "the Great".	1982
Attempts by the army to be involved in election of the Prime Minister and in governing fail. The number of senators and deputies is increased to appease the generals and elections are announced for 18.4.1983.	16.3.1983
Typhoon "Kim" causes severe flooding in Bangkok and makes many homeless.	October 1983
Elections confirm President Prem Tinsulanonda in office; he is now at the head of a four-party coalition.	18.3.1984
Pope John Paul II names Archbishop Michael Michai as the first cardinal of Thailand and shortly afterwards pays a visit to the country.	May 1984
Laos brings the frontier dispute with Thailand before the United Nations Security Council.	9.10.1984
The Thai baht loses value against the US dollar; the Thai government devalues by 17.4%.	November 1984
Heavy fighting on the north-east border with Cambodia as Thais attempt to drive back a Vietnamese unit searching for Khmer Rouge resistance fighters.	12.12.1984
Thailand places large areas of its territory on the frontier with Cambodia under martial law.	15.3.1985
Unsuccessful coup by generals.	9.11.1985
Following new elections the governing coalition under President Prem is confirmed in office.	27.7.1986
The sixth five-year plan for the period 1986–91 comes into operation; its principal aims are growth in the economy and price stabilisation.	1.10.1986
1987 is declared "Visit Thailand Year".	1987
89 members of the outlawed Thai Communist party, who had for a long time remained hidden in the frontier region between	March 1987

Thailand and Cambodia and as rebels had constantly sought to attack the military forces, surrender to the police. This is seen as a great success for the Prem government which gains temporary popularity.

May 1987

After a referendum King Bhumibol receives the honorary title "the Great One", an honour which is rarely bestowed (the last time on King Rama I). Vietnamese mercenaries attack a refugee camp, killing seven and injuring 20 people. Foreign minister Savetsila meets with Shevardnadse and credits the USSR with playing an important part in resolving the conflict with Cambodia.

July 1987

Princess Chulabhorn accepts an invitation to be guest professor at the University of Ulm and gives lectures on pharmacy.

5.12.1987

The 60th birthday of King Rama IX is celebrated. On this date the new King Bhumibol Suspension Bridge across the Chao Phraya (Menam) in the south of the city is opened to traffic.

February 1988

A ceasefire with the Cambodian government puts an end to hostilities along the border, thus paving the way for negotiations towards a peace treaty.

July 1988

Prem decides not to continue in office. A coalition government is headed by Chatichai Choonhavan, son of a Chinese immigrant.

November 1988

Uncontrolled tree-felling leads to severe floods with hundreds dead and thousands made homeless.

December 1988

Tree-felling is banned by a Royal Decree. Re-afforestation is to take place on threatened slopes.

September 1989

Despite the collapse of the Cambodia peace conference in Paris Vietnam withdraws its troops from Cambodia. Continued fighting with Khmer Rouge on Thailand's borders.

November 1989

Hurricane overturns American drilling platform in Gulf of Thailand, leaving several dead. Severe damage also caused in the south of the country.

February 1990

Thailand negotiates on behalf of Prince Sihanouk, living in exile in Paris, and his former country. The Cambodian government rejects the proposals.

September/October 1990

The southern province Prachuap Khiri Khan is hit by a devastating hurricane resulting in thousands losing their homes. The Bangkok government promises a progamme of aid to finance rebuilding.

23.2.1991

A successful military coup, led by the generals, results in Prime Minister Choonhavan's removal from office and house arrest. General Sunthorn Kongsompong forms a "Committe for National Salvation" and recommends to King Bhumibol the 59 year old diplomat Anand Panyacharun as the new leader.

February/March 1991

A series of devastating fires take place in Bangkok: in early February a freight train carrying fuel explodes in the suburb of Din Daeng killing over 30 people. 6000 are made homeless by a chemical explosion on 2 March in the harbour district Khlong Toey. On 4 March a department store in Silom Road burns down, miraculously nobody is hurt. On 5 March 150 houses in Thonburi are destroyed by fire.

The new cabinet minister Meechal Viravaidya, a well known campaigner for the use of condoms, declares that "sex tourists" are no longer welcome in Thailand. A government campaign to fight the spread of AIDS is announced. In future female prostitution is to be discouraged.

March 1991

Ousted Prime Minister Choonhavan returns from abroad and announces his intentions to be active politically. Charges against him concerning embezzlement of public money are dropped; the Chart Thai party select him as their candidate in the forthcoming election in October. However, he decides to return to London as he finds the political situation in Thailand intolerable.

August 1991

Successful negotiations take place in Patthaya between the opposing factions in the Cambodian civil war.

September 1991

Bangkok in Quotations

Baedeker's "India"
"Handbook for Travellers"
(1914)

Bangkok (City of Olives), the capital and only noteworthy settlement in the Kingdom of Siam, with 630,000 inhabitants, more than one third of whom are Chinese, founded in 1768 on the site of a fishing village, is situated on latitude 13° 38' north and longitude 100° 31' east on both banks of the Menam and covers an area of 40 sq.km/15 sq. miles. All the state institutions, important temples, educational establishments, businesses and most of the foreign trade are concentrated here. The main part of the city stretches along the left bank. The Old Town with the Royal Palace Quarter and many holy places nestles in the curve made by the river on its journey west, surrounded by a partly preserved wall 10m/32ft high and 3m/10ft thick. The European quarter with its embassies, consulates and banks extends south adjoining the newer districts of the native population in the east. The entire townscape is dominated by the Wat Tscheng in the outskirts on the right bank.

Remarkable commercial activity takes place on the Menam and canals (klongs) branching off it which traverse the city in concentric circles and are linked to each other by smaller canals. Part of the population live in floating houses which are anchored or else securely moored. The wooden houses enclosed by gardens on the river bank are built on high stilts as protection against the floods. Skiffs carrying foodstuffs and household goods and even cooking-boats are surrounded by the barges of their customers as they ply the river. All this, in conjunction with the view across the temple spires and the pinnacles of the Royal Palace Quarter explains why the name "Venice of the East" has been given to Bangkok. But the comparison applies to the poorer areas and not to the splendour of that Western city of lagoons.

Carl Bock
(Norwegian explorer)
"The Kingdom of
the White Elephant"
(Leipzig 1885)

A crowd streamed in the palace grounds, the focal point of the whole inviting spectacle. In the palace garden soldiers were standing on guard and palace officials on horseback, glowing with excitement, galloped here and there as they made preparations to receive the noble beast . . .

Directly next to the royal bodyguard stood an artillery unit with field cannons. Not far away on the river bank we met a number of white-clad natives with large hats made of sugar-cane leaves encircled by a wide gold band. There were priests, earthly angels, who having fulfilled all the demands of the Buddhist faith, had reached the highest level of spiritual life attainable for mortals . . . now the hero of the day arrived, the white elephant itself, accompanied by three other so-called white elephants, compared with which he surely deserved the proud description. To describe him as "white" I would have to be accused of colour-blindness. But he was a complete albino; his entire body looked pale reddish-brown; there are a few real white hairs on his back. The irises of his eyes were pale yellow. He looked very calm, his inner peace in sharp contrast to the general excitement . . . The blessing and baptism of the elephant followed in the presence of the King and the entire aristocracy.

One of the higher priests handed the animal a piece of sugar-cane leaf on which the elephant's full name had been inscribed. It ate it willingly even though it had been overfed on sugar-cane.

Describing the Thai theatre:
When the Siamese become tired of games they visit the nearest theatre . . . (where) normally only girls appear on the stage . . . Most of the performance consists of entwining fingers, hands and arms in such a way that the limbs appear to be dislocated. In Siam the limb movements and gyrations are the same as those seen in Java, but the clothes worn are different. The young ladies of the "Lakon" wear gilt-embroidered, tight-fitting jackets with epaulettes rather like horns which, with a little imagination, can resemble wings; they wear false finger-nails extending some 12 or 15cm/5 or 6in beyond the tips of their fingers, and bent over at the end like the horns of long-horned cattle . . . The best theatre in Bangkok is the Phra Mahin and . . . I attended a performance there. The maidens were all attired in Scottish costume, but on their heads they wore a crown in the shape of a Phra Chedi . . . The Siamese are great music-lovers and enjoy European brass instruments as well as their native ones. Every man of rank has at least one band of musicians, two if possible – one playing solely European instruments . . . In (some) cases the conductors are German or Italian, but the players are all Siamese.

Describing Phra Thinang Summer Palace:
. . . a beautiful pool in the middle of which rises the loveliest of truly Siamese pavilions with its triple-layered roof, tapered gable-ends and slender spire . . . The effects of this very special building so clearly mirrored in the still waters is so arresting that I betook myself to photograph it . . .

. . . The King retires to his summer palace from time to time when he wishes to be free of the cares of State. Some three years ago while on such a visit to Bang Pa In His Majesty (King Chulalongkorn) suffered a painful loss through the death by drowning of his first wife, Sunanda Kumaritana, and their three little girls. Her Majesty was travelling upstream on board a small pleasure-boat towed by a steam-launch. At a bend in the river the boat was set rocking by the strong current and capsized . . . The present Queen, Sawang Wadhana, is her sister . . . "

Early one morning we passed the sandbank (south of Packnam) and as the sun rose shining over the flat plain we steamed upstream along numerous curves in the river passing under the shadow of the large golden pagoda and reached the outskirts of the city.

Joseph Conrad
(writer)
"Shadowline"
(1906)

There it lay, spread out on both banks of the river, this oriental capital, which has never had to bow to a white conqueror; an extensive, wide area of brown bamboo houses, a mass of interwoven mats and leaves – architecture in the style of a vegetable garden growing out of the brown muddy earth. An almost incredible thought: in this sprawling mass of human shelters there is probably not even a half pound of nails. On his visit to Europe King Chulalongkorn first set foot in Venice and it is this very city which resembles Bangkok the most. For Bangkok is also a city of canals. On both banks of the yellow waters of the Menam, which is as wide as the Rhine at Mainz as it surges towards the Gulf of Siam, an intricate labyrinth of canals criss-crosses the forty square kilometres/fifteen square miles of lowland on which, circled by white walls beset with towers, Bangkok lies. Yes, it is as if there are, so to speak, two cities: one on top of the other; first, the city of the river and canals with the thousands and thousands of floating houses and where the volume of small and large craft is so dense that it is only with difficulty and thanks to the skill of the half-naked local oarsmen that you can get through. A storey higher on the mainland towers a second city of stone and wooden houses. . . .

It is all flat alluvial land, the work of the great Menam, which here, like the Nile in Egypt, waters the land and occasionally floods large areas. So the people who live here have become sort of amphibians. Those who live on the mainland spend half their lives on or in the water, those who live in the water spend all their lives there. . . .

Duke of Phentièvres
"Voyage autour du monde"
(c. 1849)

(In the Grand Palace) groups of 15 to 20 women surprised by this unexpected visit immediately threw themselves down onto the colourful mats which covered the floor; lying on their knees and elbows they seemed very frightened; on seeing us others, probably about 160 in number, fled to the steps, balconies and recesses; others again disappeared like lightning among the shady avenues of the gardens and behind the cracks of the not quite closed doors curious black sparkling eyes could be seen. Some of them, the old matrons with wrinkled skin and withered charms moved aside; others, delicate chocolate-coloured nymphs, young languid sultanas wearing only a narrow band around their upper bodies, short blue skirts and diamonds adorning their necks, arms and legs huddled together in surprise.

First the King headed towards a group of older queens, and taking one by the hand he pulled her towards us, shaking with fear. Holding her in his right hand he reached for one of our hands with his left which he placed in her hand . . . "Good woman" said the King, as he dismissed her after this forced handshake, "she gave me three children". Then he went to fetch another equally ugly one; the same handshake with Madame No. . . . "Very good woman" continued the King, "she gave me ten children. . . ."

Ernst von Hesse-Wartegg
"Siam" 1899

"Bang-pa-in is Siam's Versailles . . . How did it ever come about that a fairy-tale castle like this was placed here in the jungle amidst primeval forests where the elephants roam? And yet here it is. Even after seeing the magnificence of the royal palace precinct in Bangkok I scarcely believed my eyes when I saw Siam's Versailles. King Chulalongkorn, a second "roi soleil", created it without ever setting eyes on the model for this vast design.

The centre point of the whole plan is a broad basin with walls all around. In the middle of it there stands on stone pillars a delightful cruciform pavilion with roofs that rise out and over one another and whose gables have curious pointed finials. All this is surmounted by a five-storey tower narrowing to a slender spire.

"During the period of the King's residence here there were performances at various times of the day by the royal band of musicians while richly gilded gondolas carried the King's wives up and down the wide, mirror-smooth expanses of water or along the shady canals nearby with their flower-beds on either hand.

. . . amid a group of palm trees stands the most beautiful of all the buildings, the Chinese palace. A Chinese Croesus who had earned his millions in Siam had it built here and presented it to the King. The Emperor of the Celestial Kingdom cannot possess any palace so beautiful as this; at any rate, I have never seen its like in China . . .

The whole building, from the wonderful porcelain roof which crowns its second storey to the wooden balustrade which surrounds the lowest verandahs, is all in the purest Chinese style with magnificent wood-carvings, paintings and gilding . . . "

(Speech on the opening of a railway line)

Rama IX
(Bhumibol)
King of Thailand
(b. 1927)

The construction of a railway network not only has the greatest influence on a country's development but is at the same time the most impressive proof of such development. To unite the different regions of a country the railway requires a capable administration for which clear oversight and vision are essential. In creating a means of transport that is both fast and comfortable it brings real investment for the country and manufacturing. Wherever it operates it takes with it enlightenment and encourages a sense of national identity which is such an important element for the well-being of the country.

(From a letter to his son)

The only reason and the point in sending you to England to be educated is the acquisition of knowledge. Therefore do not make it known that you are a prince! . . . Apply all your efforts and enthusiasm to your studies instead, so that one day you will be able to serve your country usefully . . . Were you to think that as a prince you would not need to work, then your life would only be that of an animal.

(On the office of a ruler)

I have never liked "history" and I would like to add to that I have never had the ambition to be a "great" king who "goes down in history". It has been proven that the reigns of such kings were always times of war . . . That is not for me. I hope that as long as I am on the throne my people may live happily and peacefully, without war.

(From a speech on his constitutional role as "defender of all faiths")

Every faith has its philosophical and religious principles. Philosophy is a world of ideas and imagination which has to do with the origin and progress of the world and with our own happiness. Every religion has its own path to the goal which may be summarised by concepts such as fortune, heaven or success . . . . and for every religion it is an ideal for everyone to help each other to reach this "peak" in the same manner. Along this path we must beware of arguing over what is the best route, just because we have different ideas about what is right. Religious disputes could be described as the route to hell. All religions teach love and compassion for others and advocate respect for others convictions instead of threats and violence.

Bangkok from A to Z

Note

The nature of the Thai language is such that in transliterating into Roman script the spelling of place names can vary.

Itineraries

For visitors spending only a short time in Bangkok see Practical Information, Sightseeing for suggested itineraries.

Buses

The numbers of the bus routes given in the margins against the individual places are those served by air-conditioned buses (see Practical Information, Transport for general time-table). There are also a number of bus companies who run vehicles without air-conditioning but, as these are cheap, they are usually hopelessly overcrowded, and it is strongly recommended that only the air-conditioned buses are used.

Temples

For an explanation of the terms used in describing Buddhist temples see Facts and Figures, Temples and A to Z, Wat.

Amphorn Gardens

C3

Location
Dusit

Buses
3, 5, 10

The district of Dusit, with its square grid of tree-shaded avenues, is the only part of the city which has managed to retain the feeling of a garden city, and its elegance remains unspoilt by heavy traffic, slums and high-rise concrete.

The pretty park here, Amphorn Gardens, is open on public holidays and is the venue for many folk festivals, charity events, cadet parades and promenade concerts. The Vajiravudh Boys' College within the park was founded by King Rama VI (1881–1925) along the lines of an English public school. His bronze statue is in a raised pavilion on a carefully tended lawn close by an artificial pool, its waters reflecting the blue and yellow Siamese roofs of the classrooms.

The equestrian statue of King Chulalongkorn (1853–1910) dominates the large square in front of the park which becomes a parade-ground for schoolchildren, students and armed forces on Chulalongkorn Day, 23 October, when the former King, still very much revered by the people, is afforded their highest sign of respect in typical Thai fashion, namely, the form of obeisance known as "Mop Krap", involving touching the ground with forehead, hands and the whole of the lower part of the body.

The statue, cast in the style of the Belle Epoque, was funded by popular subscription during the King's lifetime.

Ancient City (Muang Boran)

Location
33km/20 miles south-east of Bangkok, in Samut Prakam Province

Covering some 500 sq.km/200 sq. miles, Ancient City is one of the biggest open-air museums in the world, amounting to exactly one-thousandth of the surface area of the whole of Thailand. Known as Muang Boran, it was financed by a rich

◀ *Ancient City, Phra Buddha Bat (Saraburi)*

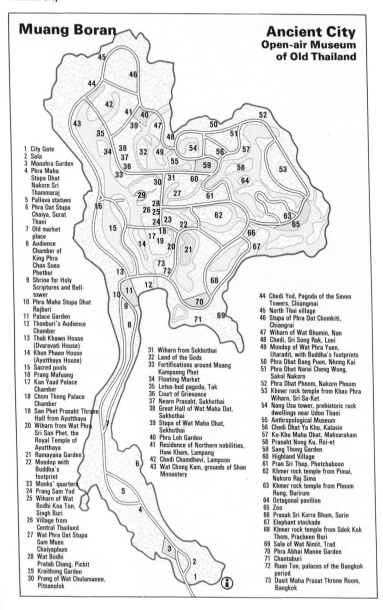

Muang Boran

Ancient City
Open-air Museum of Old Thailand

1 City Gate
2 Sala
3 Manohra Garden
4 Phra Maha Stupa Dhat Nakorn Sri Thammaraj
5 Pallava statues
6 Phra Dat Stupa Chaiya, Surat Thani
7 Old market place
8 Audience Chamber of King Phra Chao Suea Phetbur
9 Shrine for Holy Scriptures and Bell-tower
10 Phra Maha Stupa Dhat Rajburi
11 Palace Garden
12 Thonburi's Audience Chamber
13 Thab Khawn House (Dvaravati House)
14 Khun Phaen House (Ayutthaya House)
15 Sacred pools
16 Prang Mafuang
17 Kan Yaad Palace Chamber
18 Chom Thong Palace Chamber
19 San Phet Prasaht Throne Hall from Ayutthaya
20 Wiharn from Wat Phra Sri San Phet, the Royal Temple of Ayutthaya
21 Ramayana Garden
22 Mondop with Buddha's footprint
23 Monks' quarters
24 Prang Sam Yod
25 Wiharn of Wat Bodhi Koa Ton, Singh Buri
26 Village from Central Thailand
27 Wat Phra Dat Stupa Sam Muen Chaiyaphum
28 Wat Bodhi Pratab Chang, Pichit
29 Kraithong Garden
30 Prang of Wat Chulamanee, Pitsanulok

31 Wiharn from Sukhothai
32 Land of the Gods
33 Fortifications around Muang Kampaeng Phet
34 Floating Market
35 Lotus-bud pagoda, Tak
36 Court of Grievance
37 Nearn Prasaht, Sukhothai
38 Great Hall of Wat Maha Dat, Sukhothai
39 Stupa of Wat Maha Dhat, Sukhothai
40 Phra Loh Garden
41 Residence of Northern nobilities, Haw Kham, Lampang
42 Chedi Chamdhevi, Lampoon
43 Wat Chong Kam, grounds of Shan Monastery

44 Chedi Yod, Pagoda of the Seven Towers, Chiangmai
45 North Thai village
46 Stupa of Phra Dat Chomkiti, Chiangrai
47 Wiharn of Wat Bhumin, Nan
48 Chedi, Sri Song Rak, Loei
49 Mondop of Wat Phra Yuen, Utaradit, with Buddha's footprints
50 Phra Dhat Bang Puen, Nhong Kai
51 Phra Dhat Narai Cheng Wong, Sakol Nakorn
52 Phra Dhat Phnom, Nakorn Phnom
53 Khmer rock temple from Khao Phra Wiharn, Sri Sa-Ket
54 Nang Usa tower, prehistoric rock dwellings near Udon Thani
55 Anthropological Museum
56 Chedi Dhat Ya Khu, Kalasin
57 Ku-Khu Maha Dhat, Mahsarakam
58 Prasaht Nong Ku, Roi-et
59 Sang Thong Garden
60 Highland Village
61 Pran Sri Thep, Phetchaboon
62 Khmer rock temple from Pimai, Nakorn Raj Sima
63 Khmer rock temple from Phnom Rung, Burirum
64 Octagonal pavilion
65 Zoo
66 Prasah Sri Korra Bhum, Surin
67 Elephant stockade
68 Khmer rock temple from Sdok Kok Thom, Pracheen Buri
69 Sala of Wat Nimit, Trad
70 Phra Abhai Manee Garden
71 Chantaburi
72 Ruan Ton, palaces of the Bangkok period
73 Dusit Maha Prasat Throne Room, Bangkok

Bangkok citizen and cost more than 200 million US dollars. It took ten years to construct, and is laid out in the shape of the country, with some features copied in their original size, as well as 65 miniatures of the most beautiful and important temples and other historical monuments built to a scale of 1:3. The latter include copies of some buildings long since destroyed, such as the Sri Sanphet Prasat or Royal Audience Chamber of the ancient Ayutthaya.

The individual places of interest, most of which mirror the actual geography of Thailand, are served by wide roads where the visitor can drive his own car or hire a bicycle. Cars can be hired also by arrangement with the office in Bangkok, at 78 Ratchadamnoen Avenue (near the Mercedes-Benz premises by the Democracy Memorial, tel. 222–8145). They will provide a well-illustrated booklet in English and a map of the area which dispenses with the need for a guide.

Access
On the Sukhumvit Highway to Samut Prakam and then follow the signs along the main road.

Open:
Daily 8.30am–6pm

Admission fee

The Anthropological Museum in the northern part of the grounds differs from the rest in that it houses finds from all over Thailand. These are on view in farmsteads and courtyards such as exist in villages in Central Thailand. The museum exhibits span over a thousand years and include musical instruments, pottery, fishing equipment, rice-farming tools and utensils, baskets, jugs and bottles with woven bast covers for storing or fermenting palm wine, fishing-nets and fish-traps, wheelbarrows and carts.

Anthropological Museum

The upper floor of the Ho Kham (i.e. Gilded Hall) houses an art collection consisting of stone and bronze sculpture, ceramics and wooden and mother-of-pearl objects from periods when Thai culture was at its peak.

The highlight of the exhibition is the most modern item, a representation of some 70 episodes in the life of Buddha carved in seven panels of teak which together make one whole. The artist is said to have been about 80 years old and to have taken ten years to create this piece of work.

The Ho Kham building is an exact replica of the former Governor's residence in Lampang, an example of the extraordinary skill displayed by Thai craftsmen. It is built entirely of wood, and without a single nail. The biggest problem was finding and then acquiring the hefty tree-trunks needed, particularly for the massive pillars that support the building, as teak-felling has been forbidden for a number of years.

Ho Kham

Besides reconstructions, the Ancient City also has buildings that were brought here from their original locations. These include, for example, some houses from the Bangkok "Floating Market" which had to be sacrificed for road building in the seventies. The only reconstructions – some reduced to one-third, others in their original size, but all, after decades of research, authentic down to the smallest detail – are of major buildings, such as temples or palaces, the originals of which now either lie in ruins (see Ayutthaya's Throne Hall, San Phet Phrasat) or have been Westernised (e.g. the Dusit Maha Prasat in the Grand Palace – see entry).

Original buildings

San Phet Prasat, the reconstruction of Ayutthaya's Throne Hall, is especially remarkable for its lofty interior with magnificent wooden ceilings, gilded walls of mirror mosaics, and stucco ornamentation.

San Phet Prasat

Ancient City

The Ancient City's San Phet Prasat (Throne Hall)

Dusit Maha Prasat

The faithfully depicted murals in Dusit Maha Prasat are particularly worth seeing, especially as very few of these paintings from the early Bangkok period have been preserved, as a result of the deleterious substances in the atmosphere. They depict state ceremonies, religious festivals, military parades and life at the court of King Rama I (1782–1809). Particularly fine are the carvings and ornamentation on the doors and windows.

Khao Phra Wiharn

In the north-eastern part of the grounds (corresponding to what is now the "no man's land" between Thailand and Kampuchea) there is a 54m/175ft high artificial mound on which stands Khao Phra Wiharn, a re-creation of a Buddhist shrine visited by Thai kings and pilgrims for a thousand years (until 1974). In that year the International Court in The Hague awarded it to neighbouring Cambodia, since when it has been the subject of bitter struggles between border troops of both countries. Recently, however, there have been negotiations aimed at making the shrine accessible once again to Thailanders and foreign visitors. Rising up from a small river at its foot, the four terraces on the sides of the hill, which is best tackled in the cool of the morning, carry stone ruins which used to be crowned with beautifully crafted gable roofs in the Khmer style of Angkor Wat, and there is an authentic reconstruction of one of these roofs here. The top of the hill offers a superb panoramic view to help the visitor plan how to visit the rest of the many sights that make up the Ancient City.

Gardens

Dotted around the whole area are seven gardens where it is possible to relax and enjoy the scenes, among the waterfalls, rocks and tropical flowers, from Thailand's myths and sagas.

78

The "Garden of the Gods", for instance, portrays the Indian moon god Chandra's team of ten bronze horses virtually flying over the waterfall. Farther on the "Manohra Garden" has a respresentation of the pretty girl with birds' legs pictured among her sisters.

Near the entrance is a Brahman shrine called the "Royal Stand", from which Queen Elizabeth II of Great Britain formally opened the Ancient City in 1972 while a guest of the Thai royal couple, declaring it – in accordance with the wishes of its founder – to be a unique cultural gift "for the world of the future and against the growing materialism of our age".

Brahman Shrine

The grounds also hold an elephant stockade and a zoo full of game, monkeys and many species of birds in natural habitats. This is highly recommended for children visiting the Ancient City.

Elephant Stockade and Zoo

More a tourist attraction than a genuine part of rural life is the Floating Market in Ancient City.

Floating Market

**Ayutthaya (Phra Nakhon Sri Ayuthya)

The old capital of Ayutthaya, now one of the most impressive ruined towns on the continent of Asia, lies on the wide, fertile plain of the Menam Chao Phraya where this, Thailand's most important river, forms a natural loop. The Menam and two other rivers, the Lopburi in the north and the Pasak in the east, form the town boundaries; an artificial canal links the two river courses, forming a favourably situated island in between.
By car, the best way to get to Ayutthaya is from Bangkok along Highway 1. After 86km/53 miles turn off left at Wang Noi onto the 309 and follow the signs. Coaches from Bangkok to Ayutthaya depart from Bangkok North Bus Station several times a day, and the larger travel agents in the city arrange organised tours which visit the major points of interest; a full-day tour is recommended.
Ayutthaya lies on the rail route running north, has its own station and is only 1½ hours from Bangkok. A very pleasant way of getting there is along the Menam Chao Phraya river, with the choice of either the regular river-boat service (board at the Tha Tien landing stage behind the Thamasat University) or organised trips, such as the "Oriental Queen" from the Oriental Hotel.
It has to be said that anyone who is really interested in the history of Ayutthaya ought to allow at least two days and also take in Lopburi and Sukhothai, royal towns in Central Thailand which are both closely associated historically with the country's former capital.
Most of the organised tours allow only an hour or so in Ayutthaya, plus the fact that arriving in the heat of the day means not seeing this ancient ruined city at dawn or dusk, when it is at its most magical and impressive – and photogenic, too.

Location
72km/45 miles north of Bangkok

Rail
From the Hualampong Main Station

Buses
From the Northern Bus Terminal
Bus tours

Boat
Along the Menam Chao Phraya river.

For more than 400 years, between 1350 and 1767, Ayutthaya was the capital of the Kingdom of Siam; visitors enthusiastically described it as the most beautiful place they had ever seen. North of the present railway, near the Wat Khudi Dao, is where Khmer founded a small outpost of his kingdom in the

History

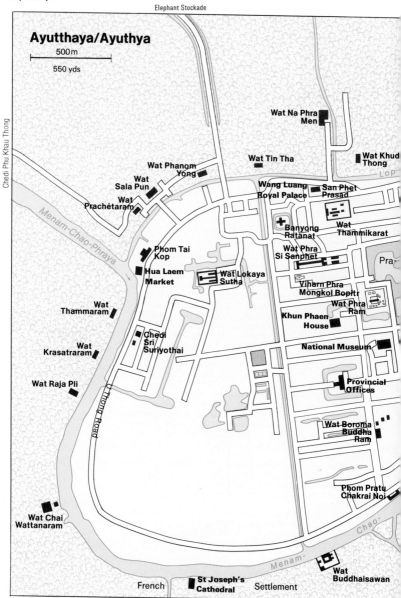

Ayutthaya/Ayuthya

500 m

550 yds

Chedi Phu Khau Thong

Elephant Stockade

Menam-Chao-Phraya

Wat Na Phra Men

Wat Khud Thong

Wat Tin Tha

LOP

Wat Phanom Yong

Wat Sala Pun

Wat Prachétaram

Wang Luang Royal Palace

San Phet Prasad

Banyong Ratanat

Wat Thammikarat

Phom Tai Kop

Wat Phra Si Sanphet

Pra—

Hua Laem Market

Wat Lokaya Sutha

Viharn Phra Mongkol Bopitr

Wat Thammaram

Khun Phaen House

Wat Phra Ram

Wat Krasatraram

Chedi Sri Suriyothai

National Museum

Wat Raja Pli

Provincial Offices

Klong Road

Wat Boroma Buddha Ram

Phom Pratu Chakrai Noi

Chao-

Wat Chai Wattanaram

Menam-

Wat Buddhaisawan

French

St Joseph's Cathedral

Settlement

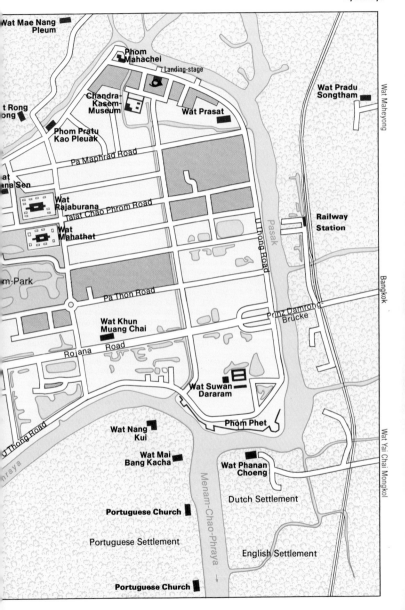

Wat Mae Nang Pleum

Phom Mahachei

Landing-stage

Chandra-Kasem-Museum

Wat Prasat

Wat Pradu Songtham

t Rong ong

Phom Pratu Kao Pleuak

Pa Maphrad Road

at ana Sen

Wat Rajaburana

Talat Chao Phrom Road

Wat Mahathat

Railway Station

Pasak

U Thong Road

m-Park

Pa Thon Road

Wat Khun Muang Chai

Prinz Damrong Brücke

Rojana Road

Wat Suwan Dararam

Wat Nang Kui

Phom Phet

U Thong Road

Wat Mai Bang Kacha

Wat Phanan Choeng

hraya

Dutch Settlement

Portuguese Church

Menam-Chao-Phraya

Portuguese Settlement

English Settlement

Portuguese Church

Wat Maheyong

Bangkok

Wat Yai Chai Mongkol

11th c. In the 13th c., after the Thais had conquered and cultivated the land of the Menam plain, Ayutthaya and Lopburi were
absorbed into the principality of U Thong, and then this in turn
became a vassal state of Sukhothai. After disastrous plagues in
1347 had decimated the population by more than a half Prince
U Thong was forced to leave. Ayutthaya, enclosed as it was by
rivers and with its defensive core favourably placed south of
the Menam, was chosen as his new capital. The fresh division
of the Kingdom of Siam into several principalities following the
death of Ramkhamhaengs also led U Thong to separate himself
politically from the the rulers in Sukhotai; he dismissed the
ruling retinue there and in 1350, as King Somdej Phra Rama
Thibodi (although usually called King U Thong in history books),
he declared his own state, naming it after his capital city.

The name Rama Thibodi reflects the godlike status of the kings
of Thailand at that time. Rama Thibodi regarded himself as the
reincarnation of the god Vishnu and the hero of the Indian epic
of "Ramayana", and had his superhuman status and divine
omnipotence legitimised by eight Brahmans from the holy
Hindu city of Benares.

The history of Ayutthaya was carved out by no fewer than
thirty-three kings. It developed into a flourishing cultural and
commercial centre, and many European trading companies
established branches there. Traces of the latter can still be seen,
such as the foundations of a large Dutch store and the recently
restored French Cathedral of St Joseph.

There were four customs posts, the one south of the city on the
eastern bank of the Chao Phraya being the biggest; warships
and the royal barges anchored on the northern bank of the
Lopburi near Wat Tin Tha opposite the royal palace. King U
Thong surrounded the city with an earth wall and stockades;
not until 1549 was it protected by a permanent wall of plastered
brickwork. In 1580 the northern defensive wall was moved
nearer to the river; remains can still be seen by the Pa Maphrad
Road.

Of the six large forts which were built into the wall only some
fragments of Fort Phom Phet, where the Pasak joins the Chao
Praya, still remain. After the destruction of Ayutthaya stones
from the remaining forts, like those from various other fortifications, were used to build Bangkok's city wall.

The destruction of Ayutthaya in 1767 is an example of the
temporary decline of the Siamese monarchy. Rival members of
the royal household, including a number of princes, exhausted
themselves in intrigue and battles for power, in which they
called for assistance from compliant soldiers and from members of the religious nobility. King Ekatot, the last reigning
monarch of the Ayutthaya dynasty and also the weakest, was
incapable of mediating between the factions. When the Burmese arrived yet again at the gates of the city but apparently
without much hope of taking it, one of the rival factions opened
a gate and let the enemy in. From that day onwards they
occupied the city for more than fifteen years, and it was only
after some hard battles that the Thais won it back once more.

The Burmese vandalised the country. No temple escaped their
ravages; most, together with the royal palace of Wang Luang,
were razed to the ground. The final capture of Ayutthaya was
symbolised by the destruction of thousands of figures of the
Buddha; since, according to the Buddhist religion, the spirit
dwells in the head, the invaders rendered the figures worthless
in the eyes of the faithful by smashing the heads off. Some of

these beheaded statues can still be seen at various places in the ruined city of Ayutthaya.

Today Ayutthaya is just a giant collection of ruined remains of temples and palaces, which initially proved of little interest to archaelogists. Since 1956, however, the ruins have been not only officially protected but are also being reconstructed, although there are no plans at present for a complete rebuilding of the city. Meanwhile, the foundations of some temples have been exposed in such a way as to give an idea of the original size. Some one hundred or so buildings and ruins have been declared national monuments by the Department of Fine Arts, and it is expected that more will be added to the list, depending on the progress made in their restoration.

Sights

On the island alone, which formed the core of the old Ayutthaya, there were at one time three royal palaces, 375 temples, 29 forts and 94 city gates. To visit the main places of interest and to get an idea of the size of Ayutthaya as it once was, it is suggested taking the following route, commencing and ending near the Prince Damrong Bridge. This tour will take in ten temple sites, two museums, two palaces and various other interesting buildings; at least half a day is required to do it justice, more if a visit to both the museums is made.

The Prince Damrong Bridge was erected in memory of Prince Damrong Rajanubhab, to whom we are indebted for much of our knowledge of the history of art in Thailand. Cross the bridge and continue to the U Thong Ring Road; follow this to the left for some 700m/770yds.

There, framed by three small lakes, lies Wat Suwan Dararam, built around 1700 by the grandfather of Rama I and extended by the rulers of the Chakri dynasty, who also carried out restoration work and decorated it with numerous paintings. It will be noticed that its foundations lean towards the centre; this is also the only temple on Ayutthaya Island which is still inhabited by monks.

Worthy of attention are the large bot with portico, the wood carvings in the tympanum, the internal frescos from the Early Bangkok period, the artistic coffered ceiling and a statue of Buddha in the Ayutthaya style. The Wiharn was built by Rama II (1809–24) and decorated in 1931 with modern murals depicting scenes from Thailand's history.

Leave the temple area and on the bank of the Menam River opposite can be seen remains of the only preserved fort, that of Phom Phet. Now follow the U Thong Road to the left once more; after about a half an hour leave it at Fort Phom Pratu Chakrai Noi and proceed northwards. After 400m/440yds take the Si Sanphet Road to Wat Boroma Buddha Ram.

Wat Boroma Buddha Ram, of which only the walls remain, was built in 1683 during the reign of King Narai. In about 1740 the doors were inlaid with mother-of-pearl. Following the sacking of Ayutthaya these exquisite works of art were moved to Bangkok, one being installed in Wat Benchamabophit (Marble Temple) and another in Wat Phra Kaeo, in the Grand Palace. The

Note

Wat Suwan Dararam

Fort Phom Phet

Wat Boroma Buddha Ram

third door was made into a bookcase which now stands in the National Museum in Bangkok.

Chao Sam Phraya National Museum

Open
Wed.–Sun. 9am–noon,
1pm–4pm

Admission fee

After passing the Ayutthaya provincial government offices we arrive at the Chao Sam Phraya National Museum, founded by King Bhumibol in 1961. It houses some valuable and interesting exhibits in the Lopburi, U Thong, Ayutthaya, Dvaravati and Sukhothai styles, including finds from Ayutthaya, sculptures in bronze and stone, terracotta work, ceramics, wood-carvings, lacquer work, votive panels and gold jewellery decorated with precious stones. Outstanding among many earlier works of art are an 11th c. seated Buddha and a collosal bust of Buddha in the U Thong style.

**Phra Mane Ground
(Sanaam Luang)**

Keeping to the left after leaving the National Museum a short walk leads to the Phra Mane Ground (also known as Sanaam Luang), in the western corner of which stands the Wiharn Phra Mongkol Bopitr. Prime Minister Pibulsonggram had it built in 1956 in a style close to that of the original building, which had been burned down in the sacking of Ayutthaya and eventually collapsed. The much revered and artistically valuable bronze statue of the Buddha, one of the largest anywhere in Thailand, was thus restored to the place where it had stood since 1603. Little is known of its early history; its U Thong and Sukhothai features suggest that it was probably cast during the reign of King Boroma Trailokanat (1448–88). He introduced the Sukhotai style into Buddha statues and Chedis in Ayutthaya, replacing the Khmer style which had been in vogue until then. Over the years the figure has been heavily restored but little changed in appearance. Some years ago hundreds of small figures were discovered inside it. The ornamentation on the base was added in 1931 and is less artistic than the original.

Wat Phra Ram

Most impressive are the nearby Elephant Gates of the Wat Phra Ram; surrounded by a pond, this wat was begun by King Ramesuen in 1369 and has been restored and enlarged over the years. Of particular interest is the gallery with Nagas and Garudas and the numerous figures of the Buddha to be found on the wide terrace.

Khun Phaen House

Nearby stands Khun Phaen House, built in the traditional Thai style on a plot of land surrounded by a moat, where the prison once stood. The house, one of the few buildings in this style which still remain, was constructed in 1940 from pieces saved from old houses. It is somewhat similar to Jim Thompson's House in Bangkok (see entry).

Wat Phra Si Sanphet

By following the Si Sanphet Road as far as Naresuan Road and then turning left we come to Wat Phra Si Sanphet, the most beautiful and important of all the temples in old Ayutthaya. With its three large chedis and numerous smaller ones on a long terrace this temple – also known as the King's Temple – today presents one of the most impressive sights to be found in the town ruins.
Two of the chedis, the eastern and central ones, were built by King Rama Thibodi II in 1492 to house the ashes of his father and elder brother. His own ashes are buried in the third chedi, which was built by his son and successor to the throne, King Boromaraja IV in 1530. All three chedis were opened up and plundered by the Burmese, but they failed to find hundreds of

small statues of the Buddha in bronze, crystal, silver, lead and gold, which are now on display in the National Museum in Bangkok. The building in the west of the terrace was once crowned by a chedi and has many entrances with small Prangs which, like the smaller chedis and chapels around it, probably contain the ashes of members of the royal family. The buildings between the individual chedis were presumably Mondhops; in front of the terrace, roughly in the centre of the temple grounds, can be seen remains, in the form of pillars and walls, of the great wiharn, which once contained a figure of the Buddha 16m/52½ft high and encased in gold. The ruins of this statue, from which the Burmese removed the gold casing, were removed by King Rama I to one of the large chedis of Wat Pho in Bangkok. Other smaller Buddhas were also taken to Bangkok and placed in Wat Buddhaisawan (which now forms part of the Bangkok National Museum) and in the western wiharn of Wat Pho.

Leaving the Royal Wat (note the memorial to King U Thong on the opposite side) a turning on the left leads to Wang Luang Royal Palace, not to be confused with the Kanthara Kasem Palace, built in a later period and also known as the "Old Palace". Nothing remains of a third palace, Klang Suan Luang, built by the western city wall near the Chedi of Queen Suriyochai.

Wang Luang (Royal Palace)

The walls of Wang Luang extend right up to the banks of the Lopburi River, but apart from them and the well-restored foundations little remains to be seen. In this quarter of Ayutthaya the Burmese really went on the rampage, so little has survived of the numerous old Thai houses. Nevertheless, a good idea of

The splendour that was Ayutthaya, the Royal Palace

the extent of the complex, which also embraces Wat Si Sanphet, can be obtained. This part of the town can be compared to
the Great Palace complex in Bangkok since, unlike the former
Ayutthaya royal residence, it was built using a number of different styles. The oldest building in Wang Luang was constructed
by King U Thong in 1350, when he named Ayutthaya as his
capital city.

Sanphet Prasad Palace

In 1448, under King Boromaraja II, Sanphet Prasad Palace was
added. Situated opposite Wang Luang, some of the remains of
tall pillars can still be seen.

Wihara Somdet

Wihara Somdet was built in 1643, under King Prasat Thong. It is
recorded that it had two quite large, tower-like porticos at front
and rear and two smaller ones on the sides, and was the first
building in Ayutthaya to be panelled in gold (which led to it
becoming popularly known as the "Golden Palace").

Chakravat Paichayon
Building

King Prasat Thong also built the Chakravat Paichayon Building
in 1632, and it was from here that royal processions and military parades rode out.

Banyong Ratanat Building

The Banyong Ratanat Building, built c. 1688 under King Prasat
Thong's son Narai and completed during the reign of King
Petraja, is situated on an artificial island in the western part of
the complex, and served as King Petraja's residence during the
whole of his reign (1688–1702).

Trimuk Building

King Chulalongkorn had the Trimuk Building rebuilt in 1907. It
is in the form of an open pavilion on a broad terrace, and has
been the scene of a number of ceremonies held by a succession
of kings, including the present King Bhumibol, in honour of
former rulers of Ayutthaya. A former building on the site, of
unknown age, was burned down in 1427.

Suriyat Amarindra Building

Built by King Narai after the middle of the 17th c., only a high
wall remains. Close by lie the stables of the royal white
elephants.

Passing by Wat Thammikarat, the overgrown ruins of an
extremely large temple (all that remains being parts of the
terrace, the portico pillars and a chedi with a crooked spire), we
return to U Thong Road. On the opposite bank of the Lopburi,
reached by a small bridge from U Thong Road, stands Wat Na
Phra Mane, which is worth a visit.

Wat Na Phra Mane

Wat Na Phra Mane is one of the few temples which somehow
managed to survive destruction by the Burmese. It is not
known when it was built; records merely state that it was
restored under King Boromakot (1732–58) and again later during the Early Bangkok period. The Bot is a large, imposing
building with some beautiful wood-carving in the tympanum
and door panels. The triple-tiered roof and large portico,
flanked by two small but graceful porches, are evidence of the
artistic skill of the Thais. In the interior a richly carved ceiling
gives the impression of even greater height as a result of being
supported on two rows of octagonal columns. Most unusually,
the large Buddha wears royal garb.
The small but well-proportioned wiharn houses a seated stone
Buddha in the European style, one of the best-preserved stat-

ues from the Dvaravati era (6th–10th/11th c.) An inscription in the wiharn states that the statue comes from Wat Phra Mahathat in Ayutthaya, but this must be incorrect. In fact it has been established that this figure, together with three other identical ones, once stood in Wat Phra Mane of Nakhon Pathom, where the richly ornamented stone frame forming its base was found. Parts of this frame are today in the Bangkok National Museum.

Returning over the bridge and turning left again the road follows the Lopburi River and, after about 800m/875yds, reaches Wat Yana Sen, a temple with a high chedi with niches. Its fine, well-balanced structure is typical of the Ayutthaya style.

Wat Yana Sen

From Wat Yana Sen can be seen two of the most important ruined temples in Ayutthaya, Wat Rajaburana and Wat Mahathat.

Wat Rajaburana was erected by King Boromracha II (1424–48) in memory of his two elder brothers Ay and Yi, who killed each other in a duel for succession to the throne. Columns and walls of the wiharn still stand, as well as the ruins of some chedis surrounding the prang and parts of the surrounding walls with lancet gateways. Very well preserved is the large prang with its finely figured stucco-work portraying, for example, Garudas supported on Nagas. The two crypts in the lower part of the prang boast some very interesting wall-paintings, which were probably the work of Chinese artists who settled in Ayutthaya and had the skill to combine such differing styles as those of the Khmer and Burmese with those of Lopburi and Sukhotai to

Wat Rajaburana

Striding Buddha

Ruins of Wat Rajaburana

form a harmonious whole. When excavating in the prang between 1956 and 1958 archaeologists found more than 100,000 votive tablets (known as "phra phim" in the Thai language); these were sold and the Chao Sam Phraya National Museum built with the proceeds. Such votive tablets were usually modelled from clay and carried by pilgrims. They usually bore pictures of holy places of pilgrimage or simply of the Buddha. Works of art were also uncovered in the prang, including wide arm-bands with intaglio decoration, headwear in gold filigree and one in solid gold inlaid with precious stones, a five-part service for betel nuts, two spittoons and gold coins with Arabic lettering. Most of these finds are on display in the Chandra Kasem National Museum.

The prang of Wat Rajaburana is historically interesting in that it combines the Indian (Ceylonese) and Burmese styles and merges them into a new architectural form. At the top some of the stucco work has been well preserved, and a small chedi stood at each corner of the square platform. Two more chedis at the road junction contain the ashes of the royal brothers, a third is in memory of Queen Sri Suriyothai who, during a battle with the Burmese about 1550, dressed as a man and rode a white elephant to save her husband's life at the cost of her own. Near this chedi, at the totally destroyed Wat Lokaya Sutha, can be seen a giant reclining figure of the Buddha.

Wat Mahathat

Only a road separates Wat Mahathat from Wat Rajaburana. Tradition says that it was built by King Ramesuen in 1384. He is said also to have constructed the central prang in order to house a relic of the Buddha. However, that is rather improbable, as a more reliable source states that the first buildings on the temple site, including the abovementioned Pang, had been erected by King Boromaraja I (1370–88). The prang, being 46m/150ft high, is also one of the most imposing buildings from the old capital. About 1625 the top portion broke off and was rebuilt in 1633 some 4m/13ft higher than before. However, it collapsed once more and only the corners survived. In 1956 a secret chamber was uncovered in the ruins containing a number of treasures, such as gold jewellery, a golden casket containing a relic of the Buddha and some artistic tableware.

Scattered in the temple can be seen some important remains of variously shaped prangs and chedis, in particular an octagonal Chedi with a truncated spire in the Ceylonese style. On the ground nearby lies the head of a still-revered statue of the Buddha.

Chandra Kasem Museum

Open
Wed.–Sun. 9am–noon,
1pm–4pm

Admission fee

The U Thong Road now follows the Lopburi as far as the Chandra Kasem Museum, which is worth a prolonged visit. Its exhibits include statues of Buddha and Boddhisattwa, gold, jewellery and carvings, tympana and domestic and religious objects from the 13th to the 17th c. It is housed in a palace rebuilt by King Mongkut (Rama IV) and originally occupied by the heir to the throne. Later it was used as a residence for royal visitors to Ayutthaya. The objects on display give only a slight impression of the full power of the earlier Thai kings, but nevertheless provide a basic insight into the lives of the inhabitants of Ayutthaya.

Passing Fort Phom Machachei and the landing-stage the U Thong Road continues via the comparatively uninteresting temple of Wat Prasat to the starting point of the tour

Further places of interest

Anyone with the time to spare and who wishes to delve more deeply into the city's history would do well to make a detour to the French Cathedral of St Joseph on the far bank of the Chao Phraya. This church, restored only a few years ago, is in memory of the large group of French people who settled in Siam. There are a number of other Wats situated outside the city wall, which are best visited by boat along the Menam; these depart from the landing-stage and the trip takes about two hours.

It is also worth paying a visit to the Elephant Stockade about 3km/2 miles outside the city. This is a square enclosure constructed in its present form by King Rama I. It was used for catching, taming and showing off elephants, and is the only place of its kind still in existence.

**Bang Pa In

The large island of Bang Pa In, formed by a loop in the Chao Phraya River, was the family seat of King Prasat Thong of Ayutthaya (1629–56), who was also born here. Following the death of his mother, he had a temple, Wat Chumphol Nikaya-ram, and a summer palace built for use in the hot season on the island (40m/130ft wide and 400m/1300ft long) near the bank of the lake. All his successors spent their summer vacations here until, following the fall of Ayutthaya, the capital was transferred first to Thonburi and then to Bangkok. After that, Bang Pa In seemed too remote and the palace was abandoned for 80 years until, with the coming of steamships, King Rama IV (Mongkut, 1851–68) rediscovered this island lake, and he and in particular his son Rama V (Chulalongkorn, 1868–1910) built a new palace, which has been carefully restored in recent years.

When Rama VIII came to the throne he chose Hua Hin by the sea as his new summer residence. However, Bang Pa is still favoured by King Bhumibol today for state receptions. Although comparatively small in area, it is a typical example of the romantic idyll so dear to the hearts of the people, who visit it frequently and enjoy sitting in the shade of one of the giant trees and gazing out over the lotus-covered ponds.

The island is described by Ernst von Hesse-Wartegg in his book "Siam" (1899; see Quotations)

Location
About 55km/34 miles north of Bangkok

Rail
From Hualampong Main Station

Buses
From the Northern Bus Terminal
Bus tours

Boat
Along the Menam Chao Phraya river.

The whole palace precinct is surrounded by a high wall, the line of which is broken up here and there by massive towers in the Neo-Classical style. In fact Bang Pa In is made up of two palace complexes, an outer and an inner. At one time the inner was accessible only to the royal couple and the male courtiers. No women were admitted.

Palace precinct

Styles are mixed here without inhibition; the gardens have bridges with Rococo curves and Greek statues, there is a Buddhist temple in Gothic ecclesiastical style (complete with pews), a Chinese-style observatory with wonderful and extensive views and the Chinese "Vehat Chamroon" palace, with specimens of the best Japanese art in its interior.

Features of interest

Interesting buildings in period styles

The Chinese palace was a gift made to the King in 1889 by rich Chinese merchants who hoped thereby to gain his favour.

**Vehat Chamroon (Chinese Palace)

Bang Pa In

Bang Pa In's Summer Palace and Phra Thinang Pavilion

Chinese workers were brought to Thailand to carry out the building. The glass windows provided King Chulalongkorn with protection from heavy rainfall.

Worthy of note is the magnificently carved furniture to be found in the palace, including King Vajiravudh's writing table carved in the Chinese style and the bookcases in the study, which contain old Chinese manuscripts from various periods.

Wat Chumpon Nikayaram

Located near the bridge as seen from the railway station, this temple is the only one of King Prasad Thong's buildings which, despite much restoration at the hands of his successors, retains its original 17th c. style. The walls are decorated with magnificent murals from the reign of King Mongkut displaying scenes from the life of Buddha. The two polygonal Chedis belonging to the temple are also well worth seeing.

**Phra Thinang Summer Palace

The purest Thai style is to be seen in the former Aisawan Tippaya Pavilion in the middle of the lake, although in fact it is only a faithful copy of the Phra Thinang Aphonphimok Prasar Pavilion built by Mongkut in the grounds of the Great Palace in Bangkok. This graceful building has served as a model for Thailand's exhibition pavilions at world fairs.

Originally built completely of wood, the floor and supports were replaced in 1920 by reinforced concrete. In the centre of the pavilion stands a life-size statue of King Chulalongkorn by an unknown sculptor.

The royal palace buildings behind it, known as Phra Thinang Warophat Phiman, were built by Kings Rama IV and V, and are a mixture of Italian Renaissance and Victorian styles. The largest hall was used as a royal audience chamber. It contains a royal

90

throne with a baldachin (suspended canopy), and on the opposite wall hangs an oil-painting showing King Chulalongkorn dressed in state robes. On the other walls will be found illustrations of the Tales of Inao, Phra Aphaimani and from the "Ramakien". A covered bridge links the audience chamber with a round building, the doors of which lead out on to a wide terrace with wide stone steps leading into the lake.

The vivid description by Hesse-Wartegg still holds good regarding the magnificent overall picture now presented following recent expensive restoration, a sentiment reinforced in 1885 by a Norwegian explorer on a visit to Chulalongkorn (see Quotations)The same chronicler, Carl Bock, also tells of the tragic consequences of the strict ban at that time on anyone touching a royal personage (see Quotations). Needless to say, it was King Chulalongkorn who did away with this ban on touching members of the Royal family which had been responsible for preventing his drowning wife and children from being saved.

Mention must also be made of the open-air theatre, a small wooden pavilion near the Uthayan Phumi Sathian Palace, and a Prang under a large Bodhi tree on the edge of the lake, which King Chulalongkorn had built in place of a shrine dedicated to King Prasat Thong. Inside it stands a statue of Prasat Thong. On a small island between the two palaces stands a tower built during the reign of King Mongkut and which he, being a keen amateur astronomer, used as his observatory. A stone staircase leads up to a platform from where there is a fine view of the countryside.

Further places of interest

To the south of the royal residence, on an island in the Menam River, lies Wat Niwet Thamapravat. Built in a strange Gothic style, it was a gift from King Chulalongkorn to the monks of the Dhramayutika sect which he had founded. The large statue of the Buddha in its Bot is a masterpiece by Prince Pradi Vrakam, who was court sculptor during the reigns of King Mongkut and King Chulalongkorn.

Wat Niwet Thamapravat

A trip on the "Oriental Queen", which sails daily from the Oriental Hotel, will be found most delightful.

Bangrak

See Floating Markets

Bang Saen (beach resort)

This beach resort lies nearer to Bangkok and is much quieter than Pattaya (see entry) at about half the price. Since it is a favourite with the Thais it is advisable to book ahead for weekends from February and during the holiday period from mid-March to June.

Location
93km/58 miles south of Bangkok

Access
Along the Sukhumvit Road Highway 3

Buses
From the Ekamai bus station (several times a day)

It has over 1km/½ mile of beach with water-skiing, sailing and angling. Close at hand is Thailand's biggest golf-course, with motel and swimming pool attached. Nearby attractions include the orchid gardens and the Khao Khiao National Park, situated between Bang Saen and the neighbouring town of Chonburi. Covering an area of 145 sq.km/56 sq. miles, it is the home of 133 protected species of animals, including butterflies, monkeys, apes and leopards. Some extremely rare species of birds can be observed in an aviary.

Rock-apes

Other special attractions include the rock-apes to be seen on the Sammuk Mountain, the handicraft centre at Ang Sila, oyster farms along the coast and the shrine of the patron saint of fishermen, Mae Khao Sammuk. These can all be reached from the old panoramic coast road or by minibus or taxi.
Bang Saen has a wide choice of restaurants catering for Thai, Chinese and European tastes, as well as specialist fish restaurants where lobster and mussels are served.

Ocean World Leisure Park
Open Daily 8am–8pm
Admission fee

To cater mainly for week-end holidaymakers from nearby Bangkok Ocean World, a leisure park on the promenade designed on American lines and complete with swimming pools, was opened a few years ago.

Tip

The TAT hotel here, with its tropical gardens and swimming-pool adjoining the beach, is recommended for a longer stay. It also has bungalows catering for 1–7 people, complete with refrigerator, cooking facilities, air-conditioning, veranda, etc. as required.

**Luk Sam Po (Fishermen's Shrine)

Another attraction is the Luk Sam Po Chinese temple, shaped like a ship, which is best reached by the coast road. It is said to have been built in memory of a catastrophe which occurred off the Thailand coast, when a ship containing Chinese immigrants sank in a heavy storm. The sole survivor built the temple in gratitude and founded a religious order with very strict rules, which probably accounts for its failure to attract novice monks for a number of years now.
Around the central pagoda are grouped some little houses, symbolising ships' cabins, in which a few monks and nuns still live. Note the monks' dwellings grouped outside the actual complex, and built in the form of small fishing boats. The monastery contains two small-scale reproductions of the chedi at Nakhon Pathom (see entry), the most revered Buddhist shrine in the world.
Today this temple is visited by Buddhists from all over the world, but visitors are nevertheless welcome if they behave correctly.

Koh Sichang (island)

Another interesting excursion is to take a boat to the island of Si Racha, only a few miles from Bang Saen, and from there by ferry to Koh Sichang, an island inhabited only by fishermen. One of its attractions is the unfinished summer palace of King Rama V (Chulalongkorn) situated in pleasant parkland.There are also some bungalows built on Koh Sichang.

Chao Phraya (Menam)

See Klongs

Chatuchak Week-end Market A5

About halfway between the city centre and the airport lies the
spacious Chatuchak Park, with large lawns, shady trees, ponds
and bridges. On its south-eastern edge, on Phahonyothin
Road opposite the bus station, lies a large market, where on
weekdays between about 6.30am and 10pm fish from rural
co-operatives, plants, animals, basketwork and much more is
offered for sale.

Saturdays and Sundays are rather special, because it is then
that the big week-end market, formerly held at Sanaam Luang
in the city, takes place here. As early as Friday evening the
locals pour in from near and far by bus, train or boat to look for
bargains or indulge in the favourite Thai pastime of gambling
and games of chance.
Goods on offer on the various stalls range from antiques (not
always genuine), wood-carvings, masks, ceramics, metal
goods, especially knives, musical instruments and music-
boxes playing Thai or Western music, textiles, leather, cane
and basketwork, decorations made from mussel shells, toys
and souvenirs of all kinds and qualities, to plants, flowers and
animals (pets, fish, birds, etc.), as well as food and pretty bird
cages.
The market is strictly divided up according to types of goods, so
it is fairly easy to find particular articles.
There are also a number of hot-dog stalls, some selling noodles
and rice, a restaurant offering Thai specialities and a super-
market for food and other necessities.
Even though betting is officially prohibited, regular cock-fights
and fish-fights are in fact held.

Moving the week-end market from Sanaam Luang was a positive move: whereas the old market place was often overcrowded and rather hectic, the new one is far more spacious.

Location
In the north-east area of the
city, on the western side of
Phahonyothin Road, opposite
the Northern Bus terminal.

Market days
Fresh goods: daily from
6.30am
Weekend market: Sat. and
Sun. 8.30am–approx. 9pm

Chidralada Palace (Chirlada-Pra'Radschawang) C3

Once King Chulalongkorn's summer villa, Chidralada Palace
stands in about 1 sq.km/250 acres of parkland with a number of
artificial lakes. At each corner of the park stands a fountain
playing over Late Baroque legendary figures, illustrative of the
keen aesthetic sense displayed by the rulers of Thailand. The
moat around it hit the headlines in 1973 when students on the
run from police during the revolution of that year sought – and
found – refuge here on the far side of the railings.

The grounds of Chidralada Palace do not look very much like a
royal park but more like an experimental agricultural station.
Generally closed to visitors, the palace is in fact an experimental station which provides an additional source of income
to rice-growers in the north in the form of fish-breeding stock

Location
In Dusit, bounded by Rama V
Road, Rajawithi Road,
Sawankhalok Road and Si
Ayutthaya Road

Buses
3, 10

Admission
Through diplomatic channels
only (possibility of royal
audience)

Chidralada Palace

Chidralada Palace, home to the Thai Royal Family

which is distributed to them. Thus it will be seen that the royal fish-ponds are much more than just a hobby. There is also a beef-farming unit, an experimental dairy and agricultural research stations. The first fish-farming tanks were installed in 1963; in 1965, when on a visit, the Crown Prince of Japan donated 50 related fish species, including the Tilapia rainbow perch, which turned out to be very well-suited to conditions in Thailand. In recent years attempts have been made by German scientists near Ayutthaya to rear fish from here. They introduced the giant gourami fish into the country, an "easy-care" species which should also soon enrich the often monotonous diet of the rice-farmers.

White elephants

Also accommodated at the palace, as befits their royal status, are the famous royal "white" elephants, after they have spent some time in the nearby Dusit Zoo (see entry). With sixteen white elephants, Kinh Bhumibol far surpasses the number owned by any of his predecessors; never before has a ruler been given so many Albino elephants during his reign.

The "white" elephant, even though – strictly speaking – there is no such thing in zoological terms, enjoys reverential status in Thailand. There are 32 special features which differentiate it from its fellows. For instance, it has twenty toe-nails instead of sixteen and has red eyes. Contrary to popular opinion, however, it is not completely white, but in fact differs only in having largish or smallish white patches on head and ears. The more such animals are found during the period of a king's reign the luckier these years are supposed to be for the ruler and his people.

*Chinatown

Chinatown is simply a particularly concentrated assortment of Chinese businesses, workshops, banks, temples, restaurants and people. On Chinese festivals (especially Chinese New Year) it is possible to see Chinese opera or puppets. Chinese shops, restaurants and cinemas (screening films made in Hongkong and generally very bloodcurdling) are to be found in every other part of Bangkok, and the Chinese are, in fact, dispersed throughout the city. However, the "Sampheng" district, around Yaowarat, is where the descendants live of the first Chinese to be settled here in 1782, by King Rama I, when their tin- and silver-smiths, shoemakers, tailors and traders lived in what is now the entire Palace district, or had their homes and workshops in junks and houseboats moored six abreast on the river-bank.

Modern Chinatown is thronged with people and tightly packed with jewellers, banks, pawnshops, workshops and shops of every kind. There are hardly any sightseeing attractions here, but the chemists' shops and restaurants offer everything a health-conscious Chinese gourmet could desire, including hundreds of sorts of tea and herbs, antelope horn, cobra venom in Chinese rice wine, crocodile, lizard and python meat, bats, bear's bladder and, of course, birds' nests (Rang-Nok-Gin) for the famous birds' nest soup. However, the latter come not from China but from the Thai islands of Phee-Phee to the south. Here you may also come across Chinese or Vietnamese Mahayana Buddhist monks. They are easily recognised

Location
Yaowarat Road and Sampang Lane in south-eastern Old Bangkok

Buses
1, 7

Bangkok's Chinatown

because they wear orange jackets and trousers, unlike the long, yellow robes of the Theravada-Thai Buddhists. These Chinese monks are in fact allowed to marry, but may only eat strict vegetarian food prepared in one of their monastery temples, of which there are about eight in Chinatown. Their main task is taking care of the burial rites in the Chinese cemeteries.

*Wat Don (Chinese Temple)

The best-known temple in this quarter is Wat Mongkon Malawat, but there is little doubt that the most interesting one for the tourist is Wat Don, where the traditional "Quingming Festival" – a ceremony in honour of those gone before – is held in every third month of the lunar year. Skeletons of the dead are disinterred, laid out once more, suitably adorned and then finally cremated. The celebrations are conducted in a very lively atmosphere, with shops selling devotional objects, and small Chinese restaurants, souvenir shops, soothsayers and palmists all plying for trade.

More practically-minded people, however, see the Quingming Festival as an opportunity to obtain a space in the rather narrow cemeteries in the centre of the city.

Everyone here understands Thai, and most understand English as well, especially the younger generation who long ago renounced the wide black satin trousers and drooping moustaches affected by their grandfathers and great-grandfathers; the women, too, have given up the little bun perched on top of sleeked-back hair. The State schools only provide instruction in Chinese for from six to eight hours a week in the first four years of primary education, and it is left to the parents to pay for any further study. However, they clearly succeed in this, since there are still three Chinese daily newspapers with a total circulation of about 200,000.

Tip

Wat Traimitr also stands in Yaowarat Road and should be visited in order to see its massive statue of the Buddha cast in pure gold.

Chulalongkorn Equestrian Statue

See Amphon Gardens

Chulalongkorn University (Mahan-Whit'jalai Dschulalongkorn)   E4

Location
Between Henri Dunant Road
(east entrance) and Phya Thai
Road (west entrance)

Buses
1, 2, 7

This university (Mahan-Whit'jalai Dschulalongkorn) is traditionally the one rated most highly in the country, and when King Vajiravudh (Rama VI) founded it in 1917 it was the only one. Nowadays it tends to be in competition with Thammasart University which was founded in 1934 and which in recent times has been the inspiration of most of the movements towards reform and democracy. It was called Chulalongkorn by Rama VI in honour of his father, Rama V.

Popularly known as "Chula", the extensive campus with its stylish traditional pitched-roof buildings is a modern university housing virtually every faculty.

The Graduation ceremony is especially impressive when, as at all the country's universities, the King personally presents each degree – and nowadays there are hundreds of them – to each student.

This highly colourful ceremony takes place between mid-June and September and occupies the entire campus. The famous Chulalongkorn Hospital is attached to the university; and the Thai Red Cross and the Pasteur Institute (see Snake Farm) are in the immediate vicinity. These, too, owe their origin to King Vajiravudh.

*Crocodile Farm and Zoo (Dsch'ra'ke)

About 35,000 crocodiles including, it is said, the longest one in captivity, measuring 5.9m/19ft 4in., live here in what is the second largest crocodile farm in the world. "Out of the tiger into the crocodile" is an old Thai proverb, meaning much the same as our "out of the frying pan into the fire". It comes from the time when people travelling along jungle paths had to be careful not to fall prey to a crocodile when trying to escape a tiger.

This vast zoo, as popular with those researching animal behaviour as it is with tourists, was started by its owner in 1950 with only a dozen animals, with the avowed aim of saving the threatened species from extinction. Since then, of course, reptiles have enjoyed worldwide protection under the Washington Agreement, enabling them to multiply to a considerable extent. Several interesting shows a day are put on, and there are also now tigers, chimpanzees, snakes and elephants, with the chance to ride on the latter.

The crocodile farm is on the itinerary of many tour operators, and provides an eventful addition to a trip to, say, the "Floating Markets" (see entry) of Damnoen Saduak or to the city.

Location
777 Taiban Road, Samut Prakam (Paknam), 30km/18 miles south-east of Bangkok

Buses
Bus tours

Open
Daily 8am–6pm

Guided tours
Mon.–Fri. 11am, 1pm and 3pm
Sun. and public holidays: 6 tours

Admission fee

Damnoen Saduak

See Floating Markets

Dusit Zoo   C3

Bangkok' Dusit Zoo is one of the largest of its kind in south-east Asia, and will bear comparison with any other zoo anywhere in the world. It has most animals found in a European zoo except polar bears and penguins – keeping them cool simply costs too much!

The shady park with its little boating-lake is a favourite picnic site for Bangkok people from all walks of life. The visitor may occasionally be lucky enough to see a white elephant here before it is moved to the Chidralada Palace stables.

The Dusit district, one of the most desirable residential quarters of the city, with shady tree-lined avenues and beautiful old villas, has succeeded in retaining much of its old charm. Here too can be found the Chidralada Royal Palace, the Marble Temple of Wat Benchamabophit, the Amphorn Gardens and the National Assembly Hall (see entries).

Location
In the Dusit district of the city; between Ratchawithi Road and Si Ayutthaya Road, the main entrance being on Ratchawithi Road.

Buses
3, 10

Open
Daily 8am–6pm

Admission fee

Emerald Buddha

See Grand Palace, Wat Phra Kaeo

Erawan Waterfall

See Kanchanaburi

Floating markets (Dalaad-Naam)

General

Very little remains of the "floating markets" which once gave Bangkok the nickname of the "Venice of the Far East". The main reason for this was the order issued by the government and civic authorities to fill in the narrow canals so that roads could be built. Those that remain form what can only be called a giant sewer. However, the absence of any clear, clean water does not deter those who live nearby from continuing to use it as they have always done; naked children, men and women can still be seen performing their daily ablutions. Life on the Klongs of Bangkok is not what it once was.

Nevertheless, a trip through the Thonburi Klongs should be included in any itinerary (see Klongs). With a little effort the visitor will perhaps be able to imagine what things were like a few years ago. However, the Thonburi Floating Market, so popular a few years ago, now boasts very few traders.

Damnoen Saduak

Location
About 100km/62 miles south-west of Bangkok.

Access
On Highway 4 as far as Ratchaburi, then to Damnoen Saduak landing-stage and continue by water-taxi or water-bus.

Buses
By bus from the Southern Bus Terminal (Thonburi) to Damnoen Saduak landing-stage and continue as above.

Tours
Organised tours from Bangkok

One of the markets, however, has remained, even though the Thailand tourist authority has a hand in its preservation and it is some distance away. This is Damnoen Saduak, a market situated about one and a half hours by car or bus from the capital and which gives some idea of how market life in Bangkok used to be.

To get the best from a visit an early start must be made, either in a hired car (a driver is recommended) or by bus, in order to arrive when the traders are almost the only people there. Participants in organised bus tours usually arrive about 9am, and then it is too late to capture the real atmosphere of the floating market.

In order to accommodate the hordes of tourists the market was moved in 1984 from its original site at Klong Ton Khem (where it had stood since 1856) to the Damnoen Saduak canal.

The canal-system around Damnoen Saduak is very confusing; there are some 200 canals in all, most of them interconnected by subsidiary canals. Floating markets did more than simply trade in foodstuffs and other daily needs; as centres of communication they also performed an important social function, and traders came from near and far. On narrow Klongs lively trading (sometimes even the time-honoured art of barter) is carried on. Women row skilfully past noisy motorboats, their frail little craft loaded to the brim with produce of all kinds. Every conceivable type of country produce is on sale here: vegetables

Marketing afloat in Bangkok ▶

▲ *The Sacred Precinct of the Grand Palace: Wat Phra Kaeo*

and fruit, fish and meat. There are unlimited subjects for the photographer.

Golden Buddha

See Wat Traimit

**Grand (or Great) Palace, Wat Phra Kaeo
(Phra Borom Maha Rajawang; Temple of the Emerald Buddha)   D2

Location
Main entrance Wiseedschairi Gate, on the southern side of Na Phralarn Road

Buses
6, 8, 12

Landing-stages
Thaa Thammasart and Thaa Tschang

Open
Daily 8.30am–11.30am and 1pm–3.30pm
(Pavilions closed Sat. and Sun.)

Admission fee

Suitable clothing should be worn

The palace city (218m/720ft by 400m/1312ft), with more than a hundred individual buildings, offers visitors a panorama of over 200 years of Thailand's history. Each of the important sights is an expression not only of the life and style of a period but also, and more importantly, of the King who was reigning at that time and who was responsible for it.

The Grand (sometimes called Great) Palace has been extensively renovated in recent years, at great expense. Most of the murals in particular, even though many appeared lost for ever as a result of damage by the weather and the environment, were in fact successfully restored, under the skilled guidance of international experts, with much of the actual work being carried out by final-year students from the Bangkok Universities.

The following suggested route for sightseers is such that there are some disappointments and incongruities to start with but also some individual high points with, as the grand finale, the sacred precinct of Wat Phra Kaeo.

Entry is through the Gate of Wonderful Victory (Wiseedtschairi Gate), and a wide street leads on through the outer courtyard. On either side stand modern buildings housing offices, archives and parts of the Ministry of Finance. The Museum of Royal Regalia and Coins (extra admission charge) is in a side street; it contains many individual items that are worth seeing.

At the end of the street by which the visitor enters lies the Great Chakri Palace, the centre-point of the so-called Chakri complex and of the central courtyard. It was designed by an English architect in the Italian Renaissance style. King Chulalongkorn had the pink-coloured palace built as a reminder of his European tour. He insisted, however, on the typical Siamese stepped roofs surmounted by their "Mondops". The highest one, which is also in the middle, contains an urn filled with the ashes of the Chagri kings who have reigned to date. The ashes of royal princes are in the two lower ones.

Chakri Maha Prasad

A stairway across a two-section arch leads to a terrace and the entrance to the reception rooms. Beyond lies the Audience Chamber with the nielloed silver throne under a nine-tier umbrella, where on special occasions the King still receives ambassadors from Bangkok's 50 or more embassies.

In earlier times the kings occupied the east wing, while the queens had their quarters in the west wing. Lit by crystal chandeliers, all the rooms are decorated with splendid portraits of kings and queens and pictures of ambassadors being received at the Courts of, for example, Napoleon I and Queen Victoria. Entry to this building is, however, allowed only when special tours are arranged by the Fine Arts Department or on application to the visitor's own embassy.

The incongruities in the style of the exterior of the palace led an Englishman, who had come to Thailand in the 1960s to advise

101

on town-planning in Bangkok and Thonburi, to write the following comment under a photograph of the palace in 1966. "Maha Chakri Palace, built 1876–80 . . . Not even the charming idea of replacing a dome with a Thai roof is enough to tone down the hideousness of the 19th c. European Building" (Larry Sternstein, "Bangkok at the Turn of the Century: Mongkut and Chulalongkorn entertain the West").

Anybody who is fortunate to take a helicopter flight over the palace will grant, however, that King Chulalongkorn must have had some inkling 140 years ago that later generations would fly through the air as a matter of course, for "harmony with the environment" is the principle behind his pattern of roofs.

Dusit Maham Prasad

West of the Chakri Palace lies Dusit Maham Prasad. This white building, erected by Rama I in 1789, seems graceful, despite its size, with the fourfold curved roofs clad with red and green glazed tiles. The plan is so laid out that the roofs cross over the gables with their gold ornamentation and rise up to their golden Mondop which surmounts all this, towering up in a spire, like a chedi. The starting-point of the plan, creating the harmonious linkage of the curves of the roof, are four Garudas, mythical birds which served the god Vishnu as steeds and are symbols of royalty in Thailand.

The large inner chamber is open to visitors. It used to be Rama I's Audience Chamber. The King did not, however, receive his guests sitting on the black throne with mother-of-pearl inlay which can be seen today, but on a higher one which stands in a niche in the wall of the south wing. The murals, too, depicting tevados, lotus flowers and foliage in muted colouring, were painted only later, when the chamber was used solely for the ceremonial lying-in-state of deceased kings. The richly ornamented bier and a number of other individual pieces of furniture do, however, date back to the time of Rama I, as do the timbers of the walls and ceiling, which at that period still had to be brought down from the north with enormous effort by elephants and on rafts.

Amporn Phimok Prasad

After the grandeur of the Dusit Maham Palace the ornamental pavilion at its exit, the Amporn Phimok Prasad, like the rich green of the propped-up ebony tree on the edge of the oval of turf, seems especially cheering and gracious. The pavilion was used by the King as a robing chamber where he changed between "progresses", whether on litter or elephant throne, and audiences. Before he alighted – the litters and the platform at the pavilion were of the same height – golden drapes were let down between the pillars while he donned different robes. The Aisawan Tippaya Pavilion at Bang Pa In (see entry) is a copy of this building.

The paths that fork to go around both sides of the Chakri Palace lead to the quarters where the women and children were once housed. At times there were over 3000 living here, including former and future concubines of all ages. Nowadays this part of the palace is private accommodation and not open to tourists.

Mahamontien and Amarinda
Vinichai Room

Near the Chakri Palace, a little to the east, stands a complex of buildings in three sections known as Mahamontien (or High Residence). The palace in the front is generally open to visitors. It is a single, vast hall called Amarinda Vinichai (meaning roughly "Divine Decision, Solemn Judgement"). It was here that the coronation ceremonies took place from the time of

Dusit Maham Prasad

King Rama I to that of King Rama IX. The hall is now used only for ceremonial State events. The paintings on the ceiling and walls are quite magnificent, but what really catches the eye is the broad golden throne in the background, shaped like a boat. In earlier times golden curtains fell around it, and they were drawn back only when the King, in strict conformity to etiquette, was to appear there. In the Buddha position, with legs crossed, he used to sit in majesty in the middle of the "boat" to receive the homage that was his due.

The present King was in fact also crowned in traditional fashion on 5 May 1950. However, he prefers to sit on the throne placed in front of it, which is far lower and allows the King to adopt the European sitting position. Moreover, each year on the anniversary of his coronation, not only are Heads of State and other high-ranking dignitaries invited here to be invested with titles and awards, but also men and women of every social class who have rendered particular service to the country and its people or have distinguished themselves in social work (see Notable Personalities).

On leaving the building visitors turn to the right round the peristyle in front of it, where royal judgements used to be proclaimed. The red and gold individual posts were "parking places" for the royal elephants. In the pavilion, ornamented with glass mosaics and a marble floor, the purification rites – of Brahmin origin – used to be carried out at coronations in days gone by.

The extensive stretches of lawns, with bright flowers and the vivid hues of the surounding trees, were used until a few years back for the garden party celebrating the King's birthday. Nowadays the royal couple retire to the privacy of the provinces on

Sivalaya Garden

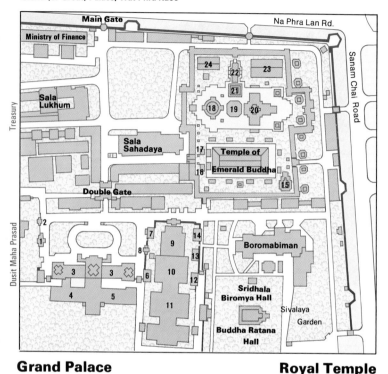

Grand Palace
Phra Borom Maha Rajawang

1 Royal Council
2 Amporn Phimok Prasad
3 Chakri Maha Prasad
4 Somut-Devaraj-Ubbat Room
5 Moonstarn-Baromasna Room
6 Hor Phra Dhart Monthien
7 Dusida-Bhiromya Room
8 Snamchandr Room

9 Amarindra-Vinichal Room
10 Paisal-Taksin Room
11 Chakrabardi Biman
12 Hor Phrasulalaya Biman
13 Rajruedi-Room
14 Hor Satrakom
15 Hor Kantnararasdr
16 Hor Rajbongsanusorn

Royal Temple
Wat Phra Kaeo

17 Hor Rajkornmanusorn
18 Phra Sri Ratana Chedi
19 Phra Mondop
20 Prasad Phra Debicorn
21 Modell von Angkor Wat
22 Phra Viharn Yod
23 Hor Monthien Dharma
24 Hor Phra Naga

that day (5 Dec.), and invitations that were once so exclusive are now handed out to thousands. In Government House the Prince and Princesses celebrate the event with guests who are by no means restricted to the "élite".

Boromabiman

Boromabiman Hall is the official name of the adjoining building with the square dome over the inner hall, from which it took its name of Heavenly Abode. Frescoes depict the four Indian gods – Indra, Yahuma, Varuna and Agni – as protectors of the universe, above plaques on which are inscribed the ten royal virtues: liberality and propriety; readiness to make sacrifices, uprightness, clemency and modesty; conscientiousness over duty; freedom from anger; freedom from suspicion; patience and, finally, right judgement in actions. Since the time of Rama VI (Vajiravudh) all the Crown Princes, including the present King, have grown up here. Nowadays the building is used only from time to time to house visiting Heads of State (as it was for the visit of Queen Elizabeth II) or high Buddhist dignitaries.

Wat Phra Kaeo

On workdays it is possible to go from the outer court of the palaces through a side gate straight into the sacred precinct. On Sundays and public holidays the main gate of the temple , on Sanam Chai Street, is also open. By this gate may be seen the beginning of the "Ramakien", depicted in murals which were last renovated in 1987, and in marble plaques with verse inscriptions, personally redrafted by King Chulalongkorn, as many of his royal predecessors had also done.

Photography prohibited

In contrast to the palace precinct the sacred precinct has, despite restorations, remained purely Asian in style. The Chinese, who were the original inhabitants of the whole quarter, must have left behind some of the menacing gigantic sentinels, the so-called "Jaks", or else have subsequently donated them.

European influence may be seen in the eight statues of kings inside the "Pantheon", which is open to visitors only one day a year, i.e. "Chakri Day", on 6 April. Everything else is Thai in appearance, some of it still profoundly influenced by Ayutthaya, and other parts (in the chedis and Prangs) by Singhalese and Cambodian sacred styles.

The four corners of the Phra's Mondop will be recognised by those with a knowledge of Javanese art as belonging to the Borobudur style. They are said to date from the 14th c. For once the Mondop is not high up above the roof; in fact it seems comparatively lowly placed between its two neighbours, the Pantheon (Phra Debidorn) and the relic chedi (Phra Sri Ratana) with its massive gilded tiles. It normally houses a magnificent black lacquered bookcase with mother-of-pearl inlay, in which are kept the Sacred Scriptures (Tripitaka or Triple Basket). The Mondop floor is pure silver.

The various numbers of elephant figures with crowned heads symbolise the amount of "good fortune" possessed by Rama I, II and III in white pachyderms.

As in every wat, here, too, there are shady Salas under sheltering roofs intended as places of rest for worshippers, as well as a library with a particularly beautiful west front and a wiharn.

In Phra Wiharn Yod is to be found the most ancient sight in the entire precinct, a stone throne of Ramkamhaeng (13th c.), the founder of Thailand. It was discovered by King Mongkut (Rama IV) in the course of his years of wandering when he was a monk, and he had it brought here. From the time of Rama IV also comes the model of Angkor Wat in Cambodia – which at that date still recognised his suzerainty. Even though it lacks the impressive size of the original and the primal forests that surround it, all students of archaeology find it a most rewarding educational model to visit.

Phra Wiharn Yod

The elephant figures nearby have a special importance for visitors to Bangkok: even though signs ask you not to touch them, you can watch and see both Thais and foreigners stroke first the head of one of the animals and then their own heads. Legend says that, if you do this in the correct order, it will not be

Frescoes in Wat Phra Kaeo

your last visit to Bangkok or to Thailand. Try it if you like – preferably when you are not being observed!

The way to the Holy of Holies – not just for the palace and city, but for the whole country – leads past the Assembly Hall with recently restored murals by In-Khong (Rama IV's Court Painter), then past a row of colourful Stupas with the ashes of deceased members of the royal families. After duly removing their shoes visitors mount the stairway flanked by bronze lions and come to the marble platform of the bot where photography is strictly prohibited. Passing through golden pillars which have lotus-flower capitals and are decorated with glazed earthenware tiles, visitors come to the main chapel, but not by way of the central aisle, as this is reserved for the King. The pair of lions guarding the entrance come from Cambodia and were brought here by Rama I, the builder of the temple. The other two pairs of lions are from a temple at Ayutthaya (see entry).

Bot (Temple of the Emerald Buddha)

Photography forbidden

Inside the bot stands the tall plinth with the Emerald Buddha under a nine-tier canopy. It was carved out of a piece of jade in Patalibutr (India), according to legend. Another source says its home is in Vientiane in neighbouring Laos, where it is said to have stood in the Wat Phra Kaeo and where it is still mourned today. However, it certainly came by way of Ceylon and Cambodia to North Thailand, where it was discovered in Chiangmai in 1436 when its plaster and gold-leaf ornament flaked off as it was being transported. The King of Chiangmai wanted to take it to his residence, but the elephant chosen to carry it refused to

Emerald Buddha

◀ *In the grounds of Wat Phra Kaeo*

107

Kinnaris and Nagas

do so. Consequently it remained for years in the Wat Phra Kaeo of Lampang before it was taken to Chiangmai.

When the King of Laos conquered Chiangmai in 1551 he in turn took it to his residence, that is first to Luang Prabang, then to Vientiane where it is still sadly missed from their Wat Phra Kaeo (see above). In 1778, when King Taksin ruled in Thonburi, his general Chao-Phaya took Vientiane and handed over the Phra Kaeo – by now venerated throughout the Buddhist world – to his King in Thonburi (Wat Arun).

Then, after he himself had been proclaimed King as Rama I, he brought the statue to its present site.

The beautiful lines of the statue are seen to best advantage in the rainy season (mid-May to October) or, failing that, in the hot period (February to May). During the cold season (November to February) it is almost totally concealed under a covering of gold netting. The changing of the statue's raiment according to the season of the year is always carried out by the King himself in solemn ceremonies based on Thai tradition; the King climbs up a ladder to reach the holy relic.

On the front of the richly ornamented plinth are three remarkable statues. The two standing Buddhas were named after Rama I and Rama II and date from the reign of Rama III (1824–51). The third, which is seated, was cast by King Mongkut (Rama I) in person. It stands under the smaller canopy in the centre. The small gold and silver trees were a tribute presented by the Princes of Laos and Malaya respectively.

Both to the right and the left over the entrance are depicted scenes from the life of Buddha, while the universe is portrayed on the back wall in Buddhist astrological representation. Epi-

Buddha in the raiment proper to summer, the rainy season, and winter

sodes from the "Ramakien" are related both in pictures and simple rhymes on the doors and window-shutters.
After leaving the temple it is well worth walking round the plinth with its graceful bird-maidens (Kinnaris) and the golden Nagas – symbolic snakes which hang down in great numbers from the Garudas as if in triumph, looking like skipping-ropes.

**Kanchanaburi (Menam Kwai Yai)

Until some fifty years ago Kanchanaburi was one of Thailand's least interesting regions, only its rural charm and variety together with its relative proximity to Bangkok made it a favoured leisure spot. However, archaeological digs have shown that there were settlements here back in prehistoric times, and that the rivers flowing down from the mountains in the west formed an important part of the trade routes between Southeast Asia, Burma and Cambodia.
The Three Pagodas Pass near the source of the Menam Kwae Noi River also provided the gateway through which poured the Burmese hordes when finally, in 1767, they defeated Ayutthaya and razed the country to the ground. Thus the provincial capital of Kanchanaburi grew up at a strategically important site; there, where the two rivers, the Kwae Yai (the "River Kwai") and Kwae Noi join at Mae Klong and the wild and rugged mountains open up into a broad plain leading down to the Gulf of Siam, the Siamese armies were in a good position to defy the enemy.
Perhaps even then Kanchanaburi attracted inhabitants to it because of its fertile soil. Sugar cane, tobacco, cotton, maize and cassava thrive here, but today the main crop grown is rice. Also of great economic importance are the numerous mines from which are obtained the precious stones used in Thailand's famous jewellery industry. In the limestone mountains, which

Location
130km/75 miles north-west of Bangkok

Rail
From Hualampong Main Station via Nakhon Pathorn
Day trips arranged by SRT (Thai Railways)

Buses
From the Southern Bus Terminal
Bus tours

Best season
September to early Feb.

For river hotels
Anti-malaria, anti-mosquito protection

For caves
Pocket-torches

rise to as high as 1800m/5900ft and are covered with thick rain-forests, there are many imposing waterfalls and numerous magnificent caves and grottos. The Erawan National Park (see below), 67km/55 miles from Kanchanaburi, is also well worth a visit.

The first organised digs and explorations were commenced in the 1950s under the guidance of the Dutchman Dr van Heekeren who, as a POW, was forced to work on the Bridge on the River Kwai (see below), and stayed here at the end of the Second World War. They really began as a result of some chance finds of prehistoric stone implements in, for example, Bo Ploi to the north of Kanchanaburi and Sai Yok to its west. In caves and under bushes along the river bank in Sai Yok were found implements dating from the Neolithic Period (New Stone Age). An Iron Age grave was found perfectly preserved; the manner in which the deceased was interred is now normally followed in Kanchanaburi, i.e. facing north, with the legs bent and the upper body weighed down with a stone. The latter is to ensure that the spirit of the departed remains in the grave, and cannot escape to confuse or distress the living.

In spite of the many digs and finds there still remains much to be done. Further excavations are taking place under the generous auspices of UNESCO in an attempt to bring to light evidence which will provide a picture of the ancient history of Thailand, much of which is still shrouded in mystery.

Sights

Apart from being a lively, almost effervescent place with a busy harbour, the town itself has little to offer in the way of places of interest, but is nevertheless a good choice if you are seeking an idyllic place to stay far from the hustle and bustle of Bangkok.

The Bridge on the River Kwai

The main tourist attraction in Kanchanaburi is the notorious Bridge on the River Kwai, made famous by the novel of the same name by Pierre Boulle (1956) and by David Lean's spectacular 1958 film (which was in fact shot in Ceylon). Visitors today to this bridge situated some 5km/3 miles outside the town do in fact see a modern steel and concrete construction which has replaced the original, having been built after the Thailand State Railway (SRT) took it over. Only the supporting pillars (apart from the two central ones which were destroyed by bombing) remain from the old bridge. It formed the central part of the 415km/260 miles long "Death Railway", which was built over the Three Pagodas Pass in only sixteen months by more than 300,000 prisoners of war of the Japanese. During the dry season about 100m/110yds downstream can be seen the remains of a bamboo bridge which was used temporarily while the new bridge was being built.

Bridges and railways were considered by the Japanese to be a safer link between Ban Pong and Burma, the shipping route through the Strait of Malacca being far more dangerous. Those forced to work on the railroad included 61,000 British, Australians, Americans and Dutch who had mostly been taken prisoner after the fall of Singapore on 15 February 1942; there were also some 250,000 slave-labourers and workers from the Japanese-occupied countries including Thailand, Burma and Malaysia. Over 16,000 Allied POWs perished here, dying for the most part of malnutrition and tropical diseases as well as in

Allied bombing raids. The names and precise numbers of the coolies who died (estimated at about 100,000) were never recorded by their taskmasters. Once the bridge was completed most of the survivors were shipped off to Nagasaki in Japan to work in the mines, where thousands more died.

The sad story of the Bridge on the River Kwai is perhaps best illustrated by means of a visit to the little POW museum in Kanchanaburi, known as the JEATH War Museum; the name is made up from the initial letters of some of the countries of origin of those who were forced to work on the railroad, Japan, England, America, Thailand and Holland. Situated near Wat Chai Chumphon on the bank of the Mae Klong River, it is housed in three huts made of leaves similar to those in which hundreds of prisoners lived. Looking at the old photographs, notes and pictures painted by the prisoners themselves, together with the makeshift surgical instruments devised by the doctors to treat their injured comrades, it is not difficult to imagine the suffering and privation they endured.

The JEATH War Museum

Open daily 8.30 a.m.–4.30 p.m.

Apart from the Americans, whose bodies were taken back to their homeland after the war, the Allied dead lie buried under simple stone tablets in two very carefully tended military cemeteries surrounded by luxuriant greenery, one quite near the bridge, the other, smaller Chong Kai cemetery being on the bank of the Kwai Noi (Little River). The latter, with the graves of 1700 dead, is likely to impress the visitor more than the larger one; a small boat can be hired at the Kwai Bridge for the fifteen minute trip upstream. At the foot of a knoll in the cemetery is a memorial, at the entrance to which a book is sometimes open to inspection, containing the names of those who died.

War Graves

Kanchanaburi: the Bridge on the River Kwai

111

Kanchanaburi

Kanchanaburi War Cemetery

From Kanchanaburi to Nam-Tok by rail

While you can of course cross the famous bridge on foot or on a hired bicycle, it is far more rewarding to make the 77km/48 mile train journey from the bridge to the present rail terminus. It is also possible to take a train from Bangkok; it leaves Thonburi main station each day, with additional trains on Sundays and public holidays.

After the track had been taken over by the Royal Thailand Railways the section lying in Burma was closed. The most interesting section of the journey, about an hour out from Kanchanaburi, goes along a steeply falling ridge, above the river rather than by its bank, and passengers will be pleased that the train travels slowly here, for reasons of safety as well as for the view. During the journey you will pass a grotto which is now a shrine – it used to provide accommodation and also served as an air raid shelter for the prisoners.

Nam-Tok Khao Pang Waterfall

Less than a mile from the bridge is the Khao Pang Waterfall, in the basin of which it is possible to bathe.

Mangkom Thong Grotto

A half an hour's boat trip on the Kwai Noi will bring you to the Mangkom Thong Grotto; boats can be hired in Kanchanaburi. Two brightly coloured dragons guard the entrance; 95 steps lead down to a temple in the cave, and a tunnel takes you to the mountain peak, with a broad grotto containing some beautiful stalactites.

Ban Kao Archaeological Site

Ban Kao, by the Kwai Noi, used to be one of the most important archaeological digs in Kanchanaburi province. However, the finds – implements, animal bones, ceramic pots and the fully preserved grave mentioned above – are now housed in Bangkok National Museum, together with statues in the Lopburi style, a subsidiary form of the Khmer style, 7th–13th c., which were found in Prasat Muang Singh, the "Town of the Lions", 34km/21 miles from Kanchanaburi.

Prasat Muang Singh was built as a stronghold against the Burmese; parts still survive of the town wall which once covered a square measuring 1000 by 600m/3300 by 2000ft, and also of a shrine and four Gopuras, or defensive towers. The shrine with its brick Prang is well-preserved; the inner courtyard measures 18 by 26m/60 by 86ft, and a large number of inscriptions were found in the library on the right-hand side. Behind the restaurant at the entrance to Muang Singh stands a hut in which more recent finds are stored waiting to be catalogued. Nearby under a palm-leaf lean-to are exhibited some well preserved statues and the like.

Prasat Muang Singh

The adventurous boat trip to the Sai Yok Waterfalls passes over rapids and between high rock-faces, and will leave a lasting impression. Torrents cascade down into the Kwai Noi. During the rainy period the Kwai Noi is navigable as far as Songkhla. From there a path leads through relatively virgin jungle to Three Pagodas Pass, where some mountain tribes have settled and eke out an existence by laboriously clearing the jungle to plant crops or by smuggling.

Nam-Tok Sai Yok Waterfalls

This pass gets its name from the three pagodas situated along the road which winds its way up to heights of some 1400m/4600ft, the highest mountain in this region reaching 1950m/6435ft. Today the pass is a favourite route for smugglers between Burma and Thailand, and is not recommended.

"Three Pagodas Pass"

The province of Kanchanaburi owes part of its wealth to its productive mines, some of which near the little town of Bo Phioi are still worked today. Gold, silver, wolfram and tin are found here. There are also a large number of mines producing sapphires, star-sapphires, rare rubies and semi-precious and other stones used in jewellery, such as garnets, agate and amethysts. In the Bo Phioi shops it is possible to buy uncut or polished stones and jewellery more cheaply than elsewhere in Thailand.

Bo Phioi Mines

About 95km/60 miles from Bo Phioi (turn left at Ban Nong Preu) lie two grottoes which are well worth a visit. In the first, Talad Noi Grotto, many finds were made which showed there had been a prehistoric settlement there. In the caves, wide in parts and high in others, you can see some impressive stalactites and stalagmites.

Talad Noi Grotto

In the second cave, Talad Yai ("The Great Grotto"), which lies about 2.5km/1½ miles past the Nam Tok Trai Treung Waterfall, live two hermits.

Talad Yai grotto

Other sights

Other worthwhile places to visit in the Kwai Yai valley include Wat Kanchanaburi, a temple on the site of the old town of Kanchanaburi, where a Chedi and a Prang from the Ayutthaya period still remain, and also the Erawan Waterfall; the latter is

Klong Toey market

situated some 55km/34 miles from Kanchanaburi, and can be reached by car along the 3199, a good road, or by way of a three hour boat trip.

Erawan Waterfall

The waters of the Nam Tok Erawan plunge down from the rocks above in fifteen cascades from level to level. The rocks are thought to resemble the three-headed elephant of the god Indra, hence the name Erawakan. The best time of year to go is during the rainy season.

National Park

The whole area, covering 2024 sq.km/745 sq. miles, has been declared the Khao Salop National Park, merging into the Thung Yai Nature Reserve. It is best to visit them during the week, as they are usually thronged with people from Bangkok at the week-ends.

Pong Teuk Archaeological Site

East of Kanchanaburi, by the No. 323 road to Nakhon Pathom – probably a very old trade route – lies the famous archaeological site of Pong Teuk. The foundations of several buildings which probably formed part of temples have been unearthed here. A quite sensational find was made in 1928, a bronze Roman oil-lamp probably cast in the 2nd c. A.D. in Alexandria in Egypt. Its handle is in the shape of a stylised palm leaf surrounded by dolphins, while the lid is decorated with the head of a Silenus. This find provides proof that commercial relationships must have existed between the Roman Empire and Southeast Asia.

Wat Dong Sak

Other buildings to visit include Wat Dong Sak, built of teak and containing a beautifully carved gable and a 6th c. figure of Vishnu, and also Wat Phra Taen Dong Rang, which is reached via roads 323 or 324, in which, according to legend, Buddha is said to have lain in a manger in order to enter into the state of beatitude known as Nirvana. A short distance away on a hillside stands another shrine where – again according to legend – Buddha's corpse was cremated.

Klong Toey market

See Markets

*Klongs (Canals)   A–G 1–3

General

For over 500 years, since the first Europeans came to Ayutthaya and later to Bangkok, one of Thailand's most exotic sights as far as they were concerned – apart from the pomp and ceremony at Court – was the life on the waterways. However, now that almost all the Klongs in Bangkok itself and many on the opposite bank of the Menam Chao Phraya in Thonburi have been drained and turned into roads, the end of this way of life in the Thailand capital is not only in sight – it is imminent.

While the opportunity still exists of getting to know this aspect of Thai life, one should not shrink from venturing quite a long way out of Bangkok for once.

Even the locals make no distinction between whether it is a Klong (or canal) or a natural watercourse, just as nobody distinguishes between waterways as places where you live your everyday life on the one hand, and routes for transport and trade on the other.

The two possibilities described here – a third is a visit to the Floating Market of Damnoen Saduak (see under Floating Markets) – offer individuals as well as groups of tourists, whatever their means, as wide a choice as possible. Those who are able to do so should make a point of taking a trip along the waterways in the early morning and a second one in the late afternoon.

The map of the Klongs provided by the Thailand Information Bureau TAT – and also available in Europe – is most helpful in finding your way about, and information on which to base your own individual combination of Klong trips can be obtained from the TAT in Bangkok (see Tourist Information).

Anyone who intends to go independently would be well advised to start at one of the landing jetties by the river where there are usually boat-owners waiting for custom. It is advisable to negotiate the fare before you climb aboard; about 500 to 600 baht should be about the right price for a two-hour trip.

Independent Klong Tours

The most interesting feature of all Klong trips (best made in a rowing-boat for two to four people) is observing the everyday life of the people living on them. The smaller the Klong, the more charming and unspoilt it appears, although the smell may well offend a sensitive Western nose. However, it is worth bearing in mind the words of Somerset Maugham, who described the many smells of Bangkok as a mixture of sewage and orchids. If it gets too bad there is only one thing to do – hold your nose and press on regardless!

In order to reach the Klongs of Thonburi the visitor will have to cross the Menam Chao Phraya river. Starting from the landing stage near the Oriental Hotel (Tha Orientään), first row a fair way downstream, then cross the Menam to one of Thonburi's wide waterways. Between these Klongs there is an intricate network of medium-sized canals leading into smaller and then even smaller ones, the narrowest being as little as three or four metres/ten to thirteen feet wide. They are lined with bright-hued tropical blossoms, and the few remaining original Klongs are shaded by a vaulted roof of green foliage formed by the palm trees growing along the banks.

What there is to see depends on the time of day. In the early morning there are monks rowing from gangplank to gangplank in their solo craft with their alms-bowls; dozens, if not hundreds, of students and schoolchildren in their gleaming white uniforms; market-women in boats selling fresh fruit, vegetables, charcoal and cooking utensils. Sometimes a postman in his snugly fitting uniform can be seen carefully keeping his balance in his cockleshell craft and on the swaying gangplanks and trying to deliver his letters, addressed in Thai, Chinese and English, without, if possible, getting them splashed with water. Sometimes, however, he merely pushes the post into the mailboxes alongside the canals. Perhaps he will change over from a larger boat into a smaller one, and then he will be the best person to act as a guide to the smaller and most beautiful Klongs.

In the late afternoon a truly "foaming" spectacle can be observed: between 4 and 5pm things really start "bubbling up" in the Klongs, in every sense of the word, as people get going with soap, shampoo, toothpaste and washing-powder. The very

Departure points
Either Bangkok Yai or Bangkok Noi Klongs, as a way into the smaller Klongs

Landing-stages
See map on page 116

Best times
6–10am and 4–7pm

115

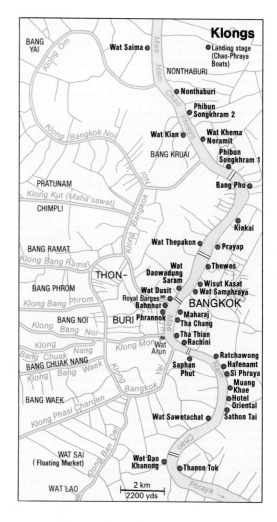

young and the very old sit half in, half out of the water on their bottom doorstep, while others stand, paddle or wade around with just their heads above water. Stark-naked boys and girls indulge in water-fights, while not forgetting to wave cheekily to passers-by. Whilst it is true that the Bangkok authorities now deliver fresh water daily to the Klong-dwellers, this tends to be used mainly for cooking. However murky the water may appear to Western eyes, the Thais feel perfectly clean and refreshed once this pleasurable evening exercise is completed.

New splendour for an ancient Royal Barge

In an unprepossessing hangar at the mouth of the Bangkok Noi Klong are kept the Royal Barges, duly restored in time for the King's 60th birthday in 1987. For many years they were unused and seemed to have been almost forgotten. At one time they were used to transport the ruler of the day across the Menam Chao Phraya to Wat Arun, where he took part in a religious ceremony on a certain day in early April. For a time King Bhumibol used the land route to Wat Arun; it was not until preparations were in train for his jubilee celebrations that the magnificent old barges were remembered. Restored with a loving attention to detail, they were enthusiastically received at a grand birthday parade on the Menam Chao Phraya, attended by hundreds of thousands of visitors gathered on the banks of the river.

*Royal Barges

Sometimes there is the opportunity to watch sailors from the Marine Academy practising their rowing.

It is worth while to stop briefly at some of the interesting temples to be seen along the canals, for example, Wat Kalaya at the mouth of the Bangkok Yai Klong, which was founded and restored by King Mongkut (Rama IV) over 130 years ago. Its wiharn has the highest and longest temple roof in Bangkok, and the library of the Holy Scriptures (Hor Trai) is well worth seeing. A monk or novice will willingly show the interested visitor around. Never offer a personal tip, however; put the money in one of the glass collecting-boxes instead.

Wat Kalaya

Anyone who prefers not to risk trying to get there by boat can take an early morning taxi or the bus to Thonburi Railway Station or straight to Wat Suwannaram. The railway station lies

Wat Suwannaram

opposite the Royal Barges, on the south bank of the Bangkok Noi, and the wat precinct, just a few minutes' walk away, has a landing-stage on the Klong.

The wat has a bot and a wiharn which date back to the time of Rama I (c. 1800) and exhibit many features of the Ayutthaya style, such as the elegant harmony of the roof, the antechamber buttresses, and wood-carvings which are plainer than those in the temples. Visitors entering the bot will be impressed by the particularly fine frescos of Rama III's time; many connoisseurs consider them to be the finest in all Bangkok. The triumph of Buddha over Mara (the temptation of evil) above the entrance is depicted far more imaginatively than in the many statues which symbolise it merely through gestures of the hands.

Klong Chak Phra/Bang Kun Sai

From the temple landing-stage take a pradscham (a boat providing a scheduled service) which goes off to the left, i.e. away from the main river. Bearing left once again, opposite Wat Suwan Khiri, the boat turns into Chak Phra Klong which runs past some very pretty onshore houses and here and there the villa of a rich Bangkok citizen. This Klong is now called Bang Kun Sai, and there is a choice of either taking the Klong forking off to the left which goes straight on to Wat Arun (see entry), or of staying on the boat and continuing along this Klong, which soon widens out into Bangkok Yai, returning to Wat Pak Naam.

Wat Pak Naam

It is possible to leave the boat for a while at Wat Pak Naam and to find an English-speaking "Farang" or foreigner in monk's robes or possibly even a young "Metji" in her white nun's garb, since this temple is one of the city's great centres of meditation,

Nuns (Metji) in Wat Pak Naam

enjoys an extremely good reputation and attracts many visitors from the West wishing to learn more of the teachings of Buddha.

From here there is again a choice between going by road and taking the bus back to Bangkok via the Memorial Bridge, or re-embarking on the boat to continue in the same direction as far as Wat Kayala (see above) with its great roof, where on the left Wat Po (see entry) can be seen on the opposing bank. Scheduled boats of all kinds ply from here to Wat Po, to Sanaam Luang (see entry), back to the start of the tour, the Oriental Hotel (Tha Orientään) or, staying on the west bank, to Wat Arun (see entry).

It is of course possible to follow the route that has just been described in the opposite direction. Equipped with a map and the names of the klongs and wats mentioned, you can get by with a minimal knowledge of the language and very little expense, and yet not miss out on the sights or lose independence.

Tip

Rice Barge Tours

These afternoon trips are beginning to replace more and more the former evening Dinner Barge Tours, although the latter continue to be offered in a particularly grand style by the Oriental Hotel on the elegant "Ayutthaya Princess" and "Ayutthaya Queen", and can be booked at the Oriental Hotel reception desk. The hotel reception will also provide details of the Rice Barge Tours, which take you further away from Bangkok; when booking, make it quite clear that you want to see a Fishermen and Farmhouses Klong, and avoid over-large groups; about 20–40 people is ideal.

The particular tour described here starts by taking a very small boat (it is also possible to go overland by bus) to the Phra Weed Klong Barge. This waterway is about 8m/26ft wide and free of big tourist steamers and cargo boats, so that the peasants and fishermen at the water's edge can be seen, as well as the paddy-fields nearby being cultivated using water-buffaloes.

A stop can be made on the way to inspect a typical peasant dwelling, with cooking utensils and farm implements, and to see the very entertaining fish feeding at Wat Yang with its village on a bridge, Saen Saeb.

The prospect of catching one of the thousands of Blaa-got (a kind of catfish) with bare hands seems highly unlikely, but it can be done, although this is not the time of day to try, since feeding them is a typical Thai Buddhist tambuun, i.e. an act of acquiring merit for the after-life, which also happens to be Sanuk, or great fun. These may well be the fish that gave rise to the popular saying "dschabblaa song my" (catching fish with both hands), which is used to make fun of any man who tries to hang on to two women at the same time, since the chances are that, like the fish, both of them will get away.

The barges, with their typical curved tarpaulin roofs, have enough freeboard to allow passengers to give their eyes, cameras and above all their lungs full rein, since the air here is not yet laden with exhaust fumes. Apart from a narrow wooden

bench and a miniature WC the boat does not pander to Western tastes, but is very much a typical Thai model, complete with delicious local fruit and drinks, with or without alcohol, and the nut cakes, usually free of charge, which every Thai hostess has on hand for her guests.

Kwai Bridge

See Kanchanaburi

Lak Muang (shrine)   D2

Built around the city's foundation and boundary-stone, this shrine is the point from which all distances are measured. According to popular animistic belief, however, this little "house of spirits" is the home of the real but unseen landlords of the whole city.
The throng of people carrying flowers and joss-sticks around the Lingam, which is the phallic symbol in the middle, are hoping it will bring them good luck in all kinds of earthly ventures, especially in the lottery, for which tickets are on sale close by (see Facts and Figures, Religion, Animism). Performances of Thai opera can quite often be seen to the left of the entrance.

Location
Opposite the south-eastern end of Sanaam Luang, near the Ministry of Defence

Buses
3, 6

Open
Daily 6am–10pm

Lumpini Park (Suan Lumpini)   E/F 4

Every morning between six and eight o'clock Lumpini Park in the centre of Bangkok is the meeting-place for many people practising shadow-boxing (Thai-Dschi-Tschüen), with groups and individual fighters performing in a sort of open-air ballet under the luxuriant trees with brick-red blossoms in among little artificial pools and streams. At week-ends and public holidays in particular the "Lumpini" is one of the few green "lungs" in Bangkok where people can go to relax – and they go in their thousands! However, the visitor should not be put you off but, on the contrary, take this opportunity of enjoying Bangkok life to the full and experiencing the friendliness and hospitality of the Thailander.
In the late afternoon and evening the park is a favourite spot for sports and games, and the garden restaurants are very popular.
Thousands gather in the park on May Day, and when there are strikes or elections, as well just before Christmas for the international bazaar organised by the Scouts and Guides and the foreign embassies.
The park gets its name from Buddha's birthplace. The statue in Rama IV Road, in front of the main entrance, is of Rama VI (1910–25).

Location
In the south-east of the city, bounded by Rama IV Road, Ratehadamri Road and Wit Thayu Road

Buses
4, 5, 7

Open
Daily 6am–10pm

Marble Temple

See Wat Benchamabopit

◄ *Floating takeaway on a klong*

*Markets

General

Every day, from sunrise to sunset and even on into the night, numerous markets are set up in Bangkok and all around to meet most of the townspeople's demand for fresh vegetables, live animals such as chickens and fish, clothing, textiles and other daily needs. As well as the big week-end market (see Chatuchak Week-end Market), visitors to the capital will find these daily markets just as interesting; nowhere else in Bangkok will you experience such noise and bustle so typical of life in south-east Asia. The markets are usually at their busiest on Fridays and Saturdays.

Those listed here represent only a small proportion; you will easily be able to find many more for yourself.

Klong Toey   F5

Location
Rama IV Road

Bus
44

Klong Toey market is one of the cheapest, if not the cheapest, in Bangkok, but the goods are displayed in a rather haphazard fashion, with fish next to clothing, for example. There is, nevertheless, plenty to choose from. As the market is not centrally situated it serves as an open-air shopping centre for poorer people.

Nakhon Kasem (Thieves' Market)   E3

Location
Chinatown, Charoen Krung Road

Buses
1, 7

This market, in the middle of Chinatown, still profits from its traditionally bad reputation, having at one time been notorious as a place for disposing of goods obtained in dubious circumstances..That may well have been the case many years ago but today "Thieves' Market" should certainly be visited because its rich variety of goods for sale is unparalleled. Anyone who is patient enough may well succeed in discovering amongst the numerous reproductions a genuine antique worth far more than its asking price. Nakhon Kasem is at its busiest in the evenings.

Tha Thewes (Flower market)   C2

Location
On the bank of the Menam Chao Phraya, near the National Library

Bus
6

Landing stage
Tha Thewes

The whole range of flowers grown in Thailand will be found displayed in Tha Thewes market. In the early mornings many children lovingly and skilfully make the garlands of flowers for which Thailand is famous. They then offer these for sale until late at night to tourists, taxi-drivers and even the locals for just a few bahts, thus contributing at a very early age to the household budget. This Flower Market, one of the few markets to be found on the very bank of the river, is well worth a visit. Orchids in rare abundance, jasmine, hibiscus and lotus blossom are a joy to the eye and the senses, their scent drifting over the whole market. Numerous varieties of garden and jungle plants are also to be found. The morning is the best time for a visit.

Daily activity in Bangkok's market

Extensive variety of produce at the Chatuchak week-end market

Markets

Bangrak   F3

Location
Between Sathorn Thai Road
and Silom Road, near the
Shangri-La Hotel.

Mutton on the hoof can be found for sale at Bangrak market
only in the early hours of the morning, but it is still an interesting place to visit later in the day. Most of the fruit and
vegetables are snapped up by the larger Bangkok hotels, who
take full advantage of the wide range of fresh produce
available.

Pratu Nam   D4

Location
Petchburi/Ratchadamnoen
Road

Buses
12. 13

This is a very extensive market providing everything the average Thai needs for everyday existence, and as a result it is
always busy from morning till night, and therefore is one that is
well worth a visit. Craft workshops and other shops have
sprung up around the market stalls and covered halls making
the whole into a large shopping centre. Furthermore, it is very
favourably situated, being only about ten minutes' walk from
the Siam Hotel.

Pak Klong Talaad   E2

Location
Chakrapet Road

Also well worth a visit is Bangkok's big market, the Pak Klong
Talaad on the banks of the Menam Chao Phraya. This is where
retailers and hotel chefs obtain supplies of all descriptions.

Silom Road   F4

Location
Silom Road, between the
Narai Hotel and Silom Village

Not only are the shops along Silom Road open in the evenings,
but a lively street-market has established itself here as well. It is
worthwhile taking a stroll along this street, even though the
goods on display are limited to the normal run of cheap reproductions and the like. In some side streets (Sois) can be found
open-air restaurants and hot-dog stalls.

Pat Pong   F4

Location
Between Silom Road and
Surawong Road

Since Pat Pong Roads I and II have been closed to traffic from
5pm both the owners of amusement arcades and street traders
have realised that this is a profitable site for a night-market.
Admittedly about the only things on sale are the usual tourist
items at prices even higher than on other markets. Bartering is
almost obligatory! Sometimes the visitor may witness one of
the – albeit rare – police raids when imitation fabrics, watches
or pirate videos are seized, unless the trader happens to be
quicker than the arm of the law!

Floating Markets

See entry

Menam Chao Phraya

See Klongs

**Nakhon Pathom

Although historically unproven, it seems likely that at one time the city of Nakhon Pathom actually stood on the coast of the Gulf of Siam. Extensive silting-up resulted in the sea being pushed back more than 50km/30 miles, a factor which has contributed in no small measure to some of Bangkok's present-day problems; for example, the sandy, even muddy sub-soil has put great difficulties in the way of constructing an underground system which is urgently needed to combat Bangkok's serious traffic problem.

In spite of its changed geographical position, however, Nakhon Pathom remained a flourishing trading centre, and within its walls stands the most important building in the Buddhist world – the Phra Pathom Chedi.

Although much of the early history of Nakhon Pathom lies clouded in legend there is no doubt that it is one of the most ancient settlements in all Thailand. Its origins go back to the 2nd c. B.C., when King Asoka (273–231 B.C.), the Indian Gupta Emperor and a disciple of the new Therawada-Buddhist religion, ruled over a large kingdom. He sent monks to what is now the region around Nakhon Pathom to spread the teachings of Buddha. It was at that time, too, that a forerunner of the Phra Pathom Chedi is believed to have been built, although nothing is known of the form it took.

It is historically certain that Nahkon Pathom first became a settlement in 675 A.D. when, known as Nakhon Chaisi, it was the seat of government of King Chaisiri (or Chaisi or Sirichai) and of the kingdom of the same name. Most of the population were descended from the Mons, whose culture – as evidenced by numerous finds from this period, including stone Wheels of Law and paintings which are clearly meant to be Buddha – was strongly influenced by the Indo-Buddhist Gupta style. It is also certain that Nakhon Pathom succeeded U Thong as the capital city, and that a powerful Dvaravati Empire flourished at this time.

It can be safely concluded that Nakhon Pathom must have been a wealthy city because it was licensed to mint its own coinage. Silver coins from the 7th–8th c. have been found, the obverse of which carry symbols depicting prosperity (a cow with calf or a vase of flowers) and the reverse the Sanscrit inscription "Srid-varvati Svarapunya", or "In the service of the King of Dvara-vati".

Whether the Kingdom of Dvaravati and its capital Nakhon Pathom were conquered by the Burmese King Anuruddha is also uncertain. Historians tend to think that it was destroyed either by King Suryavarman I (1002–50) or by Yayavarman VII (1181–1218). After that Nakhon Pathom became forgotten as

Location
54km/34 miles west of Bangkok

Access
On Highway 4 (Petchkasem Highway)

Rail
From Hualampong Main Station (1 hour)

Buses
From Southern Bus Station (Thonburi):
Bus tours

most of its inhabitants moved away and founded the new city of Nakhon Chaisi on the right bank of the Ta Chin River, where it remains to this day.

It was King Mongkut (Rama IV) who, during the long period he spent as a monk before becoming King, came on a pilgrimage to the Phra Pathom Chedi and saw that it was in danger of being completely overgrown by the primeval jungle. When he came to the throne in 1851 he arranged to have it restored, but it was found to be in such a bad state that he decided to have the original Prang which dated from the Khmer period replaced by a new Chedi. However, a part of the new buildings collapsed in a storm and sadly it was not completed until after his death, when his successor Chulalongkorn was on the throne.

The City

Although officially the city has less than 50,000 inhabitants, rail and bus links mean that more than 10,000 students and professors at the university and teacher training colleges add to the bustle by commuting daily from Bangkok. Originally founded as a branch of the Bangkok Fine Arts Department, the university now has many other faculties, including Departments of French and German, as well as numerous famous figures in the field of fine arts on its staff.

Every Buddhist festival brings tens of thousands of pilgrims to the city from all over the country. Anyone who gets the chance should try to visit Nakhon Pathom for one of these festivals (see Practical Information, Events).

A particularly attractive event is the pilgrims' festival and annual fair in November (the dates change each year; information from the TAT, see Tourist Information). This is when theatrical performances, shadow plays and all kinds of other entertainments take place on the terraces of the temple, and a fair is held on the large square at the foot of the chedi. The chedi itself is illuminated with garlands of lights.

Since Mongkut's time kings and their families have often been numbered among the pilgrims, and Chulalongkorn's son and successor Vajiravudh (1910–25) built himself the Sanam Chand Palace just 2km/1½ miles south of the Pathom Chedi. It has a bronze monument which comes as a surprise for anyone familiar with Thailand, since it is dedicated to his favourite pet dog, Yaleh. Vajiravudh's years as an Oxford student may have had something to do with this very un-Thai-like expression of affection and respect for a dog.

Sights in Nakhon Pathom

Approaching the city along Highway 4 from Bangkok the first thing seen is a whitewashed prang standing on a square base. It is said to be the oldest building anywhere in Thailand, older even than the Phra Pathom Chedi (see next entry). Nearby archaeologists have uncovered foundations and a terrace which formed part of a religious building, as well as fragments of friezes decorated with figures and also statues of the Buddha, which are now housed in the Nakhon Pathom National Museum.

Phra Pathom Chedi

Phra Pathom Chedi, (Most Venerated First Chedi) stands 118m/387ft high (or 127m/415ft including the base), making it the tallest Buddhist edifice in the world, taller even than the famous Shwedagon, the Golden Palace in Rangoon, which stands 99.36m/326ft and was built in 1773.

Phra Pathom Chedi in Nakhon Pathom

A figure in the wiharn on the north side is said to be that of King Phya Kong who – according to legend – played a part in the building of the chedi. It is said that he consulted an astrologer about his son's future, only to learn that the latter would one day slay him. He thereupon sent his son out into the forest, where a woman found him and brought him up. When he, now named Phya Pan, grew up he entered into the service of the King of Ratchaburi, who owed a feudal duty to the King of Nakhon Chaisi. Phya Pan's wisdom and prudence became known far and wide, and the King decided to adopt him. Phya Pan persuaded him to declare war against the King of Nakhon Chaisi, and in the battle Phya Pan killed his natural father. After the victory, as was then the custom, he married the Queen (his mother). When she told him the story of his origins he attempted to atone for his sins by building a Dagoba – the precursor of the present Phra Pathom Chedi.

On its circular base stands the great dome or Anda, 98m/321ft in diameter, shaped rather like a huge inverted bell or the alms-shawl of a Buddhist monk. Note the decorated, smooth and rounded ledges which taper upwards and form the base. This is surmounted by a square superstructure, regarded as a shrine looking down on the whole Buddhist world, and is in turn topped by a spire-shaped cone consisting of a number of rings one above the other, symbolising the protection and worthiness of Buddha.

Around the base of the chedi runs a colonnade, with the four wiharns at the cardinal points. The whole of this holy precinct is protected by a railing. The main entrance lies on the north side, where a wide flight of steps leads up to the first terrace, surrounded by a balustrade. The banisters are richly embellished with ornaments and seven-headed Nagas framed in beautifully sculptured decoration and faïence.

Several buildings stand on the terrace; in the bot, to the south of the entrance, will be found a most beautiful statue of the Buddha in bright quartzite, decorated in gold and lacquer. In the Dvaravati style, it depicts The Enlightened One enthroned in a European position. Three exact replicas of this statue exist and once belonged to the Wat Na Phra Men in Nakhon Pathom, of which only a few bricks now remain. One of the copies is now in Wat Phra Men in Ayutthaya, the other two are in the Bangkok National Museum.

Temple Museums

Open Wed.–Sun. 9am–12 noon and 1pm–4pm

Admission free

The wiharn to the north of the east entrance houses the old temple museum, with a number of stucco and stone statues in the Mon style. More interesting is the new museum near the south staircase, outside which stand the Wheels of the Law dating from the earliest period of Nakhon Pathom. Inside will be found statues of Buddha, including some particularly beautiful ones in the Mon style, stone and terracotta sculptures and a reconstruction of a bas-relief from the Chulapradit Chedi and an original from Wat Sai (south of Nakhon Pathom) depicting Buddha preaching to some of his first disciples. Note also the various coins and articles from everyday life.

By the south staircase stand a model of the Khmer Prang, above the ruins of which King Mongkut built the present chedi, and a reproduction of the famous chedi of Wat Mahathat (see entry).

By the northern staircase steps lead up to the upper terrace, where there are two salas in the Javanese style. We then come to the colonnade with its four wiharns, made up of an inner and and outer ambulatory. Through red-painted round-arched doorways we pass to the inner terrace with its 24 towers containing bronze bells. On the two terraces will be found several Chinese stone figures which served as ballast on junks, two tall Chinese chimneys, numerous finds dug up around the temple, as well as trees, plant-containers and several salas. This leads through to the monks' quarters in the south-east of the temple precincts.

Wiharns

The four wiharns are made up of an open portico and an inner chamber. In the portico of the North Wiharn you will find the 8m/26ft tall statue of a standing Buddha in the Sukhothai style, the hands and feet being originally part of a stone figure found about 1915 in Sawankholok, near Sukhothai. The gilded statue, known as the Phra Ruang Rojanarit, is much revered. An inscription on the wall of the wiharn states that the ashes of King Mongkut are said to be interred in the base of the statue. The wiharn also contains two groups of figures; one shows two princesses paying homage to the newborn Siddharta (Buddha's original name), the other depicts one of the most important mythical scenes in the Buddha's life, when animals from the jungle brought him food and drink after a fast of forty days.

The South Wiharn houses some beautiful stone sculptures, and a niche in a wall contains the figure of Phya Pan (6th–7th c.). In the portico of the West Wiharn lies a 9m/30ft long reclining figure of the Buddha, with another smaller one inside.

Sanam Chand Palace

In 1910, before he actually came to the throne, King Rama VI built the Sanam Chand Palace in extensive parkland to the north-west of the city. A wide avenue leads up to it from the chedi. Some of the buildings are in a mixture of European and Thai styles, while the Audience Chamber is in the Bangkok style. A small shrine pays homage to the Hindu god Ganesha, whose symbol is an elephant's head on a multi-armed human body. Some local government offices are now housed in these buildings.

Wat Phra Gnam to the west of the Nakhon Pathom Railway Station is also deserving of attention; it was built in the Bangkok style by King Chulalongkorn on the foundations of an old shrine from the Dvaravati period.

Wat Phra Gnam

National Assembly

C3

The National Assembly Building stands in the Dusit district, where the Royal Family and the nobility have tended to live (see also Chidralada Palace and Wat Benchamabophit). Built of white Italian marble, the National Assembly Hall is in the Neo-Classical style with a dome. It was begun in 1907 by Rama V to commemorate his 40-year jubilee and completed under Rama VI in 1916. After being used as a throne hall it became the seat of the National Assembly in 1913, one year after the adoption of Thailand's first democratic constitution. Since the Assembly moved into a more suitable and modern air-conditioned building some years ago, visitors have been allowed to view the hall during the working week; opening times vary, and you should check with the TAT – see Tourist Information.

The murals will particularly attract those interested in Thailand's history: they depict Rama I mounted on an elephant

Location
In the Dusit district, not far from Wat Benchamabophit (Marble Temple)

Buses
3, 10

Open
At varying times (check with TAT)

The National Assembly Hall specially illuminated

founding the city; Rama IV proclaiming freedom of religion; Rama V abolishing slavery; and homage being paid to Rama VI on the occasion of his coronation.

Vimammek Palace

Open
Daily except Sun. and public holidays, 9.30am–4pm

Admission fee

At the back of the park stands Vimammek Palace, a four-storey building made of teak which can now be visited again following extensive restoration. It houses the extensive Royal Art Collections of furniture, paintings and jewellery, much of which was collected by Rama V.

National Museum   D2

Location
4 Na Prathat Road, on the western side of the Royal Square (Sanaam Luang)

Buses
3, 11, 12

Open
Tue.–Thur., Sat. and Sun. 9am–4pm (except public holidays)

Admission fee

Photography fee (prohibited in some departments)

Guided tours

The National Museum is Thailand's largest and most important, and its vast collection is housed in over 20 buildings and courtyards. Because of its incredible range of exhibits it is a good idea, before beginning a visit, to consult the catalogue which is available at the entrance and is excellent value, so that a selection can be made of items which are of particular interest. English-language tours are available.

The Museum was founded by Chulalongkorn (Rama V) in 1884 in the palace of Prince Wang Na, who was a kind of viceroy usually appointed to succeed the reigning king; this 400-year old office was abolished by King Chulalongkorn. Exhibits which prior to 1884 had been on display to the public in the Concordia Pavilion in the Grand Palace were then transferred to the National Museum. The new north and south wings were opened by King Bhumibol in 1967 and are arranged according to art historical periods.

The old Wang Na Palace built by Rama I remains essentially as it was, as does the ground floor of the collection made up of Chulalongkorn's bequest and what was left from the Wang Na household: regalia, religious and ceremonial artefacts, ceramics, games, weapons, musical instruments, the Viceroy's throne, etc. The Fine Arts Department is nowadays responsible for selecting and adding to the original collection, and its

Old Buildings
1 Sivamokkhapiman Hall (prehistory)
2 Pavilion of King Vajiravudh
3 Red House (Tamnak Daeng)
4 King Rama IV's Pavilion (Samran Mukhamat)
5 Pavilion of the Heir to the Throne (Ek Alongkot)
6 Throne Hall
7 Mukha Krasam (Gold Treasure from Ayutthaya)
8 Phimuk Nonthien (palanquins and elephant howdahs)
9 Thasina Phimuk (stage properties, games, etc.)
10 Presents to kings
11 Vasante Phimani (furnishings with mother-of-pearl inlay, porcelain, ceramics)
12 Models
13 Stamps, coins and medals

14 Patchima Phimuk (royal barges)
15 Pritsadang Phimuk (weapons)
16 Vayusathan Amaret (royal regalia)
17 Wood-carvings
18 Uttara Phimuk (models of barges)
19 Ships, boats and fishing equipment
20 Curios
21 Phrommet Thada (costumes and religious objects)
22 Banners
23 Burapha Phimuk (musical instruments)
24 Photographs
25 Royal cremation carriage

New South Wing

GROUND FLOOR
26 Buddhism in Asia
27 Lopburi
28 Hindu deities
29 Lopburi

UPPER FLOOR
26 Dvaravati
27 Dvaravati
28 Java
29 Srivijaya

New North Wing

GROUND FLOOR
30 Coins
31 Statues of Buddha
32 Textiles
33 *Objets d'art*
34 Bangkok

UPPER FLOOR
30 Chiang Saen
31 Sukhothai
32 Sukhothai
33 Ayutthaya
34 Ayutthaya

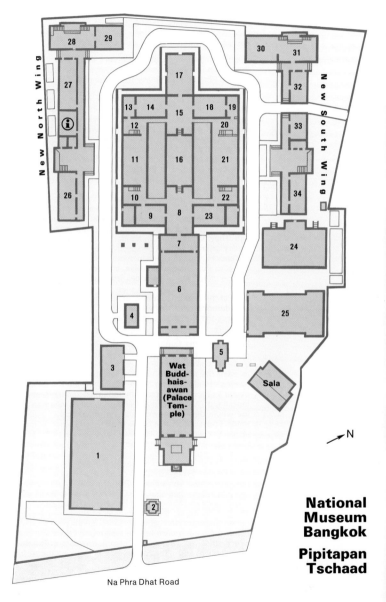

National
Museum
Bangkok

Pipitapan
Tschaad

Na Phra Dhat Road

archaeological staff play an important part in this, particularly as far as the prehistoric collections are concerned.

In front of the palace stand two particularly interesting buildings – the Buddhaisawan, one of the oldest temples in Bangkok, and the Tamnak Daeng, or Red House.

Wat Buddhaisawan

Apart from the blue mosaic gable wall, which was added later, this typical Thai temple dates from 1795 and was built by Rama I for the Phra Buddha Sihing, the statue of Buddha sitting on a throne under a canopy. This highly venerated image is carried through the streets of Bangkok in solemn procession on the Feast of Sonkran, the old Thai New Year's Eve in April. According to legend it came originally from Ceylon, but modern historians attribute its style to Sukhothai where they think it was found. It does show signs of Singalese influence, but these are also typical of the Sukhotai period. It is thought that the statue was made about 1250 and that, like the Emerald Buddha in Wat Phra Kaeo (see Grand Palace), it was much travelled as the spoils of war before Rama I brought it to Bangkok from Chiangmai.

The murals in the interior on all four walls from ceiling to floor prove to some to be even more fascinating than the statue; they are originals, unlike those in Wat Phra Kaeo, and are splendid examples of the art of Rama I's time, nearly 200 years ago. They were painted in tempera colours with mineral and earth pigments, without perspective and in historical costume. It is easy to distinguish aristocrats and saints from the ordinary folk who alone have expressive, often drily comic faces.

The paintings are of episodes from Buddha's life on earth, beginning with his parents' marriage (on the right near the door at the back). The partly Indian-inspired celestial beings and demons over the windows are all reverently looking towards the Buddha symbol, a stupa (shrine) over the back entrance.

Tamnak Daeng

Rama I built the Tamnak Daeng, the Red House, towards the end of the 18th c. for one of his elder sisters, Princess Sri Sudarak. It takes its name and colour from a plant pigment used to paint the teak from which it was built. The number and placing of the pillars on the veranda proclaim the rank of the owner and provide, just as with traditional middle-class dwellings in old Thailand, a shady and dry place in which to spend the whole day. The inward-sloping prefabricated walls also made it possible for this house to be moved several times.

Inside, the carved and gilded wooden bed, dressing-table and towel-stand are particularly indicative of the royal life-style in the bedroom, which one should imagine filled with the perfume of fresh jasmine from a posy that was replaced every day; even nowadays Thai mothers often tenderly place a sprig of jasmine on their son's pillow. The lacquered wardrobes in the living quarters – one Thai, one Chinese – used to be filled with silken robes and five-coloured Bencharong porcelain.

The two rooms by the outside wall of the house served as bathrooms where the bathers would ladle the perfumed water out of the great bronze tubs in little round bowls and pour it over themselves, a practice still common in many of Thonburi's Klong houses and in the countryside, but without the perfume and bronze tubs.

Sculptures

The largest square building contains the most interesting exhibits, the Dvaravati sculptures from Nakhon Pathom and Suk-

Exhibits in the National Museum . . .

. . . and murals

133

hotai objects. These great historical works of art include the Striding Buddha, whose gently flowing contours and delicate garb almost make one forget that it is cast in bronze (Rooms 6 and 2 in the New South Building and Rooms 7 and 8 in the New North Building).

Hindu-influenced reliefs and busts can be found classified under "Srivijaya" (Indonesian-Southern Thai, 8th–13th c.) or "Khmer-Lopburi" (Khmer style, north-east Thailand, 10th–12th c.).

Weapons

Those more interested in practical and worldly items will be attracted to Room 10, where the collection of arms and armaments includes not only lances, spears and an unused cannon from the time of King Mongkut, but also the apparently insignificant yet effective precursors of the modern minefield. These little spikes of iron or bamboo were scattered in the mud of the battlefield to impede the progress of elephants and barefooted warriors. There is a life-size war-elephant on display, carrying the king and his aide-de-camp on its back. Occasionally the king would change places with his bodyguard in front of him, either because he thought he could fight better from there, or because he recognised that his opponent was worthy of the honour of personal combat with a royal personage.

Musical instruments

Room 15 contains traditional musical instruments of the kind still used today. The basic orchestra consists of cymbals, a curved wooden xylophone which plays the melody, another xylophone made of ebony and the Pi-Nai flute which imitates the human voice.

Besides drums and stringed instruments, and complete Cambodian and Indonesian orchestras magnificently decorated with ebony and mother-of-pearl that were presented to the Court, the collection also has simple folk instruments from the Northern Highlands. Everything is labelled in English.

Coaches and palanquins

State and mourning coaches as well as litters and palanquins for kings and Buddhist patriarchs are housed in their own hall. Attention is also drawn to some exibits on the right near the entrance which illustrate the tradition, still cultivated today in Southern Thailand, of shadow-games.

Inscriptions in stone

Also worth inspection are the remains of stone inscriptions brought to Bangkok from all over the country, especially the "Government Declaration" by King Ramkhamhaeng dated 1293, which suggests the intention to form a democratic Thailand (Room 12 in the Main Building).

Textiles and Weaving

In Room 14 of the same building can be seen textiles and woven goods produced by all sections of the Thai population. There is also an explanation of the origin of the clothing worn by Buddhist monks.

*Nonthaburi

Location
About 50km/30 miles from Bangkok in Nonthaburi province.

The town of Nonthaburi lies less than 50km/30 miles from Bangkok on the banks of the Menam Chao Phraya, and to sail to it along the river in the early hours of the morning is a very impressive experience. As the river winds its way along there are numerous waterfalls and Klongs to be seen all around, and a large part of the city life takes place here on the river. On the banks of the canals, surrounded by lush vegetation and houses built on stilts, stand a number of fine temples.

Wat Chalerm Phra Kiat, situated a little way up river from Nonthaburi on the opposite bank of the Menam, can be reached either by boat hired on the spot, or by the regular ferry. The Wat was built in the first half of the 19th c. during the reign of King Rama III (1824–51); two high walls encircle the site, one topped with battlements, the other with small Chinese towers. Note the ceramic bricks probably made by Chinese labourers, and the fine proportions of the main temple and the Chedi behind. Only ruins remain of an old Wiharn, on which a less interesting one has since been built. The whole site is under the protection of the Ministry of Arts and is to be further restored.

Continuing by boat and turning left into Klong Bang Yai we reach the picturesque village of Bang Yai, set in the midst of several Klongs. The waterway south to the village of Bang Kruai passes some fine and charmingly situated temples of later construction. Wat Prang Luang, on the right bank beyond Bang Yai, dates from the Ayutthaya period. Another beautifully-shaped prang has been very well preserved.

Wat Prasat, set back somewhat from the left bank of the Klong, was built c. 1700 in the Ayutthaya style. The massive main temple has two porticos and is rich in sculptures and decorative carvings. The later frescoes in the interior are most vivid, and strongly painted in a manner typical of the First Bangkok period. On the right bank can be found the ruins of two more temples, and near Bang Kruai stands Wat Chalo, all from the Late Ayutthaya period.

An unusual place to visit is Nonthaburi Prison, which is still used as such today. In a small museum belonging to the Correctional Staff Training Division, which is linked to the prison and where prison warders undergo training, old instruments of torture are exhibited. They were used by court officials during the Ayutthaya period to force confessions. Also of interest are pieces of apparatus used to execute those condemned to death. Particularly gruesome are the large hollow balls woven from cane and lined with nails, in which the poor wretches who had been condemned to die were locked and then elephants played "football" with them.

From Nonthaburi it is only some 20 minutes journey north to Pak Kret (see entry).

Access
North-west either on Chakrapong Road or Samsem Road

Buses
From Thonburi Bus Station

Boat
Fast boats from Oriental Pier

Bang Yai

Wat Prasat

Nonthaburi Prison

Tip

---

*Oriental Hotel   F3

This, the first and oldest of Bangkok's hotels which from the day of its opening in 1887 came up to European standards and expectations, was actually known for decades as "The New Oriental", since it took the name, place – and most of the customers – of an earlier seamen's lodging-house. Since then it has welcomed countless crowned heads, heads of state and many other famous people and kept all its glamour. The fact that it is on the river yet also close to the main post office and the commercial centre has contributed to its lasting reputation.

Location
48 Oriental Avenue (near New Road)

Buses
1, 2, 3, 5, 9 (Charon Krung Road or end of Silom Road)

Landing-stage
Taa Orientään

The large-scale yet tasteful restoration of the main building has helped, too; it still presents a delightful combination of Art Nouveau and Old Viennese elegance, and has been regarded for years by businessmen as one of the best hotels in the world. Two traditional "named" suites remind guests of writers who have been especially closely connected with this hotel – William Somerset Maugham (1874–1965) and Joseph Conrad (1857–1924). Maugham, who had become famous in 1915 thanks to his novel "Of Human Bondage", made a journey to the Far East in 1922. On November 6th of that year all Bangkok was cheered by the tidings that "Mr Maugham, the novelist and playwright, has come to Rangoon from Ceylon and plans an extended tour through the Shan states, after which he will come by way of Chiangmai to Bangkok" ("The Bangkok Times").

Unfortunately Maugham was taken ill with malaria four days after his arrival. He was, however, able to recuperate on the terrace by the river, which is still a healthy place, and then embarked on a boat for Saigon. He left a literary impression of this experience of the East in "A Gentleman in the Parlour".

His next visits were altogether more fortunate, the last being in 1960 when he came out east to celebrate his 86th birthday. Several of his prose works contain evocations of the terrace by the river where he often liked to linger.

Maugham was not, however, the first famous writer to have a suite that still bears his name. On the sunny morning of January 24th 1888 Joseph Conrad, then a Polish emigrant, landed at Bangkok to take over the captaincy of his first ship, the "Otago". He put up at the Oriental, where he was lodged "well and at a reasonable price" by its proprietor, Captain Andersen. He, too, often described this period of his life, almost as if he were homesick for it. The film "Ashes and Diamonds" is in fact based on Conrad's book "The Shadow Line" and its director, Andrejez Wajda, selected the Oriental Hotel in Bangkok as the setting. The hotel has also dedicated a new "pink" suite to the author Barbara Cartland.

Anyone unable to or not desirous of spending a night at the Oriental can at least soak in the atmosphere evoked by these authors by taking afternoon tea in the Old Lobby or enjoying a "sundowner" on the famous terrace above the river. In any case it is worth paying a visit to the foyer of the old building partly hidden in the trees, on the pillars of which hang aged photographs of the families of King Chulalongkorn and King Vajiravudh.

The Taa Orientään landing-stage near the hotel is a good setting-out point for boat trips, for example to the Thonburi Klongs on the opposite bank, to Wat Arun or to Ayutthaya on the "Oriental Queen"; details can be obtained at the hotel reception.

Pak Klong Talaad

See Markets

Pak Kret

Location About 60km/37 miles from Bangkok

Lying near a bend in the river, Pak Kret is best known for its excellent pottery. Only 20 minutes from Nonthaburi or an hour from Bangkok, Pak Kret is an old Mon settlement in Thailand's central plain. An interesting and quite quick way to get there is along the Menam Chao Phraya river, and this also provides a good opportunity to observe Thai river life (see Klongs: Independent Klong Tours). The areas around Pak Kret and the place itself are still inhabited by Mons, although they are rapidly being absorbed into the Thai population.

Buses
From Thonburi Bus Station

Boat
Along the Menam Chao Phraya river

On the southern tip of the island of Pat Kret stands the graceful white Chedi, built in the Mon style, belonging to the ancient Wat Chim Phil, in front of which ships and ferries moor. Behind the bot can be seen an old weathered edifice.

Wat Chim Phil

Pottery has long been a tradition in Pak Kret, and the workshops can be seen as the boat sails along the river. Although the products are not particularly artistic as far as decoration is concerned they are well known for their perfect form.

Potteries

A boat trip along the many klongs west of the Menam Chao Phraya, such as one to Bang Bua Thong, for example, is an exotic – albeit sometimes rather smelly – experience.

Trips on the Klongs

Only some 20km/13 miles north of Pak Kret is the town of Pathum Thani, with its Stork Temple (see Wat Phailom) lying within a protected bird sanctuary. It is reached quite easily either along Road No. 306 or by boat further along the Menam.

Tip

Pathum Thani

See Wat Phailom

Pattaya

Pattaya is Bangkok's seaside playground. The original village snuggled up close to a natural bend in the coastline is now separated by the 6km/4 miles of coast road from the many hotels that have sprung up in the past thirty years or so. Also now a favourite tourist resort, with the inevitable hotels, is the Yomtien Beach area south of Pattaya itself, where sunshades, deck-chairs and water-sports equipment may be hired.

Location
About 145km/90 miles from Bangkok

Access
On Highway 3

Rail
From Hualampong Main Station; to Pattaya (weekends and on public holidays), then bus shuttle service from Pattaya Station into town.

For many years Pattaya was just a quiet, sleepy fishing village. A few trippers may have come from Bangkok at week-ends but that was all, until it was "discovered" during the Vietnam War by GIs on "Rest and Recreation" leave from the US Air Force camp of U Tapao near Sattahip about 30km/20 miles away. In the 1970s the little village rapidly developed into a fashionable resort and modern hotels shot up and continue to do so until this day. The gap left by the Americans when they went back home was quickly filled by German (mainly male) visitors, followed by Japanese, Westerners in general and finally tourists from all over the world.
The hotels and restaurants are as international as their clients, with everything from German beer-gardens to French, Mexican and Arabic restaurants, and from self-catering bungalows to top hotel chains. Pattaya continues to expand, with no end to the boom yet in sight. Visitors seeking peace and quiet may

Buses
From Ekamai Bus Station and from Don Muang Airport

Air
Bangkok Air (private airline) from Bangkok
Thai Airways regular service from Chiang Mai (one direction only)

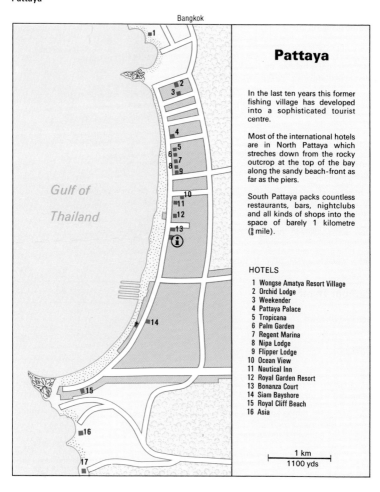

Bangkok

Pattaya

In the last ten years this former fishing village has developed into a sophisticated tourist centre.

Most of the international hotels are in North Pattaya which streches down from the rocky outcrop at the top of the bay along the sandy beach-front as far as the piers.

South Pattaya packs countless restaurants, bars, nightclubs and all kinds of shops into the space of barely 1 kilometre ($\frac{5}{8}$ mile).

Gulf of
Thailand

HOTELS

1 Wongse Amatya Resort Village
2 Orchid Lodge
3 Weekender
4 Pattaya Palace
5 Tropicana
6 Palm Garden
7 Regent Marina
8 Nipa Lodge
9 Flipper Lodge
10 Ocean View
11 Nautical Inn
12 Royal Garden Resort
13 Bonanza Court
14 Siam Bayshore
15 Royal Cliff Beach
16 Asia

1 km
1100 yds

perhaps be better suited elsewhere in Thailand, although the hotels in the north of Pattaya and on the Yomtien beaches are much better in this respect and can be recommended.

Sights and Leisure Facilities

Sun and sand are today the main assets of this, South-east Asia's largest and most popular seaside resort. Unfortunately, however, sea pollution has never been a subject that has concerned the authorities overmuch until recently; two big purification plants are now on the drawing-board, but it will be the mid-1990s at the earliest before the quality of the water sees any real improvement. Until then the discerning tourist would do well to keep to the hotel swimming pools or to beaches well away from the town.

As might be expected, all kinds of water sports play a prominent role in Pattaya: these include swimming, sailing, surfing, diving, motor-boat hire and the relatively expensive para-sailing. However, diving off Pattaya is less attractive than it was, because the coral reefs have been virtually stripped clean. Almost all the hotels have tennis-courts, some of which are floodlit after dark. Golf courses, some up to international standard, can be found at Asia Pattaya, Siam Country Club some way out of town, and in Sattahip. Other sports catered for include bowling, badminton, archery, squash and horse-riding. Motor racing is held twice a year, in spring and autumn, and there are two go-cart runs where visitors can try their skill.

However, it is at night that Pattaya really comes to life, and it is its nightlife that has given it its world-wide reputation, both good and bad. On the two main streets in particular – conveniently known as First and Second Roads respectively – are numerous bars, nightclubs, discos and other amusement places, as well as by the North Beach, where there are also plenty of opportunities for a shopping spree.

Nightlife

Among Pattaya's most notable attractions are the transvestite shows held in the "Alcazar", "Simon's Cabaret" and the "Tiffany Show".

Countryside around Pattaya

Pattaya itself boasts little in the way of interesting places to visit, with the possible exception of two comparatively modern temples on two hills south of the town, one of which has a pleasant little garden with Chinese statues. If life on the beaches begins to pall the countryside around Pattaya, both nearby and further afield, offers scope for exploration.

The little coral islands lying off the coast, such as Koh Lam, Koh Lin and Koh Krok, are about an hour away by boat. Some hotels, holiday bungalows and restaurants have already been built on them.

Coral islands

Nong Nooch village has been built on the lines of the "Rose Garden" (see entry) near Bangkok, offering similar attractions in a well-tended area of country park. Local peasant life is illustrated, as well as displays of Thai boxing, cock-fighting and elephants. Everybody, not just flower-lovers, will be entranced by the superb orchid garden, and adults as well as children will love the zoo with animals typical of the region. Excursions to Nong Nooch start from the office in Pattaya opposite the Nipa Lodge Hotel; visitors who have booked can also be collected from their own hotel.

Nong Nooch village, 15km/9 miles south-east of Pattaya

By turning off Highway 3 just before reaching the approach road to Nong Nooch and continuing for a few miles we reach the newly-built Wat Yansangwararam, a temple which the reigning monarch Bhumibol had built to celebrate his jubilee in

Wat Yansangwararam

Pattaya, once a fishing village, now a holiday resort

Monkeys pick coconuts and orchids flourish in Nong Nooch village

1988. On the right of the approach road can be seen some pretty Chinese pavilions. The shrine of Wat Yansangwararam stands on a hill, and is reached by a flight of 299 steps adorned with Naga serpents. In a pleasant park around it stand several buildings, including a round Wiharn and a group of monks' quarters.

About 6km/4 miles from Pattaya lies the elephant stockade in which there are daily displays of work with the elephants, with explanations in English; afterwards you can ride on the elephants.There is a second such stockade 5km/3 miles off the Sukhumvit Road near the Reo Ranch.

Elephant stockade

Mini Siam on the Sukhumvit Road was opened in 1989 and, as the name suggests, illustrates Thialand in miniature. It is open daily 7am–8pm; there is an admission fee. As in Ancient City (see entry), Thailand's most important sights and places of interest are modelled here on a scale of 1:25. It is especially attractive during the evening when the 80 items are all illuminated.

"Mini Siam" (Thailand in miniature)

Pattaya Pleasure Park, a few miles behind the Royal Cliff Hotel, offers giant water-chutes and large swimming pools. It is open daily 8.30am–8pm; admission fee.

Pattaya Park

Near the motorway to Bangkok stands this orphanage, which is managed by a Redemptionist padre and gives an insight into the social work being carried out in Thailand. Visitors are always made very welcome.

Pattaya Orphanage

A visit is recommended to the little township of Naklua about 12km/7½ miles away, preferably in one of Pattaya's group taxis. The best time to go is either in the early morning, when the busy fish-market can be seen, or in the evening to experience the night-market.

Naklua

There are a number of other sights within easy reach of Pattaya, such as the towns of Chanthaburi and Trat to the south, and Bang Saen (see entry) and Chonburi in the Bangkok direction. The islands of Koh Samet, Koh Sichang and Koh Chang are also worth visiting.
Anyone who, after staying in Pattaya, has not included Bangkok in his or her itinerary is recommended to arrange to go there for a day or several days if possible; bookings can made through all travel agents with offices in Pattaya.

Tip

Phra Thinang

See Ban Pa-In

Pratu Nam (market)

See Markets

River Kwai bridge

See Kanchanaburi

Rose Garden (Suan Sam Pran)

Location
32km/20 miles south-west of Bangkok, on the road to Nakhon Pathom

Access
By tour buses

Open Daily 8am–6pm

Admission fee

Show Daily at 3pm

The Rose Garden, covering 20 hectares/48 acres, is a riverside tropical park-cum-country club. It is on the route, usually in conjunction with Nakhon Pathom (see entry), of the organised bus tours that can be booked at travel agents and in most hotels (see Tourist Information). Overnight accommodation includes hotel bungalows, some with swimming pools and tennis courts, but it is necesssary to book early, especially at Christmas and during the Easter holidays. The Rose Garden has an 18-hole golf course, and every afternoon there is a show featuring picturesque Thai rural activities such as elephants at work, historic folk-dances and traditional sports and games, all made as photogenic as possible.

The gardens are laid out in the North Italian style and there are open-air restaurants by the river, specialising in Western, Chinese and Thai dishes.

Royal Barges

See Klongs: Independent Klong Tours

Sanaam Luang   D2

Location
In the western part of Old Bangkok, in front of the Grand Palace

Buses
6, 9, 12, 14

Landing-stages
Tha Thammasat and Tha Mahathat

Sanaam Luang was once the scene of Bangkok's largest market (see Chatuchak Week-end Market); now, as a consequence of the increased leisure time enjoyed by the populace, it has become a spacious park and the scene of many festivals. At week-ends in particular it is usually swarming with people enjoying a variety of leisure activities. These include spectacular kite-flying competitions, for example, and it is here that the Plough Ceremony takes place in May (see Practical Information – Calendar of Events and Public Holidays). Palmists, astrologists, fortune-tellers and lottery-ticket sellers now almost monopolise the area, and anyone who believes in such things can buy a lucky charm to guard against evil spirits. It is quite possible to pick up a rare book on the many stands doing business here, mainly at week-ends.

It was on this great oval space that in earlier times the royal cremation ceremonies took place, in which the "Nang Yai" – giant shadow-play figures dangling from tall bamboo poles in the light of the bonfires of blazing wood – were a central feature. The last ceremonial cremation in the presence of the King and Queen took place in 1974 when the coffins of students and youths who had been killed in demonstrations against the military régime in 1973 were committed to the flames.

Scattered around Sanaam Luang are a number of important buildings, including the National Museum, Wat Mahathat and the Grand Palace (see entries), as well as the National Theatre. Thammasat University, founded in 1933 and the centre of the student riots of 1976 which resulted in a degree of democratisation in Thailand, lies to the north of Wat Mahathat.

Sao Ching Chah (Giant Swing)

See Wat Suthat

*Siam Leisure Park

The love of the Thai people for water dates from time immemorial. However, it was foreign investors who first thought of making money out of it, and since then swimming-pools with flumes, water-chutes and leisure parks have shot up all over Thailand in recent years.

One of the largest of these is Siam Park in Bangkok, with pools covering a total area of some 16,000 sq.m/19,000 sq.yds where people can splash around and swim to their hearts' content. This is the place to come to wash away the dust of the city in a most pleasurable and relaxing environment.

Only a few of the attractions can be listed here: they include a 400m/1300ft long fresh-water lake with breakwaters made of rocks brought specially from Rayong, a water-chute 21m/70ft high, and an amusement park with a small zoo and beer-garden, on similar lines to Disneyland; enough to keep visitors amused all day long, especially if they have children with them.

Location
About 10km/6 miles north-east, by the Sukhaphibarn Road (No. 101) in the Bangkapi-Minburi district of the city.

Buses
1, 2, 14, 44

Open
Mon.–Fri. 10am–6pm, Sun. and public holidays 9am–7pm

Admission fee

Snake farm   E4

The exhibiting of snakes on this farm is really only a side line; all the money taken from visitors helps to finance the scientific work carried out here. Linked to the famous Pasteur Institute, the snake farm is a very interesting place to visit, especially at 11 o'clock each morning, when you will hold your breath as the poison is drawn off from the reptiles. This is then injected into horses who produce the anti-snake bite serum which is exported all over the world.

The building is owned by the Thailand Red Cross, the house itself being named after Queen Saovabha. The snakes are safely housed in large enclosures with concrete walls, but nevertheless it is difficult not to experience a shiver of fear when faced with the slithering reptiles. In an exhibition-room you can see snakes preserved in formalin, with boards providing background information.

There is another snake farm to be found on the Thonburi side of the Menam Chao Phraya River not far from Wat Arun. It is usually included in the itinerary of organised Klong tours.

Location
In the angle formed by Rama IV Road and Henri Durant Road, on the land belonging to the Thailand Red Cross

Open
Workdays, 8.30am–4pm

Suan Pakkad Palace   D4

In five fine traditional Thai rooms this little palace, the home of Princess Chumbot of Nakhorn Sawan, houses the beautiful exhibition of musical instruments, shells, bronze swords and screens and stone and bronze sculpture collected by her husband, who died in 1959. Anyone who does not have time to visit the National Museum (see entry) will find this an easily assimilated substitute in a private setting. One of the rooms contains

Location
352 Si Ayutthaya Road

Buses
2, 3

143

Sunday Market

Open
Mon.–Sat. 9am–4pm

Admission fee

a comprehensive collection of Ban Chiang ceramics from Northern Thailand.

But whether the visitor is interested in fine art and lacquerwork, history, ethnology or just love beautiful things – the most rewarding item here is the Lacquer Pavilion in the garden. Built on stilts next to a lotus pool, with a typical Thai roof and richly ornamented gable, it was originally a library brought here – like the other buildings – in a derelict state by the Prince in the 1920s from its original site far removed from Bangkok. Its interior is a real delight for lovers of graceful detail, with thousands of figures in black and gold, men and animals, in both heavenly and worldly scenes (a magnifying glass is useful).

The fact that some of its costumes, hats and wigs are European suggests that the interior at least dates from the reign of King Narai of Ayutthaya (1657–88), when ambassadors were exchanged with the French Court and the King received advice on such matters from Constantin Phaulkon of Greece.

Sunday Market

See Chatuchak Week-end Market

Tha Thewes Market

See Markets

Lacquer pavilion in the garden of Suan Pakkad Palace

Thieves' Market

See Markets: Nakhon Kasem

*Jim Thompson's House   D4

The life story of the American-born James ("Jim") Thompson
(see Famous People) reads like an adventure novel. At the peak
of his businees career, having made Thai silk famous throughout the world, he suddenly vanished on Easter Sunday 1967
when taking a short vacation in Malaysia. Numerous theories
have been put forward to explain his mysterious disappear-
ance; many believe that he is still living unrecognised somewhere in Asia and will one day soon return to his chosen home
in Bangkok.

When Thompson first came to Bangkok at the end of the Second World War he discovered three beautiful old Thai houses
near Ayutthaya, and had them brought by water to Bangkok
and re-erected. His rich collection of art was housed in them
and today it belongs to a charitable organisation; the exhibition
is open to the public and all the admission proceeds go to a
school for the blind in Thailand.

The seven wooden houses are now almost unique in the country, and contain a collection of art treasures not only from
Thailand but also from neighbouring countries. In addition, the
visitor will learn something of the history of Thai silk with the
help of guided tours with a commentary in English. The
houses, which every visitor should see, are picturesquely situated in a pretty garden by the side of a Klong, on the opposite
bank of which the silk-weavers once practised their skills.

The interior bears witness to the good taste of its former owner.
As well as old pictures in Thai silk there are numerous other
works of art to be seen. Note especially the sideboards which
once formed part of a Chinese altar, and the little palace in
which the children of the rich once raised their domestic pets,
possibly mice.

Jim Thompson, who adopted Buddhist teachings and became
a fervent member of the faith, first moved into his house at a
time deemed most favourable by the temple astrologers and
for a long time he lived there lacking for nothing. Seven years
later he left Bangkok for the last time.

Location
2 Soi Kasem San, near Rama I
Road

Bus
9

Open
Mon.–Sat. 9am–4.30pm

Admission fee

Vimammek Palace

See National Assembly

Wat (Buddhist temple)

Bangkok has over 400 temples and obviously there is only
room to list some of the most important ones here. They can,
however, be divided into four categories, the first two of which
having been founded by kings and/or containing their mortal
remains; the other two are accessible to all believers at all
times, having been built by private individuals or communities.

Wat

Apart from Wat Phailom, all the temples described here fall into the royal group of categories.

That apart, all temples can be seen as social meeting-places and they nearly all have a school and a garden playground for games, recreation, etc. Their enormously thick walls and stone floors make the buildings pleasantly cool inside.

Nowadays funerals and cremations are permitted only in temples which have modern cremation facilities (see Wat Sakhet).

"Wat Mahathat", a name which occurs twice in Bangkok and many times elsewhere in Thailand, indicates that a temple contains a relic of the Buddha.

The following account of the most important buildings found in every temple complex should prove helpful (see also Facts and Figures, Temples).

Bot

The bot is the most sacred place, the holy of holies and the equivalent of the Western sanctuary. This rectangular building, containing the finest altar to the Buddha in the temple, is where the monks take their vows. Shoes must be removed before entering the bot.

Chedi and Prang

Chedis and prangs are stone sepulchral monuments and reliquaries. Their shape can be traced back to one of the last utterances of the Buddha, who is said to have answered the question from his disciples about memorials with "little hills of sand, like a heap of rice, which everyone needs".

The chedi, with a pointed spire, is Thai-Burman in origin, while the prang, with its rounded top, originates from Indo-Brahman Khmer art forms.

Ho trai

Ho trai is the library containing the Holy Scriptures, the Tripitaka or Triple Basket (see Wat Phra Kaeo, for example), and stands on piles with a stepped pyramid roof.

Kambarien

This large hall with open sides for the preaching of sermons is not within the area of cult buildings but near the monks' dwellings. It may come as a surprise to the Western visitor to hear the congregation burst out laughing from time to time. They will be listening to the old Lokaniti, anecdotal parables rather like Aesop's fables. There is rarely any seating. People usually sit on the floor, with the monk seated at a slightly higher level reading his sermon.

Khana

The khana is the area where the monks live and is not found in temples built within a palace precinct.

There are no symbols of rank as far as the monks are concerned. They all wear the same yellow or brown two-piece habit, be they abbot, "luksit" (pupils between twelve and nineteen able at least to read and write), or "bhikkhu" (monks who may be here for just a week or until the end of their lives). Before being admitted to a monastic order (minimum age 20) young men must have shaven heads and eyebrows and once admitted they must then observe between 200 and 287 rules.

The white-robed nuns, also with shaven heads, are called Meji and have to observe only eight rules. For example, they are allowed to handle money and can therefore shop for food. Not all wats have buildings to accommodate Meji, who usually live in a communal dormitory.

Many young intellectuals in particular have tended of late to spend some time as Meji in wats known for their instruction in meditation.

In rural areas the sala still fulfils its original function and serves as a refectory-cum-dormitory for the period of great festivals. In Bangkok these small open halls are nowadays often used as classrooms; as the roof is supported on columns, they are airy and well ventilated.

Sala

"Suan" can be translated as "garden", but it is not just for people but also for poultry, stray dogs and grazing cows. A good example is at Wat Chai, on the short cut from Sanaam Luang to the Goethe Institute between Chakraphong and Phra Athit Street.

Suan

If a temple garden has a bodhi tree it is particularly popular with believers, since legend asserts this will be a seedling from the bodhi tree in northern India under which Buddha was sitting when he received Enlightenment. It is accounted a "tambuun", a merit-earning good deed, to water such a tree, which will normally be in an enclosure.

In temple complexes one frequently also comes across stone footprints like those of the Buddha. Larger than life, they tend to be full of offerings. However, the only temple with a footprint of the Buddha that is of more than local significance is the Phra Buddha Baar at Saraburi, about 80km/50 miles north of Bangkok.

The wiharn is the counterpart of the bot, but primarily intended for the lay congregation and is usually adorned with images of the Buddha. The fact that there are so many of these images may be connected with an old saying from the Lokaniti that "the shade of a tree is a blessing, that of a father and mother even more blessed, of a teacher yet more blessed again, but the most blessed of all is the shade of the Buddha . . ."

Wiharn

Many wiharns are also gateways through the external wall, in which case they are divided into two rooms, with the inner one opening into the inner court.

Wat Arun (Temple of the Dawn)

E2

Wat Arun was built about 1780, originally as the chapel for the palace of King Taksin after Ayutthaya (see entry) had been destroyed and Thonburi bacame capital in its place. Its tall central prang surrounded by four smaller ones has come to symbolise Bangkok.

During the Ayutthaya period a Chinese temple named Wat Cheng and a prang some 15m/49ft high stood on the same site. The present temple has retained the predominantly Chinese character as well as indications of Mahayana Buddhism. The height of the central prang has been given as between 67m/220ft and 104m/340ft, probably depending on whether the measurement is from sea-level or from the three terraces which form its base. It represents Mount Meru, the centre of the universe, while the four smaller towers around it symbolise the oceans of the world, and the four pavilions at the floor of the base steps stand for the four winds.

Niches in all four walls contain equestrian statues of the wind god Phra Pai, and inside are murals illustrating the main stages in Buddha's life, his Birth, Enlightenment, First Sermon and Entry into Nirvana.

The plaster facing of the prangs, which are brick inside, is decorated with fragments of Chinese porcelain, depicting

Location
On the west bank of the Menam Chao Phraya in Thonburi, Arun Amarin Road

Bus
57 (not air-conditioned)

Landing-stage
Tha Tien (ferry from Wat Po or the Oriental Hotel)

Open
Daily until dusk, public holidays until 10pm

Admission fee

China fragments decorate a prang

guardian giants (Jaks), mostly looking like jolly bearded China-men, and graceful winged maidens (Kinnaris), as well as mon-keys, birdmen (Garudas) and deities (Thevadas), supporting the giant towers on their heads and raised arms. The tiles of Chinese porcelain were paid for by public donations at the time it was built. The architectural feat that was accomplished here is on a par with the decoration: instead of pile-driving trees into the swampy ground, the logs were laid one on top of the other in grid fashion and then each "frame" was filled in with stone, brick rubble and clay. Men, and probably animals as well, then stamped this down until it set like concrete.

The bot was reconstructed by King Chulalongkorn (Rama V) after a fire in 1909 had destroyed the original; however, a Buddha image in royal attire, by the east wall, and dedicated by Rama IV to the memory of Rama II, survived. Another interest-ing Buddha image is the seated figure in Sukhothai style half-way up the main altar which Rama II brought with him from Vientiane. The Emerald Buddha, which probably also came from Vientiane, was also originally kept in Wat Arun but is now in Wat Phra Kaeo (see Grand Palace).

Despite the fascination of all this detail, Wat Arun's most mag-nificent effect actually lies in the silhouette of its central prang, viewed from the opposite bank at sunrise, when the full enchantment of the "Temple of Dawn" stands revealed, or when it is seen illuminated on public holidays in the evening.

◀ *Temple guard, brought from China as ballast*

149

Wat Arun

The hot and tiring climb up the steep steps will be amply rewarded by a superb view over the city and the river.

Not far from Wat Arun lie the monks' quarters and a more modern temple-school and wiharn.

****Wat Benchamabophit** (Benjama-bo-bitr; Marble Temple)   C3

Location
In the Dusit district, on the corner of Si Ayutthaya Road and Nakhon Pathom Road (opposite Dusit Zoo)

Bus
3

Open
Daily until dusk

Admission fee

This temple was built in 1899 by Rama V (Chulalongkorn) to replace a small older building which had to be demolished when the garden around Chidralada Palace (see entry) was laid out, but he let it keep the old name, meaning "Monastery of the Five Princes". As the King, who was crowned soon after his 20th birthday, had spent some time in 1873 as a "Bhikkhu" in the old monastery south of the actual temple, the Thais now call it "The Wat of the Fifth King").

Unusually, entrance to the temple compound is not through a gate in the wall or a wiharn; it is in fact separated from the street only by an expanse of green lawn and railings, where believers wait each morning to pass food to the monks beyond. The southern boundary is unusual, too, since it consists of a narrow canal inhabited by hundreds of turtles which the monks and visitors enjoy feeding. Note the bodhi tree transplanted here from Bodhgaya in India in 1871.

Marble temple

The temple is built of white Carrera marble brought from Italy, and has a triple-stepped roof of Chinese glazed tiles. Chulalongkorn incorporated some architectural ideas which he had gained during a visit to Europe, but nevertheless the little pavil-

Wat Benchamabophit, the Marble Temple

ions, matching the temple in colour and style, the red and gold bridges and the green of the many trees – including a bhodi tree the king brought here in 1900 – make this probably the most successful modern building which is perfectly Thai in style. The king took a personal interest in many of the details, and his half-brother Prince Naris was the gifted architect and was on site almost the whole time that the temple was being built.

The temple's cruciform ground-plan is heightened by the pavilions in the garden and simple slender marble columns; a covered walk behind the bot round a courtyard paved with square marble slabs conveys the impression of perfect harmony and symmetry through horizontal vistas. This accentuates the sweep of the roofs, all of which are triple-stepped, with their golden "Naga", stylised snake gable-ends, without this being overshadowed by the ornateness of the other old temple buildings. In the early morning and evening, when the shadows of the trees play over the white surface of the walls, there is a pleasing constant sense of movement, and this dappling of light and shade is intensified in mid-May, during the Feast of Visakha Bucha, when pilgrims dance three times round the bot with thousands of flickering candles.

The main gate of the bot is guarded by two white marble lions in the Burmese sitting position; the interior is usually entered through the marble courtyard. The golden Buddha on the main altar is a full-size copy, made on instructions from King Chulalongkorn, of the highly venerated 13th c. Phra Jinaraja Buddha – the "King of Victories" – which is to be found in the Wat Phra Si Ratana Mahathat in Phitsanulok. The pictures on the walls are of the country's most famous holy places – Sawangkhalok, Ayutthaya, Nakhon Pathom, Nakhon Sri-Thammarat, Lopburi, etc.
The ashes of Rama V are interred under the central altar.

Bot

The many statues of Buddha in the gallery round the inner courtyard represent the entire artistic development of the Buddhist religion and all the geographic and historic centres of that development, including Ceylon, India and Japan. Plaques in Thai and English in front of each Buddha give its meaning, place of origin, period and whether original or copy. In this way more than 2000 years of iconography give the visitor far more interesting information than merely the history of religion and art. Other themes covered are the origin of Buddhism and, on the carved north and east gables of the bot, there is the Hindu god Vishnu riding his Garuda, and the three-headed elephant Erawan. The west and south gables show the earliest symbols of the Buddha, the Unalom, a device representing the lock of hair on Buddha's forehead, and a Wheel of the Law.

Inner courtyard

Across the red suspension bridge, near where the monks and the Abbot live, an area known as the "khana", is a small museum which is well worth a visit. It contains a Burmese standing Buddha image in white alabaster which once stood in the open pavilion of the temple; there are also three drums, one of them carved from a tree-trunk, of the sort carried in processions in northern Thailand. This museum building is known as "Wiharn Somded" and was once the library. The Patriarch, the highest Buddhist dignitary in Thailand, also lives in this Khana.

The monks' living quarters

Wat Bovornives (Wat Bovornivet)

Location
On the Phra Sumen Road,
opposite the remains of the
old town wall, a little to the
north-west of the Democracy
Monument

Bus
11

Open
Daily 8am–5pm

Fortunately not as yet on the tourist trail, this temple has, since the time of King Mongkut (Rama IV) been the home of many kings (including the present one) and princes during their time as monks. As Prince Mongkut, Rama IV – like one of his half-brothers and over thirty of his sons – was the Abbot here for a number of years, when he founded the strict Dhammayuttika sect, the monks of which wear dark brown instead of saffron-yellow robes. Here it was that he brought the printing-press which was the first to print Buddhist scriptures rather than Christian Bibles for the missionaries. The many gardens and the clean, mostly blue and yellow buildings dating from the reign of Rama III (1824–51) make this temple a restful haven in the old city, quite apart from its art-historical value. Some of the Buddhist sermons are preached in English.

Bot

Inside the splendidly ornate bot, a relatively small building on a T-shaped plan, is the beautiful bronze Jinasiha (Gloriously Victorious) Buddha. It was cast in 1257 in Sukhotai to commemorate the country's liberation from Khmer rule and the setting-up of an independent Thailand; thus it is roughly contemporary with the famous Phra Buddha Jinarat in Phitsanuloke, a copy of which can be seen in Wat Benchamabophit (see entry). The larger seated statue "Si Sasta" behind it dates from the same period and was brought here from the north. Note also the restored wall-paintings behind the two central figures, in which King Mongkut introduced his idea of partially replacing religious themes with scenes from the daily lives of both his people and the royal family. Attention is also drawn to the figures of the worshippers on each side of the foremost figure. The paintings on the columns supporting the ceiling symbolise the progress of man on the path to Enlightenment, starting with the dark and gloomy colours of suffering and ending in brilliant whites and reds. The carved and gilded shutters and doors display the royal insignia, such as elephant, throne, horse, shoe and sword. Foreigners are not forgotten either; murals from King Mongkut's time show Englishmen at a horse-race, ships bringing American missionaries and Germans in search of minerals.
There are good examples of Dvaravati and Lopburi styles in the bell-towers to the east of the bot and the fine Srivijayan Buddha on the west side of it.

Chedi

A golden chedi stands in front of two wiharns which are seldom opened. The bodhi tree behind them is also said to be a cutting from the Tree of Enlightenment brought here from northern India during the reign of King Mongkut.

Bodhi tree

The colourful pavilion on the crenellated perimeter wall near the entrance is where kings and princes leave their robes of state before donning the yellow or brown habit of the monk. Like the gilding on the gate, the bearded demons standing on crocodiles that guard the temple were the gift of Chinese opium-dealers seeking heavenly blessing on their trade.

Illuminated Buddha in Wat Bovornives

Wat Chumpon Nikayaram

See Bang Pa In

Wat Jetubon

See Wat Po

Wat Kalaya (Church of the Rosary)

See Klongs: Independent Klong Tours

Wat Mahathat

The name Wat Mahathat implies a temple which is regarded as a particularly holy place. There is therefore a Wat Mahathat in all the large towns and cities in Thailand; the name also usually implies that the building contains a relic of the Buddha or other famous person from religious history. Normally only a small section of the Bangkok Wat Mahathat is open to the public. It was built in 1844.

Behind an entrance area paved in marble and with a statue of the founder Rama I are hidden the buildings of the oldest Buddhist university in Bangkok. The language faculty is

Location
On the western side of the Sanaam Luang square, opposite the National Museum.

Buses
6, 8, 12

Open
Daily 9am–5pm

153

renowned for its research into Pali, the prime language of Buddhism. Its students include not only Thais but also those from all over the world who come here to learn the true meaning of the teachings of the Enlightened One. Information about possibly taking part in, for example, meditations can be obtained from the office inside the temple complex.

On most days, but especially at week-ends and public holidays, sellers of herbs and homeopathic remedies set up their stalls in front of the Wat Mahathat, as well as dealers in devotional objects doing a roaring trade in animistic charms. While the wearing of such protective amulets of Hindu origin is hardly to be regarded as being in accord with the teachings of Buddha it does tally with the Thai view of religion, namely "better safe than sorry".

Wat Pak Naam

See Klongs: Independent Klong Tours

*Wat Phailom

Location
50km/30 miles north-west of Bangkok, on the east bank of the Menam Chao Phraya, near Pathum Thani in the Sam Kok district.

Access
On Highway 1

Buses
From the Northern Bus Station, then by ferry (40 mins.)

Open
Daily, dawn to late evening

Pathum Thani was founded as a provincial capital by King Taksin (1768–82) for Burmese Mon, whose language is still spoken there today. Its present name – meaning "Lotus City" – expressed the gratitude of Rama III (1824–51) to the local population who welcomed him with bunches of flowers every time he paid a visit. The life of the city is conducted almost wholly on the water and even the rice noodles that are the local delicacy are cooked on boats. A voyage of discovery, moving from boat to boat sampling this dish, is highly recommended, and quite safe since it is well cooked.

On the opposite bank of the river stands the temple, a visit to which is very worthwhile for ornithologists and bird-watchers in particular, for its treasure lies in being able to watch at close range the open-bill or clapper stork, some 27,000 of which come to nest here. The best time to study the living and nesting habits of this rare bird is in March. Be sure to bring plenty of film, since there is none available here.

Nobody knows exactly how many centuries old this rambling wooden temple complex is, but it certainly dates from the Ayutthaya period before Bangkok was founded. Its name means "bamboo temple", but the dense bamboo forest which once surrounded it now looks more like a a confusion of snow-white skeleton trees, as they are damaged by the thousands of storks which come to nest and breed between July and November every year. Although only two of the brood normally survive, since 1962 the number of storks has increased at least six-fold, possibly because they are under no threat here, as the use of fire-arms in such a holy place would unleash a storm of protest. The bird-watchers and "shooting cameras" in the hides certainly do not disturb them either. The novice nest-builders, who simply make a flat "plate" instead of the necessary "dish", are the only ones who have to watch helplessly as their eggs or hapless chicks that have fallen to the ground are eagerly gobbled up by dogs or monitor lizards. Incidentally, the latter are not dangerous to humans.

The storks feed on snails in the flooded rice-paddies to which they fly every morning. Their landing technique on their return is especially graceful as they apply their 3ft wing span, white above and black below, as brakes until they get a firm perch under their feet again. These storks are the only large birds to have survived the age of fire-arms, and this is due in no small measure to the Abbot of Wat Phailom having allowed them to breed and nest here within the temple precinct.

Killing was also not allowed in other temples, but the birds were chased away by the monks because their droppings robbed the magnificent temples of their lovely colours. Now it is only the trees that suffer as they prematurely lose their leaves.

Overpopulation in the stork colony has in fact led to several females having to share the same nest and male bird. Since the farmers have begun planting and harvesting two crops of rice a year, the birds now breed a second time, and those on the look-out for nest-sites take over the nests left empty by those that have flown off to Bangladesh and Cambodia. These late fledglings are not capable of making the long journey with their parents so they stay behind in Wat Phailom without running the risk of starving, thanks to the second crop of rice.

Wat Phra Kaeo

See Grand Palace

*Wat Po (Wat Jetubon; Temple of the Reclining Buddha)   E2

Wat Po, the local name of the temple, goes back to the Ayutthaya period (16th c.) when a prince had his residence and temple here in a little park which also contained a bodhi (hence Po) tree.

Its name "Temple of the Reclining Buddha" refers to the famous gigantic statue of the Buddha commissioned by Rama III.

Between 1787 and 1801 the original monastery was renovated and enlarged by Rama I, the founder of the capital city. It is still the largest temple complex in Bangkok and until 1970 it was also a sanatorium and pharmacy, a function which developed during the reign of Rama III (1788–1851). Most of the marble plaques and wall-paintings in the "cloisters" (Phra Rabieng), albeit somewhat fragmentary, are nevertheless an invaluable source of information on astronomy, medicine, exercises to achieve bodily control, ethical teachings and on life and culture in general dating from the reign of Rama III, who not only restored the temple but also established a kind of people's university here, "Thailand's first university", which together with this library dates from long before the country was familiar with the printed word.

Location
On Jetubon Road, south of Wat Phra Kaeo (Grand Palace)

Buses
6, 8

Landing-stage
Tha tien

Open:
Daily 8am–5pm

Admission fee

The temple area is surrounded by a wall with sixteen gates, most of which are opened only for religious festivals; three of these back on to Wat Phra Kaeo (see Grand Palace).

Surrounding wall

Near the main gate in Jetubon Road stand a number of human figures in strange postures. They are in fact also demonstrating

Figures

155

Wat Po Monastery

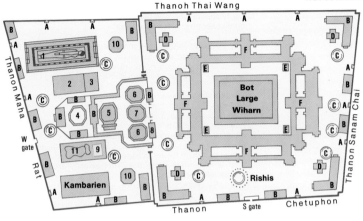

Thanoh Thai Wang

Thanon Maha Rat

W gate

Thanon Sanam Chai

Bot Large Wiharn

Kambarien

Rishis

Thanon   S gate   Chetuphon

A Closed gates
B Sala

C Rockeries
D Chedi

E Prang
F Wiharn

1 Wiharn of the Reclining Buddha
   (Wiharn Phra Non)
2 Abhidhamma School
3 Bodhi tree
4 Old Library
5 Blue Chedi (Rama IV)
6 Yellow-brown Chedi (Rama III)
7 Green Chedi (Rama I)
8 Pavilion of Thai Medicine
9 Turtle pool
10 Bell-tower
11 Rockery

exercises in bodily control and were originally intended to
illustrate the inscriptions in the cloisters. In the covered walk
surrounding the whole sacred area and joining the two courtyards are numerous sitting and (in the West Court) standing
Buddha figures, mostly now found, after cleaning, to be in the
Ayutthaya style – and some in even older styles – from all over
Thailand, including Lopburi and Sukhotai.

Just as curious to Western eyes are the many plaster figures of
animals tucked away in little tree-covered rockeries. These
have mostly been presented over the past 200 years by grateful
patients, and represent some of the many (over 500) life-forms
of the Buddha, even as an animal.

Animal figures

Everywhere there are secular figures also – stone Chinamen
wearing European top-hats, some with cigarettes in their
mouths, soldiers, ladies of the Court, as well as the religious
statues that include Buddha's foster mother and other women
who, according to Buddhist teaching, may enter Nirvana
though they may not become monks or nuns.

Secular figures

Of the 91 prangs and chedis there are four particularly large
ones which should be mentioned.
The green one was erected by Rama I over the remains of a
Buddha image from Ayutthaya, destroyed by the Burmese in
1767.
The two yellow and white chedis were erected by Rama III to
house the mortal remains of himself and his father.

Prangs and Chedis

◀ *Wat Po, the Temple of the Reclining Buddha*

157

The fourth, and probably the finest, covered in bright blue tiles, was built by Rama IV (Mongkut) in memory of Queen Suriyothai who sacrificed her own life in order to save the King, her husband, who was in danger of being killed during a duel on elephant-back (see Ayutthaya)

Visit

Any visitor to this temple complex should include the three most interesting and important buildings, namely, the bot opposite the Jetubon Road entrance, the wiharn in the west court with the great Reclining Buddha, and the Old Library.

Bot

The bot, like so many Thai temples, is guarded by seated lions. Note the 152 marble bas-reliefs in the base of the façade which come from Ayutthaya and depict scenes from the "Ramakien"; however, it remains unconfirmed whether these are actually the remains of a temple in Ayutthaya which was sacked by the Burmese, as has been suggested. Rubbings of these marbles can be bought in the temple precinct. The beautiful teak doors, also with scenes from the "Ramakien", are inlaid with mother-of-pearl.
The lofty rectangular interior, divided into three by teak columns, is very impressive, with the red and gold of the columns and ceiling reflected in the marble floor.

Wiharn Phra Buddha Non
(Reclining Buddha)

To the right of the four large chedis the path leads to the wiharn built over the huge reclining statue of the Buddha, covered in gold-leaf and 45m/148ft long by 15m/49ft high. Inside the wiharn it is difficult to gain an overall impression of the colossal figure, which is modelled in plaster round a core of brick, mainly because there is so little space between the statue and the walls around it, and it is made even more difficult by the many small altars, the signs of weathering and the flaking gold-leaf. However, representing as it does the Buddha passing into Nirvana, what is as splendid as ever is the "other-worldly" expression on the face, which makes the comparability of Nirvana and Heaven seem quite believable. The details are well worth a careful study: the long earlobes (a sign of noble birth), the flame-like curls of hair on the head, the recurring lotus-bud shape of the hand symbolising purity and beauty (the lotus grows out of the mud) and, especially, the soles of the feet which are divided into rectangles and inlaid with mother-of-pearl and fragments of chiefly red and blue precious stones, depicting the Wheel of Law and the 108 special signs by which a fine Buddha may be known.

Old Library (Ho Trai)

In the West Courtyard, in front of the four chedis, is the tower-like Old Library with its airy courtyard and three "Salas" where the lay visitor may rest and eat in the cool shade. Brightly coloured pottery mosaics decorate the main building and the scenes depicted on the door lintels are particularly worth inspection.

Monks' quarters

The southern area where the monks live, on the other side of Jetubon Road, is just as extensive as the northern part with the sacred buildings. Although it is open to the public, it is really worthwhile only to anyone with a particular interest in Buddhism.

Traditional Thai massage

A part of the great Thai medical tradition has survived in Wat Po. On the right of the entrance can be found genuine masseurs, whose skills are in no way related to what has come to be understood by the term "Thai massage". A massage, always performed by someone of the same sex, normally costs about 150 Baht.

*Wat Rajanatda (Wat Rajanaddararm)   D2

The Lohaprasat of Wat Ratjanatda (sometimes written Wat Rajanaddararm) is another temple worthy of being described as an "architectural rarity". Situated not far from the Democracy Memorial and recently restored at a cost of millions, it is well worth a visit. The locals call it the "Iron Palace", because of its metallic spires. There were only two buildings like it in the world; tradition does not say where the original, built when Buddha was still alive, actually stood. A second such palace in metal was erected in 382 in India by King Dutthakaminee, but in spite of its unusual form of construction it was unable to resist the ravages of time. Legend says that it contained one thousand rooms decorated in the most magnificent manner.
Rama III, who did not neglect the artistic side of his capital city in spite of the obligation he felt to further its economic development, was the patron and founder of the temple. The noteworthy wall-paintings in the wiharn also date from his time.

Location
Near Ratchadamnoen Road in Old Bangkok

Buses
2, 3, 9, 10, 14

Open
Wiharn: daily 9am–5pm
Lohaprasat: times vary

The Lohaprasat, square in plan and adjoining the wiharn, is classically Thai in its architecture. The building is six storeys high with seven pagodas adorning each side of the second storey and twelve smaller ones the third, before the eye is attracted to the spire which, in accordance with the Hindu concept of the world, symbolises Mount Meru.
In July 1991, during a celebratory ceremony, a Buddha which had been stored elsewhere during the fourteen years it took to carry out the renovations was reinstated in the spire.
The interior of the lohaprasat is not open to the public every day. When it is closed the visitor can climb a spiral staircase with 81 steps as far as the bottom of the highest pagoda, from where there is a superb view over Old Bangkok, Wat Sakhet (see entry) and a pretty park at the foot of the Lohprasat containing a statue of its founder Rama III.

Lohaprasat

*Wat Ratbophit (Wat Rajabophit)   D2

Wat Ratbophit, or Wat Rajabophit, is an architectural rarity among the temples of Bangkok. It is suggested that a visit is made to this peaceful oasis after seeing the nearby Wat Phra Kaeo in the Grand Palace (see entry).
When building Wat Ratbophit in the years following 1870 King Mongkut's architect based it on an extraordinary model, namely, the Great Chedi of Nakhon Pathom (see entry), which gave him the idea of constructing a circular gallery around a central chedi, the gallery being pierced by three wiharns and a bot.

Location
Between Atsadang Road and Nakhon Road

Buses
6, 8, 12

Open
Daily 8am–5pm

The figures at the entrance gates are worthy of note; they show warriors in uniform from the time of King Chulalongkorn. On entering a cemetery in which the graves, in European-Gothic styles as well as Hindu and Thai, can be seen.

Figures

Wat Sakhet

Chedi

The chedi is clad in yellow-lacquered tiles, a gift from some rich Chinese merchants who hoped thereby to earn the King's favour.

Bot

Particularly attractive is the bot to the north, the doors of which are inlaid with exquisite mother-of-pearl designs representing the five Orders of Merit bestowed by the Thai royal house.

If allowed in the visitor will be taken aback by the bot's interior, for it resembles a Gothic cathedral. It was an idea of King Chulalongkorn who, during his tour of Europe, was very impressed by Western architectural styles and tried to get them copied when he returned home. The roof is vaulted and gilded, the walls panelled in green and gold. The interior is impressive in its harmony and the way the colours set each other off. Even though the arrangement of the rooms is reminiscent of Nakhon Pathom the Bangkok temple is quite different as regards its sumptuous fittings. While the Nakhon Pathom building is sober and practical in appearance, all the walls of Wat Ratbophit are covered in hand-painted tiles. Fortunately it has not suffered at the hands of unskilled restorers so that it can still be admired more or less in all its original glory.

---

*Wat Sakhet (Kao Tong; Golden Mountain)   D2/3

Location
On the eastern edge of Old Bangkok, near the bridge over Banglampu Klong

Buses
8, 11, 12

Open
Daily 8am–5pm

When in about 1782 Rama I had the monastery built at the foot of the present-day hill, which at that time lay outside the city walls, it was intended as a place of cremation for princes and dignitaries and that was indeed what it was used for. Rama III planned the building of an artificial hill which was to have a tall, golden chedi on the summit, but the subsoil could not support it and it finally collapsed completely. The present chedi was not built until the reign of Rama V (Chulalongkorn). About 1940 the top part of the hill was reinforced with concrete. Today, at 78m/256ft high, it forms a landmark for the whole of the Old City.

Until the beginning of this century, however, people hurried past the hill as fast as they could because the former royal shrine had become a burial-ground for criminals and paupers, where vultures and ravening dogs rendered cremation superfluous. As recently as 1899 Hesse-Wartegg (see Quotations), an admirer of the Thai lifestyle and of the city, described the graveyard as the "The Place of Horror".

Nowadays that time is long forgotten, and Bangkok is proud of its Golden Mountain. Every year on the night of the full moon closest to November 20th pilgrims carrying gaily-coloured lamps stream up the sides of the mountain to the reliquaries. The next day sees the start of a gigantic fair lasting several days in the temple grounds, complete with clowns, "likay" shows, performing monkeys and, of course, "ramwong" folk-dances. The golden chedi houses a Buddha relic from India presented by the British Government to King Chulalongkorn, but this can rarely be seen, since the shrine is usually closed. However, the rather strenuous climb is worth the effort for the sake of the splendid panoramic view from the summit over Bangkok, especially the colourful roofs of Wat Po (see entry), the Dusit quarter, and Thonburi's river and gardens.

While there is nowadays no risk of the chedi collapsing as it did years ago, there is still a risk in climbing up to it on your own, because so-called "student guides" are sure to be hiding in the lush undergrowth with their eyes on tourists' purses!

Nowadays the scent of jasmine wafts around the foot of the hill where old funerary urns are buried but there is also a charming little wat here, Luang Po To, with an Ayutthaya Buddha.

Bots

The monastery and two bots on the east slope were built during the reign of Rama I, which makes them among the oldest in Bangkok. The lower of the two, surrounded by a covered walk, has frescoes of the "Ramakien", as well as murals of typical Brahman-Hindu demigods, such as the goddess Thorani washing away hordes of demons with the stream of water from her plaited hair (east wall) and representations of heaven and hell, where sinners have to suffer the torments of fire, a belief that is completely alien to Buddhism in Thailand today.

At right angles to this bot, outside the perimeter wall, lies the other bot, now regarded as a wiharn, with magnificently carved teak doors. In its centre stands an unusually tall statue of Buddha (Phra Attasa), estimated to be about 600 years old, which was salvaged from the ruins of Sukhothai by King Rama I.

Wat Suthat (Sao Chingcha; Giant Swing)   D2

In the square in front of the temple towers what looks like a tall slender Chinese gateway. This great arch of two teak logs is what remains of the former Giant Swing to which the temple owes its name.

Until 1932 this Giant Swing was used in an annual religious ceremony which took place here in mid-December after the rice

Location
In the eastern part
of Old Bangkok,
Sao Chingcha Square

Bus
8

The Giant Swing in front of Wat Suthat

Wat Suthat

Open
Temple area: daily 9am–5pm
Wiharn: only at weekends
and public holidays

harvest. Four men in three teams took turns at standing on a dangerous narrow board which was swung up at least 25m/82ft off the ground up to "Heaven" where each man on the swing attempted to grab a bag of silver coins with his teeth.

The ceremony was Indo-Brahman in origin and based on the legend that the god Shiva was sent by Brahma to visit the Earth. Brahma bade Shiva first to test the firmness of the Earth by putting his right foot on it, crossing his left leg over his right knee and waiting for a reaction. Nothing happened. Brahma then ordered Shiva to try out whether, as prophesied, the mountains would fall into the sea as soon as the Nagas (water snakes) left their homes in the mountains and returned to the seas. Shiva did as he was told, whistled the Nagas down from the mountains to east and west of the ocean into the billowing seas and waited for a reaction. The mountains did not fall into the sea, the Nagas splashed around happily in the water and thenceforth remained in their new element.

After that, every year in mid-December on the fifth day of the new moon in the second moon month, the god Shiva used to honour the earth with a ten day visit. Obviously he had to be offered something and, besides, this was precisely when the rice crop was harvested every year (there was only one crop a year in those days), so Shiva had to be thanked and his blessing for the following harvest ensured.

Four elements were crucial for this: Sun, Moon, Earth and, most important of all, Water. These carved symbols were kept in the little Hindu temple (which can still be seen) on the square in front of Wat Suthat; they were taken out and put on display when the Minister for Rice, the highest official in what was then an agrarian country, would be walking in procession with hundreds of Brahman Court Astrologers around the city walls and to the temple precinct where, at the Giant Swing, the rest of the ceremony was to take place. As the god Shiva had done, his representative would test the Earth's solidity by putting his right foot on the ground near the swing, crossing his left leg over his right knee and remaining in that position to witness the rest of the test. The mountains, symbolised by the uprights of the Giant Swing, would not fall into the sea even if the Nagas, represented by tall pointed hats, were to swing back into their new element.

While Shiva may generally have shown that he was pleased with the spectacle through the success of the harvest, his representative must have found this a tiring position for his legs and the bag of silver offerings must eventually have proved too expensive. In any event, Rama IV gave permission for the ceremony to be carried out by a different dignitary each year. What may also have happened was that the tests did not quite work out as originally intended and the bag of silver was not caught between the teeth, as it was supposed to be, but fell to the ground; or, more reprehensible still, one of the Nagas on the swing touched the ground or even the left foot of Shiva's representative. The Thai chroniclers have drawn a veil over this kind of mishap.

After several young men had paid for their foolhardiness with their lives the Ceremony of the Giant Swing was stopped in 1932.

The festival is still celebrated within the temple precinct, but inside the temple and with only 20 astrologers, After the Buddhist monks have been presented with a suitable offering before sunrise, the four elements – Sun, Moon, Earth and Water, symbolised by the goddess Torani and the god of the River Ganges – are placed, in the form of little statues, inside a golden goose known as Hinsa which is then put on a miniature swing and ridden back up to Heaven by the god Brahma.

Wat Suthan near the Great Swing is one of the oldest and most beautiful of Bangkok's Buddhist temples. The main entrance near the Swing is open only on special occasions, the usual entrance being from Thi-Tong Road.

Temple and Monastery

Three kings were involved in the building of the wat: Rama I, founder of the Chakri dynasty, started it soon after his coronation in 1782, Rama II continued the work and Rama III completed it after it had taken some ten years in all.

The whole complex covers an area of 40,800 sq.m/49,000 sq.yds, is rectangular in plan (being roughly half as long again as it is wide), and the total length of the surrounding walls is 949m/1038yds. The area is divided into two sections, the actual temple complex and the monks' quarters.

Apart from the charming architecture the wall-paintings are also very interesting. These underwent a thorough and very costly programme of restoration in the late 1980s, much of the finance being provided by the German government to celebrate the bicentenary of the city in 1982. The greatest problem was found to be the damage caused to the pictures by bat dung; The paintings covered a total wall area of 2565 sq.m/27,450 sq.ft and are perhaps the biggest and most significant of their kind in Thailand; almost a half were found to be damaged, a tenth irreparably so.

Wall-paintings

Normally, preserved Thai wall-paintings depict the life of the Buddha Gautama. The wiharn at Wat Suthat is different: the paintings show the lives of the preceding 24 Buddhas and of three of their contemporaries. This came about as a result of the slates used by the artists, which were in Pali script and designated the order of each individual section of the painting. The name of the painter is not known, nor is the exact date, but experts think they are from a transitional period, as they clearly differ in style from other works of Thai classical painters and a definite Western influence can be detected. The assumption is that part was commissioned by Rama II (1809–24), but they may have been finished off under Rama III towards the end of his reign (1824–51).

The wiharn is undoubtedly architecturally more interesting and has a finer interior than the Bot. The almost square building has splendid porches on two sides and the richly decorated gable roof is supported by six pillars on each side with gilded lotus-blossom capitals.

Wiharn

The building was purpose-built to house the Phra Buddha Shayamuni (13th c.) which Rama I brought back from Sukhothai. On its arrival in his new capital Rama I ordered seven days of festivities and the bronze figure was paraded through the streets to its new resting-place. The King himself walked barefoot in the procession and – so we are told – tired himself out so much that he fainted when he reached the temple.

The statue shows Buddha in the pose known as "pang mara wichai". The bronze body is plated in gold and stands on a stepped, ornate podium, the lower part of which contains the ashes of Rama VIII (Ananda Mahidol), the brother of the present King Bhumibol, who met a mysterious death.

Wat Suwannaram

Since it was built Wat Suthat has had several names. Rama I first called it Wat Mahasuthavat, but because of its imposing Buddha figure it became popularly known as Wat Phra Yai (The Great Temple). It stands 30m/100ft high and is divided into three naves by four pillars. Entrance to the wiharn is through two massive doorways with some famous carvings; the shutters of one of the windows was carved by Rama III himself.
The wiharn is enclosed by a balustrade with 28 Chinese pavilions, fine bronze horses and Chinese figures of soldiers.

Bot

On the far side (to the south) lies the bot, outstanding for its size rather than its architectural beauty, but what is unusual is the way the 80 statues of Buddha's disciples are naturalistically painted with white, brown, yellow and red skins. Their life-size figures are kneeling before the fine Buddha in the centre and thus appearing to listen intently to what their master is saying. Hindu gods and heroes have only modest places on the insides of doors and windows, but the 24 panels between them fulfil their purpose in a way that is easy for Westerners to understand. They are in fact a "picture-book" of 24 of Buddha's over 500 earlier incarnations and above are depicted scenes from the life of the last Buddha. Their variable artistic quality seems to indicate that different artists worked on them at different times.
All around the bot are traditional walkways with rows of gilded Buddhas.

Statue of King Ananda

The special relationship of Rama VIII with Germany led the West German government to provide financial aid in restoring the pictures. Rama VIII, whose name was actually Ananda, was born in Heidelberg and his father Rama VII received training in Germany as a naval officer. In his memory a statue was unveiled on 2 November 1974 in a corner near the main entrance. Every year wreaths and flowers are laid here on the King's birthday, 10 September.

Wat Suwannaram

See Klongs, Independent Klong Tours

---

*Wat Traimit (Temple of the Golden Buddha)   E3

Location
In Chinatown, junction of Yaowarat Road
and Charoen Krung (New) Road, just
south of Bangkok Central Station

Buses
1, 7, 17

Open
Daily 9am–5pm

Admission fee

The fame and attraction of Wat Traimit, situated in the heart of Chinatown, came about as the result of an accident; until then it had been just another of many hundreds of very ordinary temples scattered throughout Bangkok.
In the 1950s the East Asiatic Company bought the surrounding land, and a condition of the sale was that the plaster statue of Buddha should be removed. A crane was used to do this but the cable broke, the figure fell and the plaster split open, revealing the five and a half tonne pure gold image beneath.
So far the attempt to discover the origin of this priceless statue has proved unsuccessful. It is believed to date from the Sukhotai period, when marauders, perhaps Burmese, threatened the country and its treasures and it therefore became common practice to conceal such valuable Buddha images under plaster. It is also not known how the statue came to Bangkok.

The figure shows Buddha appealing to the goddess Earth, his right hand hanging down almost to his knee and the tips of the fingers touching his chair, with the left hand lying palm-upwards in his lap. His facial expression is severe, almost arrogant; the long earlobes indicate his noble descent.

The statue is on the upper floor of a two-storey building and is reached by an outside staircase next to the bot. There is little worth seeing in the other buildings of the wat.

Practical Information

Accommodation

See Hotels, Young People's Accommodation

Airlines

Tickets

Flying to Bangkok many different types of ticket are available covering a wide range of prices. "Cut-price" fares from airlines which are not members of IATA can produce savings of a hundred pounds or more, but there is often a less attractive side to these "bargains" from a tourist point of view. They may for instance involve an overnight stop spent in an airport transit lounge.

Beware of buying tickets on the so-called "grey market". Airlines belonging to IATA can simply refuse to accept them, and spot checks may be made at the airport.

In addition to the many airlines with scheduled services to and from south-east Asia (these include Royal Brunei, Thai International, Singapore, and other Asian airlines), there are also a number of UK charter companies with heavy involvement in the Thai tourist trade. Not all charter flights convey only package tours.

Internal flights

Flights within Thailand can be pre-booked in the UK through Thai International. All the major airlines with services to Bangkok have offices either in the city itself or at Don Muang Airport. These handle ticket enquiries, bookings, seat reservations, cancellations and reconfirmations.

Flight reconfirmation

Return flights must normally be reconfirmed with the airline 48 hours before departure. Passengers on charter flights should contact the appropriate tour operator's local representative (see Practical Information, Tour Operators).

British Airways
133/19 Rajaprasong Road
Tel. 252 9871–9

Air Canada
World Travel Service
1053 New Road
Tel. 233 5900–9, 234 5593

Air New Zealand
World Travel Service
1053 New Road
tel. 233 5900–9

TWA
Federal Transport Company Ltd.
142//23 Soi Sueksa Vithaya
North Sathorn Road; tel. 233 7290–1,
233 1412, 252 0664

QANTAS
14–18 Patpong Road; tel. 234 4951
Reservations: 233 8701–5

Thai Airways International Ltd.
89 Vibhavadee Rangsit Road; tel. 513 0121
485 Silom Road; tel. 234 3100
Reservations: 233 3810
Airport office: tel. 513 0022, ext. 273 and 274
Office hours: Mon.–Fri. 9am–5pm

Thai International has branch offices in the Asia Hotel (296 Phaya Thai Road) and the Royal Cliff Hotel (in Pattaya). As well as taking bookings and reservations these offices also act as assembly points for return flights (baggage check-in and seat reservation).
Telephone numbers of other airlines can be found in the Yellow Pages section of the local Thai telephone directory.

Useful tip

Airport

Bangkok's Don Muang Airport is situated about 22km/16 miles north of the city centre and handles some 15.6 million passengers a year. It lies on a modern expressway (a toll road in part) which must be judged, of course, by Thai standards. From inner city to airport generally takes about 40 minutes though it is advisable to allow longer (a good hour). The journey can be made by taxi (cabs are painted either blue and red or yellow), minibus, limousine, public bus service, or train (station by the Airport Hotel). Porters (in green overalls) vie for custom at bus stops and taxi ranks. They charge about 30 baht per suitcase. Passengers leaving Thailand check in at the "International Airport" where the international airlines have their reception desks. Internal flights within Thailand and Malaysia leave from the Inland Terminal (Domestic Passenger Terminal Building). A shuttle service runs between the two terminals which are only a few hundred metres apart (information from Thai Airways Transportation Center in the arrival hall).

*Information
Tel. 531 0022, or the appropriate airline*

Two hours must be allowed when changing flights (three hours when transferring from a Thai inland to an international flight).

Changeover times

An airport tax is levied on all passengers at check-in (currently 200 baht for international flights and 20 baht inland).

Airport taxes

Duty-free goods can be bought prior to departure at the airport duty-free shops. There are good savings to be had on tobacco products, alcohol and perfume. Thai silk on the other hand costs less in the city.

Duty-free shops

The Thai tourist organisation (TAT) has an information office in the arrival hall and will assist with finding a hotel as well as dealing with any queries.

Information/finding a hotel

"Last minute calls"

There are special telephone kiosks in the arrival and departure halls from which passengers can make last-minute local calls free of charge.

Antiques

Export

Strict regulations govern the export and import of antiques. Since 1961, around which time treasure hunting and unauthorised excavation of historic sites had become a problem in Thailand, it has been illegal to take figures of the Buddha and other deities out of the country. The ban includes the often very authentic copies to be found on sale everywhere. There are one or two exceptions to the regulations and further information can be obtained from the Director, Department of Fine Arts (Na Phra That Road, near the National Museum; tel. 221 48 17). Miniature copies of Buddha figures are exempted however. These can be legitimately exported just so long as they are clearly recognisable as exempt.
(It is only the export of figures which is forbidden, their manufacture and sale within Thailand being perfectly legal. Airport customs officials carry out spot checks on the baggage of travellers leaving the country.)

Export licences are also required for all other kinds of antiques. Processing of an application normally takes about two weeks. Approval must be sought from the Ministry of Trade and the applicable export duty determined. The regulations are intended to prevent in particular the export of any object important to the history of Thailand. If in doubt, to avoid problems, amateur collectors should seek advice from TAT (the Tourism Authority of Thailand, see Information). Professional buyers will obviously need to go through all the formalities.

Authenticity

Prospective purchasers would be well advised to be sceptical about the authenticity of any antique (it should be obvious, for example, that a centuries-old Buddha figure is unlikely to be found for sale on the beach). While the vendor may well insist on the genuineness of his wares, the truth all too often comes to light only when he and the buyer are separated by many miles. The fact is that few originals are in circulation and because of this the trade is subject to government control. Where appropriate a certificate of authenticity can be obtained from the relevant Ministry (for a fee) or from the Department of Fine Arts in Bangkok (see above).
"Genuine" copies of *objets d'art* can be purchased in the state-owned emporia in Bangkok and Chiang Mai (addresses available from TAT).

Proof of origin

Anyone bringing antiques into Thailand (e.g. from neighbouring countries) must be able to produce documentary proof of their origin. Similar documentation is required in the case of items purchased in Thailand but originating elsewhere – Myanmar (Burma) for example.

Art galleries

Thailand has been producing art of the highest quality for centuries, as the magnificent wall paintings to be found in some of Bangkok's temples clearly demonstrate.

There is also some fine, internationally acclaimed, contemporary art. Professor Preecha Thaothong is one of several Thais considered to be among south-east Asia's most talented artists.

The following galleries are worth visiting (entrance is free):

National Art Gallery
Chao Fa Road (north of the Prahmane Ground)
Open: Tue.–Thur., Sat. and Sun. 9am–4pm

Bhirasri Institute
Soi Athakam Prasit Road
Open: Tues.–Sun. 9am–4pm

Sillapakorn University
Na Phra Lan Road (opposite Grand Palace) temporary exhibitions
Open: Mon.–Sat. 9am–4.30pm

Some dealers in modern art have galleries in the major shopping centres.

Banks

Banks and money changers are found throughout the Bangkok urban area and in the tourist centres.   General

Banks in Thailand are on the whole efficient and reliable. In addition to the usual monetary transactions the useful services available to tourists include teletransfer of funds from Europe within two to three days. The two banks whose main Bangkok branches are listed below have been picked out from among the city's many financial institutions as particularly experienced in dealing with European currencies. They also have substantial branch networks covering the whole of Thailand.

Siam Commercial Bank Ltd.   Major banks
1060 Phetchaburi Road
Tel. 256 1234

Thai Farmers Bank
400 Phahon Yothin Road
Tel. 270 1122

Banks, etc. are open Mon.–Fri. 8.30am–3.30pm.   Business hours
Outside the bank there is often a separately accessible exchange bureau which remains open for business until 8pm. Passports must always be produced when changing money.

Money changers are found all over the city. Their hours of   Money changers
business are flexible, as are their rates (so up-to-the-minute knowledge of the official exchange rate can sometimes lead to a more favourable transaction than is possible with a bank).

Bookshops

Most of the larger hotels have shops ("drugstores") selling items for everyday use. These usually include books and periodicals.

The bookshops listed stock English titles (and in some cases German and French titles too):

Chalermnit Bookshop
Rajaprasong Trade Center
Specialises in travel guides and art history.

Asia Book
Soi 61, Sukhumvit Road

Best Book
76/29 Soi Lang Suan Phloenchit Road

Duang Kamoi Bookstore ("DK")
Siam Square Soi 2 and at the "Alliance Française", Sathon Tai Road (near the German Embassy)
Elite Book House
593/5 Sukhumvit Road

The Bookseller
81 Patpong Road (open till late evening)

White Lotus Co. Ltd.
47 Sukhumvit (corner of Soi 16)
Specialises in books of cultural interest including art, and illustrated books.

Business Hours

General	Government departments, post offices and other official organisations apart, commerce in Thailand is largely unfettered by regulation on such matters as shop opening hours. The smaller shopkeepers, tradesmen and craftsmen are at liberty to conduct their businesses much as they will. The information which follows, therefore, applies primarily to public institutions and larger concerns.
Banks	Mon.–Fri. 8.30am–3.30pm and Sat. 8.30–noon
Money changers	Mon.–Sat. 9am–8pm. Sun. mostly closed. Occasionally money changers run out of money to change and will then shut up shop.
Department stores	Mon.–Sat. 10am–7pm
Government offices	Mon.–Fri. 8.30am–4.30pm
Private offices	Mon.–Fri. 8am–5pm
Retail businesses	Mon.–Fri. 8am–9pm
Shops	Mon.–Sun. 8am–9pm (some even longer)
Post offices	Mon.–Fri. 8am–6pm, Sat., Sun. and public holidays 8am–1pm
Chemists	See entry
Embassies	See Diplomatic Representation

Business Trips

General	Trade between the UK and Thailand is diverse and a considerable number of British companies are already successfully

established in the country. Among Thailand's very varied exports are precious stones, textiles and a variety of natural produce and raw materials. A great deal of careful pre-planning is required if any business trip to Thailand is to succeed however, and numerous regulations apply to any foreign company seeking to set up a business there.

Further information is available from:

The Investment Board
400 Phahon Yothin Road, 16th–17th floor (Thai Farmers Bank Building)
Tel. 270 1400

and from:

The Thai Chamber of Commerce
Tel. 221 6532.

Anyone in the UK interested in doing business in Thailand is advised to contact the UK office of the Investment Board.

One, often seemingly insurmountable, obstacle the Westerner faces when conducting business in Thailand is the Asian business mentality. Nothing can be read into the Thai's proverbial smile for example: it is just as likely to accompany a "No!" as a "Yes!".

The Asian business mentality

The last thing a visitor should do is anything which forfeits respect. Thais invariably conduct themselves calmly and quietly in business negotiations; anyone who reacts angrily or raises his voice immediately loses face. Thais also respond very unfavourably to being pressurised for time; it will usually take a long while and an inordinate number of meetings before any major project is finalised. Being correctly dressed is also essential, which for men means always wearing a tie however oppressive the heat.

Thais strongly approve of punctuality, even if they are not unfailingly punctual themselves. It is important therefore to arrive for an appointment at the agreed time, though this may result in being kept waiting. In Bangkok in particular plenty of allowance should be made for the unpredictability of the traffic.

Thais also like to combine business appointments with a breakfast or a lunch. Not unusually a business associate will be invited to an evening meal, the purpose of which is for the people concerned to get to know each other better in a more informal atmosphere.

Car Rental

Any visitor who ventures onto the roads in a self-drive car should confine himself to driving in daylight. It takes a considerable time and exceptionally strong nerves to become acclimatised to the chaotic behaviour of the local traffic and the almost total disregard for safety shown by many pedestrians (see Motoring).
Traffic regulations are more often ignored than observed and failing to stop after an accident is the rule rather than the

A word of caution

exception. The general impression given is that traffic lights, for example, are little more than decoration – or a colourful form of street lighting!

Driving licence

Strictly speaking visitors require an international driving licence but in practice a national driving licence will generally suffice. An alternative to self-drive is to hire a vehicle with a driver (at an additional charge).

Insurance

Third party insurance is not compulsory in Thailand. It is usually available as part of a car rental agreement however and the option should most certainly be taken up.

Car rental companies

All the well-known international car rental companies have branches in Bangkok and Pattaya so if desired the necessary hire arrangements can usually be made before leaving the UK (contact any of the international car hire firms). In addition there are very many local firms which hire out vehicles.
Before taking over a vehicle make a point of examining its general state of roadworthiness (wear on tyres, oil level, existing damage to bodywork, etc.). Check also that it has air-conditioning and is covered by third party insurance (not compulsory in Thailand). Full comprehensive insurance cover is strongly recommended. Prices are reasonable. If in doubt on any score it is best to trust to one of the reputable car rental companies.
The jeeps available from the Pattaya car-hire firms tend not to be insured and their condition generally leaves a lot to be desired. The advice offered above applies particularly to these vehicles.
Mini-buses are relatively cheap to hire. They are ideal for small groups of up to eight people who are free to follow their own itinerary.
Heavier, more powerful motorcycles should definitely be avoided. They are positively dangerous in the unfamiliar road conditions and are frequently scarcely roadworthy. The number of serious accidents involving these machines, often resulting in months spent in hospital, has risen dramatically in recent years. Light motorcycles in contrast have proved relatively safe and reliable and are widely available for hire all over Thailand. The advice already given still applies nevertheless: inspect the vehicle carefully before completing the hire contract.

Avis

In Bangkok: 10/1 North Sathon Road, tel. 233 0397
Dusit Thani Hotel: tel. 233 5256
Princess Hotel: tel. 281 3088
In Pattaya: Dusit Resort Hotel, tel. (038) 429 901-3
Royal Cliff Hotel: tel. (038) 421 421

Hertz

In Bangkok: c/o Premier Inter Leasing 987 Phloenchit Road, tel. (02) 253 6251–4; open Mon.–Sat. 8am–5pm
In Pattaya: Royal Garden Resort 218 Beach Road, tel. (038) 42 8122, 42 8126

Chemists

General

Chemist's shops abound in Bangkok and also in tourist centres such as Pattaya. Usually opening directly on to the street those marked "Pharmacy", "Drug Store" or "Rahn Kai Jah" stock most of the medicines in common use in Europe and for which there is likely to be demand. Virtually the only difference is that here in Thailand they are a fraction of the price. This is explained by the fact that, almost without exception, such remedies are dispensed on the spot from original recipes. They have the same effect though, and often even the same name. Furthermore, all the large international pharmaceutical companies have branches in Bangkok and the prices of their products locally tend to reflect the low Thai wage levels.

There are exceptions to the rule. The so-called "British Dispensaries" sell proprietary medicines at fixed prices. The same goes for the "Drugstores" in the shopping arcades of the big hotels. They generally keep a basic selection of the pharmaceutical products most in demand.

Vying keenly with each other for business, Thai chemist's shops offer their customers much more than just the usual range of Western-style drugs. No Thai pharmacist would enjoy the confidence of his local clientele for example, were he not also to stock the traditional, ancient Chinese homeopathic remedies.

To avoid any possibility of confusion when buying medicines it is a good idea to take along the original container. In the better chemist's shops (recognisable by the cleanliness of their premises) at least one of the staff will normally speak English. Anyone who needs a further supply of a medicine prescribed at home should be wary of accepting something merely "similar". If in doubt, phone the Bangkok branch of the appropriate European pharmaceutical company (see the Yellow Pages) and check the name by which the drug is known in Thailand.

Thai doctors, even European and American trained ones in private practice, usually employ their own pharmacists. Instead of a prescription patients are given a few days supply of medicine in a small plastic bag. Certain medicines however can only be obtained on prescription.

Prescriptions

Be sure to inform the doctor of any known allergic reaction or intolerance to drugs; also ask him what any prescribed medicine contains.

Mon.–Sat. 9am–7 or 8pm, sometimes also Sunday mornings.

Opening times

Church Services

Protestant and Catholic Churches are both very active in Bangkok. The list below gives some addresses and the times of Sunday services:

In Bangkok

Holy Redeemer Catholic Church
Wireless Road, 123/19 Soi Ruam Rudi (beyond the US embassy)
Tel. 253 03 05
Sunday Mass (in English): 8.30, 9.45, 11am and 5.30pm

Cathedral of the Assumption
23 Oriental Avenue
Tel. 234 8666
Sunday Mass (in English): 10am

St John's
1110 Phahon Yothin Road
Tel. 513 4286
Sunday Mass (in English): 10am

The Evangelical Church
10 Sukhumvit Road, at the end of Soi 10
Tel. 251 9539

Beside the Chaophraya/Menam, not far from the Oriental Hotel, there is a rather unusual church, Wat Kalawa. Despite its Buddhist name the church is Catholic in denomination and Gothic in style! Services are held in Chinese and English. To attend one of the services in Chinese can be a rewarding experience, not least for the opportunity it provides for silent contemplation.

In Pattaya

Catholic mass is celebrated in English every Sunday at 9am in the Church of the Redemptionists (out of Pattaya near the orphanage on the Bangkok Highway); also at 8.30am and 4pm in St Nicholas Church (Sukhumvit Road, a little way out of Pattaya).

Cinemas

Going to the cinema in Thailand is one of many pleasures no tourist should miss. The dialogue naturally is mostly in Thai but like cinema the world over the films tend to be classic tales of good and evil, love and pain and for that reason alone will not be lost on a receptive viewer. In addition to Thai films, films made in India, China, Europe and the US are also shown, produced or dubbed in English.

Bangkok is well provided with cinemas, all with an enormous seating capacity. Queues form in front of the box office long before the performance begins so it is best to reserve tickets in advance. Programmes are advertised in the daily press (see Newspapers and Periodicals).

At the conclusion of the programme a picture of the King and Queen of Thailand is shown on the screen while the audience rises for the national anthem. The high regard in which the Thais hold their royal family is very evident.

Clothing

General

Thin loose cotton clothing and comfortable footwear are basically all a visitor will need during any of the three seasons which make up Thailand's year. A light knitted jacket is a sensible addition for the period between November and February, as well as for trips to the north of the country.

Flooding is still a frequent occurrence during the rainy seasons despite the fact that the water table is dropping a few centimetres every year as more and more unofficial wells are sunk. Avoid wearing rubber sandals in the wet conditions; they are very slippery. Cheap rubber boots are useful for negotiating floodwater but can be something of a nuisance. Anyone who favours walking barefoot through the muddy brown wash should bear in mind the risk of infection and keep a supply of disinfectant wipes (such as "Sagrotan") to hand. These are available in chemist shops both in the UK and in Thailand and can be used to wipe one's feet on escaping from the wet into a building.

Easily washable clothes, preferably made from natural fibres, are the most practical at any time of the year. Jackets are essential wear for men for business appointments and in restaurants. In the cool season or if visiting the mountainous areas in the north some warm woollens will be needed and suitable waterproofs are essential anywhere in the country during the rainy period (June–October).

Be sure to dress suitably when visiting a temple. At the very least shoulders should be covered and on no account should shorts be worn (see Thai Society and the Visitor).

Temple visits

Made-to-measure tailoring is a thriving business in Thailand, with immigrant Indian Sikhs holding something of a mono-poly. They will impeccably turn out any sort of garment to the customer's measurements. Prices are very reasonable. Bear in mind though that it will take at least three days to make a good suit for example, and that a minimum of one fitting will be necessary in the process.

Made-to-measure

While good, sometimes even excellent, ladies' and gentle-men's tailors are found in all the hotels (especially the larger ones), the innumerable tailors shops in the city have just as much to offer. The quality of the finished article can be judged from the models in the windows. Anyone daunted by the com-plexities of modern fashion can ask to see one of the European fashion magazines which are usually on display.

Thailand is justly famous for its excellent silk. Particularly pleasing to the touch, Thai silk is ideal for men's shirts as well as for ladies' evening wear. Chinese silk is rather more expen-sive but creases less than the Thai. As well as silk all the good tailors keep an extensive range of other materials suited to European fashion.

Silk

A gent's made-to-measure suit (jacket, waistcoat and trousers) costs between £60 and £100, a pure silk shirt about £10–15. Ladies' clothes cost more but the tailors will go to endless trouble to satisfy individual requirements.

Once a garment has been ordered and the initial measure-ments taken it is customary to leave a deposit (which should generally not be more than 20% of the agreed price). This gives the tailor some assurance that the finished article will be col-lected and paid for.

A list of good, reliable, Bangkok tailors is not a practical propo-sition here – recommendations usually circulate by word of mouth. That apart there is no alternative but to trust one's own judgement!

Currency

The unit of currency in Thailand is the baht, equivalent to 100 satang (also colloquially known as "dang").

Currency

Currency

The smallest coin in circulation has a value of 25 satang (= 1 salung, though the term salung is now rarely used). There are also coins of 50 satang (= 2 salung), 1 baht and 5 baht.

Thai banknotes are in denominations of 10 (light brown), 20 (green), 50 (blue), 100 (red) and 500 baht (mauve). All banknotes are also inscribed in Arabic numerals.

Exchange rates

Exchange rates of course fluctuate, and the current rate can be obtained by enquiry at a bank. At present the rate is between 35 and 45 baht to the pound sterling and about 25 to the US dollar.

Official exchange rate

The exchange rate available from banks is set by the Thai authorities and published in the daily papers. The same rate applies in the official exchange bureaux at Bangkok Airport and throughout the country. Somewhat more advantageous rates can often be secured from a "money changer". The rates offered by hotels on the other hand are generally less favourable so this form of exchange should only be a last resort.

Foreign currency regulations

Although there are no restrictions on the amount of foreign currency which can be brought into the country, sums of over 10,000 US dollars or the equivalent must be declared on the customs form. Thai currency is limited to 5000 baht per person on entry (10,000 baht for those travelling on a family passport).

On leaving the country Thai currency up to 5000 baht may be taken out (10,000 baht for families). Foreign currency taken out may not exceed the value declared on entry.

Travellers' cheques

It is best to take money in the form of travellers' cheques. As well as being more secure they usually enjoy an advantageous rate of exchange compared with cash even after allowing for the 1% insurance fee on the cheque's value. The insurance quickly repays itself if cheques are lost or stolen (though it is essential to keep the cheques and confirmation of purchase separate).
Whether to take sterling or dollar travellers' cheques is largely a matter of individual preference though on past performance the pound sterling has proved the more stable of the two.

Passports must always be produced when changing travellers' cheques. As an additional safeguard the name of the visitor's hotel in Thailand is entered on the transaction form.

Always ask for a receipt and always check the money against the receipt immediately it is handed over.

Eurocheques

The Thai Farmers Bank (branches throughout Thailand) will accept up to five Eurocheques a month. In practice however it is difficult to monitor the number cashed (an entry is sometimes made on the visa page of the visitor's passport). Eurocheque cards and passports must of course be produced.

Credit cards

All the usual credit cards (e.g. American Express, BankAmericard/Visa, Mastercard/Eurocard, Diners Club) are accepted throughout Thailand in hotels, restaurants, private shops, duty-free shops and banks. Most of those listed can also be used to settle accounts with travel agencies and airlines. Only the international car rental companies will take credit cards in payment however.

When making a payment by credit card always check to see that the cardholder's copy of the transaction agrees with the retailer's.

If a credit card is lost or stolen the cardholder should immediately inform the company in question:

American Express, tel. 253 8377
Diners Club, tel. 233 5644–5
Mastercard/Eurocard, tel. 252 2212
BankAmericard/Visa, tel. 252 2212

In addition to the normal over-the-counter services during business hours all the major Thai banks (see entry) such as the Thai Farmers Bank and Siam Commercial Bank provide automatic cash withdrawal facilities from bank machines.

Cash withdrawals

Customs Regulations

Ordinary personal effects including a camera and a movie or video camera can be taken into Thailand duty-free, as can up to 200 cigarettes or 250 grams of cigars or tobacco, and 1 litre of wine or spirits. Additional cameras are allowed but must be declared at customs.

On entry

To avoid any problems arising on departure valuable items such as video cameras, tape recorders, radios, portable computers, etc. should also be declared.

The prohibition on narcotic drugs is strictly enforced (consigned baggage is checked, sometimes by sniffer dogs), likewise the ban on pornographic literature. Firearms and ammunition can be taken in only with permission from the Police Department. The import of plants must be approved by the Ministry of Agriculture.

Antiques and *objets d'art* require an export licence from the Department of Fine Arts in Bangkok. Figures of the Buddha (even if new!) or other deities, or fragments of such, can only be exported with the authority of both the Department of Fine Arts and the Ministry of Trade.

Leaving Thailand

The duty-free allowances for travellers returning to the UK are a maximum of 200 cigarettes or 250 grams of tobacco, and 1 litre of spirits. Presents and other goods to a value of £32 are also exempt.

Returning to the UK

Diplomatic Representation

Embassies in Bangkok

1031 Wireless Road; tel. 253 0191–9
Office hours: Mon. and Tues. 8am–1 30pm. Wed. 8am–2pm
Thurs. and Fri. 2–4.30pm

United Kingdom

95 Wireless Road; tel. 252 5040–9
Office hours: 7.30–10am and 12.30–3pm

United States of America

Drugs

Canada	11/F Boonmitr Building, 138 Silom Road Tel. 234 1561 Office hours: 9am–12.30pm
Australia	37 South Sathorn; tel. 287 2680 Office hours: 9.30am–noon and 2–3pm
New Zealand	93 Wireless Road; tel. 251 8165 Office hours: 8am–noon and 1.30–4pm

Thai Embassies abroad

United Kingdom	Royal Thai Embassy 30 Queen's Gate London SW7; tel. (071) 589 2857
United States of America	Royal Thai Embassy 2300 Kalorama Road, NW Washington D.C. 20008; tel. 483 7200–2
Canada	Royal Thai Embassy 85 Range Road Suite 704 Ottawa, Ontario K1N 8J6 Tel. 237 1517, 237 0476
Australia	Royal Thai Embassy 111 Empire Circuit Yarralumiia Canberra, A.C.T. 2600; tel. 731149, 732937
New Zealand	Royal Thai Embassy 2 Cook Street P.O. Box 17–226 Karari Wellington; tel. 767864

Drugs

General	Throughout south-east Asia the attitude of the authorities towards those dealing in, possessing and taking drugs has undergone a radical transformation, not least because of intense diplomatic pressure from Europe and America. In Thailand the police are heavily engaged in combating drug related crime and a highly effective drugs squad has been specially formed for the purpose. Under no circumstances therefore should a visitor to Thailand become in any way involved with drugs, even with the so-called "magic mushrooms". Although seemingly harmless these in fact have dangerous hallucinatory properties.
Penalties	Possession of even the smallest quantity of a drug can result in many years of imprisonment – and Thai prisons bear little comparison to those in Europe. Thailand, moreover, retains and applies the death penalty. Anyone foolish enough to become involved with drugs can expect no help from their country's consulate.
A warning	Do not be talked into taking anything out of Thailand "for a friend". There have been many attempts to use unsuspecting travellers as drug couriers.

Electricity

Thailand has 220 volt 50-cycle AC power as standard. Thai plugs however are smaller than in Europe so an adaptor is needed (available from electrical shops or from hotel reception desks).

Emergencies

The Tourist Assistance Center (TAC) is a department of the Tourist Authority of Thailand (TAT) manned by English-speaking personnel from the police service. The Center is open from 8am to midnight and can be contacted by telephoning either the central number 195, or 221 6206–10 (the prefix from outside Bangkok is 02). There are also TAC offices at Don Muang Airport (tel. 523 8972–3) and Pattaya (tel. (038) 429 371).

Tourist Assistance Center

There is a TAC booklet with a blue cover which gives advice in English on the principal rules to observe while staying in Thailand. On the back is a short statement in Thai asking people to support TAC and provide information where appropriate.

The Crime Suppression Division (part of the Thai Criminal Investigation Department) performs the functions of a crime detection agency and flying squad. It can be contacted day or night (tel. 221 911 or 225 151). There may be difficulty in making oneself understood in which case TAC (see above) should be able to help.

Crime Suppression Division

The Metropolitan Mobile Police are the traffic police and flying squad for the whole Bangkok area (tel. 191 or 246 1338–42).

Metropolitan Mobile Police

The Highway Patrol Division can be contacted on tel. 281 6240, 281 6241 and 281 6250. Police patrols are usually quick to arrive on the scene of any incident, but attempting to report someone for an offence or to bring charges is likely to be complicated by language difficulties and questions of jurisdiction. It is important nevertheless to make a factual, on-the-spot statement to the police so that the TAC can later be informed accordingly. Also, get the patrolman to write down his name and police station.

Highway Patrol Division

Tel. 199 or 246 0199

Fire brigade

Tel. 252 2171–5

Emergency doctor or ambulance

Festivals and Public Holidays

Festivals and public holidays in Thailand generally have a religious dimension or are connected either with events in the country's history or with ceremonies at court. The religious festivals are movable, their dates being dictated by the lunar calendar. National holiday dates on the other hand are fixed.

General

Fixed public holidays

Chakri Day
A national holiday commemorating Rama I (founder of the

Apr. 6th

179

reigning Chakri dynasty) and the other Chakri kings. This is the only day on which the public can enter the pantheon of Wat Phra Kaeo to see the eight statues of the kings. Chakri Day also celebrates the founding of the capital Bangkok in 1782.

Apr. 13th–15th	*Songkhran Festival

Celebration of the traditional Thai new year which opens when the sun reaches the constellation of Aries. Taking place before the year's rice crop is sown offerings are made to monks, captive birds are set free, and fish are rescued from dried-up pools and returned to streams and ponds. Statues of Buddha are also symbolically bathed, i.e. splashed copiously with water. In Bangkok there is a carnival-type procession, as indeed there has been in Pattaya now for many years. On the second day, and till the festival ends, there is much throwing of water, especially by boys and girls (the water often being mixed with rice powder or even coal dust). The wave of marriages which follow the festival point to the role it performs as an outlet for Thailand's still generally straitlaced society.

May 1st
Labour Day
In addition to the usual trade union rallies and the traditional offerings to monks, musical events and plays take place in Lumphini Park. These include the immensely popular "krabi", a form of entertainment consisting largely of joke-telling and comedy sketches.

May 5th
Coronation Day
A national holiday on the anniversary of the coronation in 1959 of the reigning king and queen.

Aug. 12th
The Queen's Birthday
Marked by Queen Sirikit's participating in various religious ceremonies and distributing gifts to monks at the Chidralada Palace and elsewhere.

Oct. 23rd
King Chulalongkorn Day
Festival commemorating King Chulalongkorn (Rama V, grandfather of the present king) who died in 1910 and was held in great affection by his people. There is a parade of military cadets. Passers-by pay their respects at the equestrian statue of King Chulalongkorn, in the square in front of the National Assembly building.

Dec. 5th
The King's Birthday
The birthday of King Bhumibol (Rama IX, b. 1927), celebrated with much pomp and splendour.

Dec. 10th
Constitution Day
The day on which Thais celebrate the introduction in 1932 of the country's first democratic constitution. Monks once again receive gifts.

Dec. 31/Jan. 1st
New Year's Eve and Day
Celebrated in much the same manner as in the West. Visitors bring presents and children receive gifts.

Festivals with movable dates

January
Red Cross Day Bazaars
Stalls and refreshments, displays and entertainment (in Lumphini Park).

The Ploughing Ceremony and . . .

. . . casting offerings on the waters at Loy Krathong

Festivals and Public Holidays

Late January/early February, at full moon	**Makha Bucha** The festival commemorates the spontaneous gathering of 1250 proselytes of Buddha who came together to sit at his feet and hear his teachings. Processions take place in the evening around the various temples, bathed in the light of the full moon. Nowhere is the striking beauty of the ceremony more evident than at Wat Benjama-bo-bitr in Bangkok (see A to Z).
End of February/beginning of March	**Chinese New Year** This festival is celebrated mainly by the inhabitants of Bangkok's Chinatown where shops close for the day (some for the whole week!) Colourful entertainment with Chinese acrobats, etc. is put on by some of the big hotels (the Siam Intercontinental for example).
About May 12th	***Ploughing ceremony** A Hindu ceremony during which rice is blessed and later scattered to bring good fortune and a rich harvest. The glittering procession, headed by priests, includes high ranking public figures in white and gold as well as a bevy of girls specially chosen for their beauty who accompany the water buffalo and their wooden ploughs. As it passes before the Royal Palace on the Sanaam Luang in Bangkok the procession is reviewed by the king and queen in front of the red uniformed Royal Guard.
Mid May	**Rocket festival** Following the harvest and before the rains set in the Thais celebrate by firing bamboo rockets into the air. There are colourful processions complete with rhythmic music and singing.
May, at full moon	**Visakha Bucha** A national festival dedicated to Buddha, celebrating his birth, his Enlightenment and entry into Nirvana. In temples all over the country ceremonies are held on the night of the full moon.
July, at full moon	**Asanha Bucha** Festival commemorating Buddha's first teachings delivered to five initial disciples. Ceremonies and processions again take place all over Thailand on the night of the full moon.
July	**Khao Pansa** Start of the three-month long period of Buddhist fasting.
October	**Thot Kathin** The end of the Buddhist period of fasting to mark which monks are presented with new robes. Until 1962 the king always used to make a visit by river to Wat Arun (see A to Z), at the head of a magnificent procession of royal barges. Among the chief attractions today are the river procession and regatta at Phra Pa Daeng opposite Paknam, the site of a Mon settlement from the Dvaravati period (6th–12th c., the Mon being the original inhabitants of Thailand). An excursion is well worth while.
November	**Phra Pathom Chedi** Pilgrimage to Thailand's oldest pagoda, in Nakhon Pathom (37m/60km west of Bangkok). A big festival centred on the temple, with a fair and many different kinds of entertainment.
November, at full moon	***Loy Krathong** One of the most beautiful of all Thai festivals: Thousands of

little banana and lotus leaf rafts carrying lighted candles, incense sticks, lotus blossom and often a few coins are set adrift on the rivers and canals, a myriad of tiny lights flickering beneath the full moon. Although actually a Festival of Lights dedicated to Mae Kongka, Goddess of the Waterways, Thais also associate it with the story of a princess who, as evening fell, would send little boats with lighted candles floating across the Chaophraya/Menam to her beloved. Sukhothai and Chiang Mai are particularly good places to witness the festival but it is worth seeing in Bangkok too.

Golden Mount Fair   About Nov. 22nd
A great fair and a procession to the Golden Mount (see A to Z, Wat Sakhet) in Bangkok where pilgrims pay their respects to relics of Buddha.

Floating Markets

See A to Z

Folklore

No longer are Thai popular theatre, Thai classical dance or   General
Chinese opera part of the everyday experience of visitors to Thailand. To find out where and when they can be seen enquiries should be made at the Department of Fine Arts or TAT.

Good classical theatre and dance is performed on certain days   Theatre
at the National Theatre. Additionally there are daily performances specially for tourists at the Rose Garden (see A to Z). Thai folk music and dance also features in the evening entertainment provided by some leading hotels and restaurants.

The best-known forms of Thai classical dance are "khon"   Dance
(masked dance), "rabum" (dance with music) and "lakon" (dance drama). Despite the weight of their magnificent costumes the dancers move with the utmost grace, often in a sort of rhythmic counterpoint to the accompanying flutes, gongs and xylophones.

Food and Drink

There is surely nowhere else in Asia where the food is as varied   General
as it is in Thailand. Not only are there innumerable Thai specialities to be enjoyed but cuisine from every corner of the globe is represented as well (see Restaurants).

Thai cooking draws on traditions from China, India and Malaya.   Thai cooking
The basic ingredient in many meals is rice served with a variety of vegetables, meat and fish, all prepared in a host of different ways. A multitude of herbs and spices including chilies, coriander, garlic, basil, cardamom, curry, mint, ginger, citronella, etc. and an equally wide range of sweet, sweet and sour, salty and hot sauces, endow these dishes with their special flavours.

Food and Drink

Pork, beef and poultry, prepared with or without coconut milk and in any case very hot, are extremely popular.

Tip

The Oriental Hotel puts on regular courses in Thai cookery conducted by a top local chef. Further information at the hotel reception.

Spices

Thai cooking is typically mildly hot, and can sometimes be very hot. Soups and main courses are usually served with a choice of spices which can be varied to influence the taste. A little care is required because some of them, the small red and green peppers known as "nam prik" for example, are so strong they are best used very sparingly. Instead of salt a fish sauce called "num bplah" is often served.

Soups

Most soups are creamed and extremely tasty. As well as vegetable there are soups made from poultry, meat and fish (bplah joo-oot), often served with noodles. Soups (such as "tom yam gairng" for example, a Thai favourite enjoyed at any time of the day or night) are usually rather spicy. Anyone who prefers a milder flavour should let the waiter know when ordering, by saying "mai sai prik" (Thai for "not hot please").

Main courses

There are a great variety of typically Thai dishes to be sampled, all prepared with generous amounts of garlic and onion and garnished with different kinds of salad. Pork (moo) and beef dishes (woo-a), chicken (gai) and fish (bplah), appear frequently on the menu in all sorts of guises. They are usually eaten with rice (kao), noodles (ba-mee) and chips (mun fa-rung tort). To order pork with fried rice for example, simply say "kao put moo"; if beef is preferred to pork "kao put woo-a"; and so on.

Fish and shellfish

Fish and shellfish (lobster, spiny lobster and crab) are very reasonably priced, always fresh, and excellently prepared.

Nam prik

Som

Many restaurants display their seafood in cool-cabinets. The giant crabs which are caught fresh in the bays of southern Thailand and cooked over a charcoal fire before being served with a variety of accompaniments are exceptionally tasty.

Desserts (korng wahn) usually take the form of little puddings, very sweet and very brightly coloured, or some form of rice dish. Small, dry, raisin cakes are also a favourite. The Thais are exceptionally good at preparing sweet rice dishes (ka-nom, etc.) and have mastered the art of ice-cream making from the Americans. Their ice-cream sundaes in particular, sometimes served in a hollowed out pineapple, are superlative.

Dessert

Thais insist that food appeals to the eye as well as to the palate. As is so often the case with a tradition, the Thai art of cutting fruit and vegetables is traced back to a legend. In one of King Rama II's poems the story is told of a queen who loses the king's favour to a rival. Banished from the palace she returns secretly as a kitchen maid, revealing herself to her son by depicting incidents from her life at court in the vegetables she prepares for the soup. Recognising his mother the boy intercedes with the king on her behalf and she is at last restored to her rightful place. And so, it is said, this ancient Thai tradition was founded. Today even hotel kitchens have staff who are masters in the art of sculpting fruit and vegetables.

Thailand is a veritable orchard, a cornucopia of fruit much of which visitors may never have encountered before. Most of it comes fresh off the tree. Many Thai restaurants make a point of serving seasonal fruits. Fresh pineapples (sup-bpa-rot) for example, are available from April to July. There are no less than eleven types of this delicious fruit, all rich in vitamin C but low in calories. Some kinds are eaten when fermented.

Bananas (gloo-ay) can be enjoyed throughout the year. Thailand, the world's biggest exporter of bananas, produces fifteen different varieties. Those sold in the evenings from grills on the street are usually soaked in fresh coconut milk. Remember that the smaller the banana the sweeter the taste.

The subtle floury tasting flesh of the durian is considered a great delicacy by the Thais (available April to June). Known also as "stinking fruit" the durian is not very popular with Europeans on account of its unpleasantly strong smell. Indeed guests are often asked by management to refrain from taking them back to their hotels.

Fa-rung fruit (guavas) are usually served with sugar or a little salt. "Fa-rung" is the Thai word for a European and guavas are so called because they appear strange among the country's native fruit! They are available from September to January.

Jackfruit (ka-noon), large, round fruit weighing several kilograms, are sweet and aromatic. Ripening in August and September they are served sliced and chilled.

In Thailand no part of a coconut (ma-prao-onn) goes to waste. The coir is turned into baskets and matting, the milk provides a healthy, refreshing drink, and the flesh is eaten with a pointed spoon. Finally, in rural areas at least, the shells are used as a fuel.

Coconut

Mango

Durian

Langsats (langsard) are tasty berries, light-brown in colour, with a thin but tough skin which has to be peeled with a knife. Care is required when eating them because the sweet fruit hides a very bitter pip. (June to September).

Limes, round and green, the cheap local version of the lemon, are found all through the year. The yellow lemons familiar to Europeans have to be imported and are very expensive.

Longans (lam-yai) come from the northern provinces and are rather costly when bought in Bangkok (July to September).

Lychees (hong huay, gim-yeng, ohia) were also once a luxury, imported from China in tins. Nowadays they are grown in Thailand, mainly in the north. The three types refer to different price categories, which in turn reflect varying degrees of vulnerability to pests. All taste virtually the same however. They are fresh and ripe (with red skins) from May to August.

Mangoes (ma-moo-ung) are second only to pineapples as the tourists' favourite fruit. They need to be completely ripe before eating, the skin yellow, not green. Then they are sweet, juicy and will not keep at all. Slice them through the middle scooping the pulp out with a spoon or eating it straight from the skin. (March to June).

The purple-skinned mangosteen (mung koot) is on sale from June to November. It has white flesh and a sweet taste not unlike a lychee.

Thai oranges (som) are mostly green and thin-skinned; the yellow ones are particularly sweet (available all the year round).

Grapefruit (som-oh) are also found fresh throughout the year and are generally the delicious pink variety. The Thais enjoy them best with a pinch of salt.

Papayas (ma-la-gor) are the cheapest of all Thai fruit and can be bought on any market stall at any time of year. The hotels serve papaya halves for breakfast, sprinkled with lemon. Eaten to excess papayas are an effective laxative.

Rambutans (ngor) were christened "hairy" by the Americans on account of their spiky covering. Cut the skin with a knife and eat the juicy flesh, but avoid the stone. (May to October).

Rose apples (chom-poo) are pear-shaped, with a rust-coloured waxy skin and spongey white flesh both of which can be eaten. It has a slightly sharp taste so is best eaten with sugar or a little salt (January to March).

Weak tea (cha) served cold is always available and in better restaurants is sometimes provided free of charge. Hot tea (cha rorn) on the other hand has to be specially ordered.

Drinks

Coffee tends to be served either hot with milk and sugar (very sweet) or iced and black (oh-lee-ung). Italian-style espresso coffee is also widely available nowadays.

Fresh milk (nom sot) is sold in plastic cartons. Ask for "mai waan", otherwise it will be sweetened. Thai soft drinks also tend to be too sweet and highly coloured for Western tastes and fresh (sot) orange or lemon juice (num som or num ma-nao) is much to be preferred. Great quantities of ice are usually added as a matter of course so the words "mai sai num kairng" ("without ice please") are likely to be needed more often than "kor sai num kairng" ("with ice please"). "Soda" is generally understood as referring to mineral water.

In addition to the iced water available everywhere – sometimes the cause of stomach upsets – German-style lagers (Singha, Amarit, Kloster) are very popular. They are sold throughout the country in either small bottles (koo-ut jai) or large bottles (koo-ut lek). The price in the shops is half what it is in a restaurant. Draught beer is only to be found in one or two restaurants.

The most widely known of Thailand's alcoholic drinks is probably Mekong, a spirit made from rice (28% proof). It is usually drunk with cola or with lemon (ma-nao) and soda. It comes in three bottle sizes and is very cheap.

Imported spirits, etc. are extremely expensive!

Thai wine (lao angnun) is very sweet. Imported wines are again expensive and have often suffered in the keeping, an exception being the Australian "Seppi" available in supermarkets.

Getting to Bangkok

Given the distances involved most visitors to Bangkok arrive by air. Modern jet travel means that the long (about 10,000km/6215 miles) journey from Europe can be completed in as little as eleven hours (non-stop) and seventeen hours at most. Since the cost of flights can vary enormously it pays to shop around, not forgetting in the process what the scheduled airlines have to offer. When choosing between the various

By air

options the question of stopovers, any extras such as hotel transfers, and return flight flexibility all need to be taken into account.

Air travellers normally arrive at one of Thailand's three international airports. Bangkok's Don Muang, the country's largest, was opened as recently as 1987. Even so its capacity has already proved too limited. International airlines also fly into Phuket and U Tapao (Pattaya). Don Muang, about 22km/14 miles from Bangkok, is the busiest staging-post for air traffic in south-east Asia.

Transfer to the city

Passengers travelling with a tour company can expect to be met at the airport by the local representative (couriers wear company badges for ease of identification). As a rule they will be driven to their hotel in buses, which leave from outside the airport building.

Those who need to make their own way into the city have the choice of a taxi or the Thai Airline Limousine Service minibus (fixed fare; seat reservations at the "Transportation Center" in the main hall). The minibuses are comfortable with full air-conditioning. If going by taxi note that only vehicles with the yellow or green sign are officially licensed to carry passengers and hence appropriately insured. To avoid any possible misunderstanding with the driver ask someone at Tourist Information (in the main hall) to write down your destination in Thai. The fare should also be agreed with the driver in advance. The same means of transport are available on departure and can be booked from the hotel.

The ordinary bus service (bus stop in front of the airport building) provides a cheap alternative link with the inner city. The journey takes about an hour and there are stops at some hotels which lie on the way. The buses however are exposed to the full brunt of Bangkok's traffic chaos so this mode of transfer is best regarded as a last resort.

By rail

For anyone making their way to Bangkok from Singapore or Malaysia the Thai state railways' (SRT) Singapore-Bangkok express is a chance to embark on a truly delightful journey. The train has comfortable 2nd class couchette cars and ticket prices are very reasonable when compared with those of Europe. Couchettes and sleepers (1st class) must be reserved in advance (see Travel Agencies).

By sea

Most round-the-world cruise liners put in to Bangkok, mooring in the river (usually between Piers 9 and 12) for one or sometimes several days. Passengers are able to explore the city, or go on excursions inland. There are always plenty of taxis available at the quayside for those who prefer to make their own arrangements. Since the port of Bangkok is huge it is advisable to have a note of the ship's exact berth written down in Thai.

It is also possible to make the journey from Europe to south-east Asia by sea – quite an adventure (taking about a month).

Help for the Disabled

Information

The Thai Tourist Office in London (see Information) provides information on request for disabled people planning a visit to Thailand.

With certain qualifications transport in Thailand should not present too many problems for the disabled. Local tour operators will put together special programmes for disabled tourists if so requested.

Transport

A wheelchair is no bar to visiting buildings of interest in Thailand (such as temples). As well as hotels belonging to the big international chains the better category Thai-owned hotels in particular are fully geared to the needs of disabled visitors. It is not possible however to provide a list of accommodation specifically designated "suitable for the disabled". It is usually helpful to give details of any disabilities when booking a holiday so that any necessary preparations can be made.

Sightseeing

Hotels

Hotels in Thailand stand comparison with anywhere in the world and some are among the very best. Bangkok's famous Oriental Hotel (see A to Z) for example is already something of a legend, having for years been voted the world's top hotel by visitors travelling on business.

General

The choice of accommodation ranges from luxury hotels to the simplest kind of guest house and youth hostel (see Practical Information, Young People's Accommodation). A night in Bangkok can cost as much as 4500 baht in the Oriental and as little as 100 baht in a guest house.

A number of Bangkok's hotels are set in beautiful grounds, among them the Siam Intercontinental in a 12 hectare park and the Hilton with its lovely gardens. The big hotels on the Chaophraya/Menam embankment are in a class of their own. In addition to the Oriental Hotel (already mentioned) the Menam Hotel and the Shangri-La can be highly recommended. Business people will find the new Mansion Kempinski convenient as well as comfortable. It has large rooms (some with as much as 72 sq.m/775 sq.ft of floor area!) and its German management aims to provide a pleasant as well as practical environment in which to conduct business successfully.

There is no clearer evidence of the tourist explosion of recent years than the great number of new hotels. A few years ago Thailand could lay claim to only about 12,000 hotel beds; by 1991 that number had almost tripled. No end to the building boom is yet in sight. Japanese and Chinese investment in particular is being channelled into the construction of yet more top-class hotels.

An especially active building programme is underway in and around Pattaya. Even though the past few years have seen the opening of an already considerable number of new hotels, the further development of this seaside resort seems set to continue. There are now about 24,000 hotel beds and by the end of the century the number should have doubled. Pattaya's biggest drawback is its water supply (the proposed new purification plant is still only on the drawing-board).

Particularly in the off-peak season from April to October the hotels compete keenly among themselves for trade. If a bit of diplomacy is shown travellers can sometimes turn this to their advantage by discreetly negotiating a reduction in rates.

The "bachelor hotels" listed in some travel brochures are, as the name implies, specifically aimed at men travelling alone, often in search of the more exotic forms of Bangkok holiday experience. They are not suitable for women or families. In Pattaya and the resorts along the coast two or three bed-roomed holiday bungalows are commonly available and can represent very good value.

European-style "pensions" are unknown in Thailand. Most hotels provide a continental breakfast, but arrangements for half- or full-board are unusual and extremely expensive when they are found. Almost all the hotels listed below have coffee shops open 24 hours a day. The majority of big hotels have first-class restaurants. A stay in a private house is virtually unknown unless it can be arranged through Thai friends. Even then anyone who succeeds deserves congratulation!

Advance booking is advisable, especially during European holiday periods and around the Chinese New Year. Reservations for all forms of accommodation in Bangkok and Pattaya can be made at Don Muang Airport. A list of hotels is also available.

All the hotels provide facilities free of charge for the safe keeping of money and personal valuables (including passports). Visitors are advised to take full advantage of them.

Abbreviations

r. = number of rooms; SP = swimming pool; F = keep fit; T = tennis; TF = floodlit courts; S = shopping; WS = watersports

Hotels in Bangkok

Luxury hotels

*The Airport Hotel, 333 Chert Wudhakat Road, Don Muang (opposite Don Muang Airport), tel. 566 1020-1; 440 r., SP, F, T, S
The Ambassador, 171 Sukhumvit Road, tel. 254 0444, 255 0444; 935 r., SP, F, T, S
Bangkok Palace, 1091/336 New Phetchaburi Road, tel. 253 0500; 690 r., SP, F
*Central Plaza, 1695 Phahon Yothin Road, tel. 541 1234; 607 r., SP, F, T, TF, (the biggest shopping centre in south-east Asia)
*Dusit Thani Hotel, 946 Rama IV Road (opposite Lumphini Park), tel. 236 0450–9; 525 r., SP, T, F
*Hilton International Hotel, 2 Wireless Road, tel. 253 0123; 343 r., SP, T, F
Holiday Inn Crowne Plaza, 981 Silom Road, tel. 238 4300; 385 r., SP, BC, S
*The Hyatt Central Plaza, 1695 Phahon Yothin Road, tel. 541 1234; 607 r., SP, T, F, S
The Imperial, Wireless Road, tel. 254 0023; 400 r., SP, T, squash, S
*The Indra Regent, Ratchaprarob Road, tel. 251 1111; 450 r., SP, S
The Landmark, 138 Sukhumvit Road, tel. 254 0404, 254 0424; 415 r., SP
Le Meridien President, 135/26 Gaysorn Road, tel. 253 0444; 400 r., SP
The Mandarin, 662 Rama IV Road, tel. 233 4980–9; 400 r., SP, S
*The Mansion Kempinski, Soi 11, Sukhumvit Road, tel. 255 7200; 127 r., SP, S (just along Sukhumvit Road)
*The Menam, 2074 New Road, tel. 289 1138; 727 r., SP, T, F, S

Architectural tradition reflected in the Siam Intercontinental Hotel

Montien Hotel, 54 Surawong Road, tel. 234 8060; 485 r., SP
*The Oriental, 48 Oriental Avenue, tel. 236 0400; 394 r., SP, T, TF, (see A to Z)
The President, 135/26 Gaysorn Road, tel. 253 0444; 400 r., SP

The Rama Gardens, 9/9 Vibhavadi Rangsit Road, tel. 5/9–5400; 384 r., SP, F, T, G (the latter two in the Royal Sports Club opposite)
The Regent of Bangkok, 155 Ratchadamri Road, tel. 251 6127; 400 r., F
The Royal Orchid Sheraton, 2 Captain Bush Lane, tel. 234 5599; 775 r., SP, T
*Shangri-La Hotel, 89 Soi Wat Suan Plu (on the banks of the Chaophraya/Menam), tel. 236 7777; 700 r., SP, T, F
*Siam Intercontinental Hotel, 967 Rama I Road, tel. 253 0355–7; 400 r., SP, T, TF, golf, jogging (12 hectare park)

Asia Hotel, 296 Phaya Thai Road, tel. 215 0808; 650 r., SP
Bangkok Centre, 328 Rama IV Road, tel. 238 4848–57; 225 r.,
Bayoke Tower, 130 Ratchaprarop Road, tel. 253 0362, 255 0150; 244 r., SP, F
Century, 9 Ratchaprarop Road, tel. 246 7800–10; 89 r., SP
Fortuna, 19 Sukhumvit Road Soi 5, tel. 251 5121–6; 110 r., SP
Impala, 9 Sukhumvit Road Soi 24, tel. 259 0053; 220 r., SP
Manhattan, 13 Sukhumvit Road Soi 15, tel. 252 7141–9; 200 r., SP
Manhora, 412 Surawong Road, tel. 234 5070; 240 r., SP
Nana, Soi Nan Tai 4, Sukhumvit Road, tel. 252–0121; 325 r., SP
Narai Hotel, 222 Silom Road, tel. 233 3350; 500 r., SP, F, S
New Peninsula, 295/3 Surawong Road, tel. 234 3910–7; 113 r., SP

Comfortable hotels

191

Hotels

New Trocadero, 343 Surawong Road, tel. 234 8920; 131 r., SP
Novotel, Siam Square Soi 6, tel. 255 6888–7; 430 r., SP, F
The Plaza, 178 Surawong Road, tel. 235 1760–79; 160 r., SP
Silom Plaza, 320 Silom Road, tel. 236 8441–53; 200 r., SP
Tawana Ramada, 80 Surawong Road, tel. 236 0361; 265 r., SP, F
Collins House (YMCA), 27 Sathon Tai Road, tel. 287 2727, 287
1900; 147 r., SP
Continental, 971/16 Phahon Yothin Road, tel. 278 1385, 279
7567; 122 r.
Federal, 27 Sukhumvit Road Soi 11, tel. 253 0175–6, 253
4768–9; 93 r., SP
First Hotel, 2 Phetchaburi Road, tel. 252–0111; 220 r., SP
Florida Hotel, 43 Phaya Thai Road, tel. 245 3221–4; 107 r., SP
Golden Dragon, 20/21 Ngarm Rongwan Road, tel. 589 0130-41;
120 r., SP
Golden Horse, 5/1–2 Nana North, Sukhumvit Soi 3, tel. 280–
1920–9; 130 r., SP
Grace, 12 Nana North, Sukhumvit Soi 3, tel. 253 0651–79; 542 r.,
SP, F
Jasmin, Wireless Road, tel. 319 2421–8; 72 r.
Liberty, 215 Pradiphat Road, tel. 271–0880–1; 196 r., SP
Majestic, 97 Ratchadamnoen Avenue, tel. 281 5000; 240 r., SP
Malaysia, 53 Soi Ngam Du Phli, Rama IV Road, tel. 286 3582;
120 r., SP
Mido, 222 Pradiphat Road, tel. 279 4560–6; 220 r.
New Fiji, 299–301 Surawongse Road, tel. 234 5364–6; 66 r., SP
New Nana (South), 4 Soi 4 Sukhumvit Road, tel. 252 0121; 334 r.
Parliament, 402 Visuthikasat Road, tel. 236 0400, 236 0420; 92 r.
Prince, 1537/1 New Petchaburi Road, tel. 251 6171–6; 200 r., SP
Princess, 269 Larn Luang Road, tel. 281 3088; 170 r., SP
Ra-Jah, 18 Soi 4 Sukhumvit Road, tel. 251 8563, 252 5102–9;
450 r., SP
Ramada, 1169 New Road, tel. 234 8971–5; 62 r.
Rose, 118 Surawong Road, tel. 233 7695–7; 105 r.
Royal, 2 Ratchadamnoen Road, tel. 222 9111–16; 297 r., SP
Royal Plaza, 30 Nares Road, tel. 234–3789; 245 r.
Royal River, 670/805 Charan Sanitwong Road, tel. 433 0300;
404 r., SP
Siam Hotel, 1777 New Phetchaburi Road, tel. 252 5081; 120 r.,
SP
Tara, Sukhumvit Soi 26, tel. 259 2900–19; 200 r., S, F
Thai, 78 Prachathipatai Road, tel. 282 2831–3; 100 r., SP
Victory, 322 Silom Road, tel. 233 9060–9; 122 r.
Viengtai, 42 Tani Road, tel. 282 8119–23; 217 r., SP
Windsor Hotel, Sukhumvit Road, Soi 20, tel. 258 0160; 250 r., SP

The following hotels are under construction or nearing
completion:
Atrium Hotel (600 r.), Watergate Hotel (553 r.).

Guest Houses

Amara Court, 645/44–51 Phetchaburi Road, tel. 251 8980–81;
16 r.
Amarin Guest House, 593–595 Chakraphet Road, tel. 222 0532;
16 r.
Apple Guest House, Asia, 488 Chakraphet Road, tel. 221–4661;
19 r.
*Bangkok Christian, 123 Sala Daeng Soi 2, tel. 233 6303, 233
2206; 36 r.
Bangkok Inn, 155/12–13 Sukhumvit Road Soi 11, tel. 254–
4834–7; 18 r.

*Bangkok Youth Hostel, 25/2 Phitsanulok Road, tel. 182 0950;
20 r.
Bovornivet Youth Hostel, 395 Phra Sumen Road (opposite Wat
Bovornives), tel. 281–6387; 120 r.
Boston Inn, 4 Soi Si Bamphen, Rama IV Road, tel. 286 1680, 286
0726; 70 r.
Chart Guest House, 61 Khao San Road, tel. 281 0803; 55 r.
*Grand Tower, 23/1 Sukhumvit Soi 55, tel. 259 0380–9; 104 r. SP
James Guest House, 116/1 Prachathipatai Road, tel. 280 0362;
30 r.
K.T. Guest House, 14 Suthisarn Road, tel. 277 4035; 20 r.
Krit Thai Mansion, 931/1 Rama 1 Road, tel. 215 2582; 52 r.
Lee Guest House, 21/38–39 Soi Ngam Du Phli, Rama IV Road,
tel. 286–2069; 24 r.
Lek Guest House, 125 Khao San Road, tel. 282 6223; 20 r.
Merlin Apartment, 33 Ramkhamhaeng Road Soi 8, tel. 319
0934–37; 55 r.
Mermaid's Rest, 6/1 Sukhumvit Road Soi 8, tel. 253 5122, 253
3410; 25 r.
My Place Guest House, 34/28 Soi Si Bamphen, Rama IV Road,
tel. 287 1658; 15 r.
Muangphon Building, 931/8–9 Rama I Road, (opposite the
National Stadium), tel. 215 0033; 70 r.
Narai Guest House, 5/7 Sukhumvit Road Soi 53, tel. 258 7173;
80 r.
New Siam Guest House, 21 Soi Chanasongkhram, Pra Athit
Road, tel. 282 4554; 20 r.
Peachy Guest House, 10 Phra Athit Road, tel. 281 6471; 50 r.
Prasuri Guest House, 85/1 Soi Prasuri, Dinsor Road, tel. 280
1428; 21 r.
P. Guest House, 151–157 Trok Sa-Ka, Tanao Road, tel. 224 1967;
60 r.
Red Stone Apartment, 11/1 Soi Thantawan, Surawongse Road,
tel. 236 0108; 62 r.
Ruamchit Mansion, 1–15 Soi 15 Sukhumvit Road, tel. 251
6441–4; 50 r.
Safty Guest House, 1036/6 Rama IV Road, Yannawa, tel. 286
8904; 17 r.
Shanti Lodge, 37 Sri Ayutthaya Road, tel. 281 2497; 15 r.
*Sathorn Inn, 37 Soi Suksa-Vithaya, tel. 234 4110; 96 r.
Sri Guest House, 1 Soi 38 Sukhumvit Road, tel. 381 1309, 391
9057; 33 r., T
Suda Palace, 24 Suthisarn Road, tel. 270 0585–7; 130 r.
Sunisa Guest House, 7/10 Soi 4 Sukhumvit Road, tel. 252 5565;
24 r.
S.T. Apartment, 72/2 Soi Chantima, Nakhon Chaisi Road, tel.
243 1107; 25 r.
S.V. Guest House, 19/35–36 Sukhumvit Road Soi 19, tel. 253
1747; 20 r.
Thawi Guest House, 83 Sri Ayutthaya Road, tel. 280 1447; 15 r.
T.T. Guest House, 138 Soi Wat Maha Pluetharam Si Phraya, tel.
236 3053–4; 30 r.

Hotels in Pattaya

The Ambassador Resort, Jomtien, 21/19 Sukhumvit, Na Jomtien, Sattahip, tel. 231 501–40; reservations in Bangkok: tel. 254
0444; 2500 r., SP, T, TF, WS
*Dusit Resort, 240 Pattaya Beach Road, tel. 425 611; 500 r., SP,
T, TF, WS

Luxury and comfortable
hotels

*Orchid Lodge, Pattaya Beach Road, tel. 428 161; reservations in Bangkok: tel. 252 6118; 236 r., SP, T

*The Royal Cliff Hotel – The Royal Wing, Cliff Road, tel. 421 421–30; reservations in Bangkok: tel. 282 0999; 671 r. (+ 86 Royal Wing suites), SP, T, TF, WS

A-One The Royal Cruise, 499 North Pattaya, tel. 233 5970; 200 r., SP, F

Asia Pattaya Hotel, 352 Cliff Road, tel. 428 602–6; reservations in Bangkok: tel. 215 0808: SP, T, WS

Garden Lodge, Pattaya Road, tel. 429 109; 80 r., SP

Golden Beach, Pattaya 2nd Road, tel. 429 969; 240 r., SP

Island View, Cliff Road, tel. 428 818; reservations in Bangkok: tel. 252 0723; 209 r., SP, WS

*The Merlin Pattaya, Pattaya Beach Resort, tel. 428 755–9; 360 r., SP, T

*The Montien Pattayam 369 Mu 9, Pattaya Klang Road, tel. 428 155; 301 r., SP, T, TF, F

Nipa Lodge, Pattaya Beach Road, tel. 428 195; reservations in Bangkok: tel. 252 6045; 147 r., SP, T, TF

Novotel Tropicana, 45 Beach Road, North Pattaya, tel. 428 645–8; 186 r., SP, T,

Ocean View, 382 Mu 10 Beach Road, tel. 428 084; 112 r., SP

Palm Garden, 240/1 Mu 5, tel. 429 188; 115 r., SP

Pattaya Inn Beach Resort, 380 Soi 2, North Pattaya, tel. 428 718–9; 120 r., SP, T, TF

Pattaya Palace, Pattaya 2nd Road, North Pattaya, tel. 428 487; 261 r., SP, T

Royal Garden Resort, 218 Beach Road, tel. 428 126–7; 142 r., SP, T

Royal Palace, 215/2 Pattaya 2nd Road, tel. 425–656–9; 350 r., SP, F

Sea Breeze, 347 Jomtien Beach, tel. 231 056–9; 80 r., SP

Seaview Resorts, 500 Soi 18, Pattaya-Naklua Road, tel. 429 317; 242 r., SP

Siam Bayshore Hotel, Pattaya Beach Road, tel. 428 678; reservations in Bangkok: tel. 251 0355; SP, T, TF

Siam Bayview, Pattaya Beach, tel. 428 871–9; 260 r., SP, T, TF

Sports Garden Resort, 179/138 Mu 5, tel. 426 009; 183 r., SP, F

V.C. Pattaya, 492 Mu 10 Cliff Road, tel. 424 504–8; 100 r., SP

Wong Amat, Pattaya-Naklua Road, tel. 428 118–120; 207 r., SP, F, T, TF

Beach View, 389 Soi 2, Beach Road, tel. 422–660–4; 135 r., SP, SP

Best Inn, 420/42 Mu 9, Soi Buokaow, Banglamung, tel. 422 248; 48 r., SP

Caesar Palace, 176 Mu 10, Pattaya 2nd Road, tel. 428 607; 80 r., SP

Carlton Pattaya, 172 Soi 5, Pattaya 2nd Road, tel. 421 556–8; 70 r., SP

The Champ, 561 Mu 10, Cliff Road, tel. 428 431; 105 r., SP

Charming Inn, 119/1 Soi 3, Beach Road, tel. 428 895; 65 r., SP

Cherry Inn, 359 Mu 10, Soi White Rose, tel. 428 395; 70 r.

Coral Inn, 411 Jomtien Beach Road, tel. 231 283–7; 36 r., SP

Cosy Beach, 400 Mu 12, Cliff Road, tel. 429 344; 62 r., SP

Diamond Beach, 373/8 South Pattaya Beach Road, tel. 429 885; 138 r., SP, F

Diana Inn, 216/6–9 Pattaya 2nd Road, tel. 429 675; 87 r., SP

Holiday Corner, 175/51 Soi Diamond 15, tel. 426 072; 39 r.

Honey Inn Pattaya, 529/2 Soi 10, Pattaya 2nd Road, tel. 421 543–4; 68 r., SP

Jomtien Bayview, 192 Mu 10, Jomtien Beach, tel. 425 889–90; 55 r., SP
Koh Larn Island Resort, Loh Larn, tel. 428 422; 60 r.
Little Duck Pattaya Resort, 336/22 Pattaya Klang Road, tel. 428 104–5; 180 r., SP
Lido Beach, 236–7 – 15 Pattaya Beach Road, tel. 429 383; 57 r.
Marine Beach Resort, 131/62 Mu 12, tel. 231 129–10; 65 r., SP
Marine Plaza, 200 Mu 10, Pratamnak Road, tel. 424 817–8; 160 r., SP
Natural Park Beach Resort, 412 Mu 12, Jomtien Beach, tel. 231 561–70; 116 r., SP, T, F
Palm Villa, 485 Mu 10, Pattaya City, tel. 428 153; 67 r., SP
Pattaya City, 557 Mu 10, Cliff Road, tel. 423 300–2; 136 r., SP
Pattaya Park Beach, 345 Jomtien Beach, tel. 423 000–4; 240 r., + bungalows, SP
Regent Marina, Beach Road, North Pattaya, tel. 428 015; 221 r., SP
Siam Beach Resort, 372–11 Mu 2, Sukhumvit Road, tel. 231 490–1; 107 r., SP, T
Silver Sand, Jomtien Beach, tel. 231 030; 107 r., SP
Weekender, 78/20 Pattaya 2nd Road, tel. 428 720, 429 461; 202 r., SP
Welcome Plaza, 213 Mu 10, Pattaya 2nd Road, tel. 424 765–7; 268 r., SP
Windmill, 665 Mu 5, Pattaya-Nakiua Road, tel. 425 930, 101 r., SP, S

Pattaya has several bungalow parks, a list of which can be obtained from the TAT office in the resort. One in particular is worth special mention:
Thanaporn Bungalow and Hotel, Cliff Road (next to the Asia Pattaya Hotel), tel. 428 609; 120 r. (incl. bungalows), SP, S, WS

Sinsomboon Hotel, Songkwae Road, tel. (034) 51 3218
Prasopsuk Garden Resort, Kwai Yai Riverside, tel. (034) 513 215

Kanchanaburi

The floating hotels along the river here and on the River Kwai are rather special (information from the TAT office in Kanchanaburi).

Information

The Tourism Authority of Thailand (TAT) operates an information service from offices in Bangkok, at the international airports, and in the main resorts. As well as supplying useful brochures, etc. (either free or for a nominal charge) TAT offices will also try to help resolve any specific problems tourists may encounter.

In Thailand

Tourism Authority of Thailand
4 Ratchadamnoen Nok Avenue, Bangkok
Tel. 282 1143–7
Open: Mon.–Fri. 8.30am–4.30pm, Sat. 8.30am–noon

The address of the TAT office in Pattaya is:

382/1 Chaihat Road, South Pattaya
Tel. 428 750 and 429 113
Open: Mon.–Fri. 8am–4.30pm

Interpreters and Secretarial Services

Offices abroad   See Tourist Information

Yellow telephones   Telephones installed in conspicuous yellow kiosks at sites fre-
                            quented by tourists (e.g. the Grand Palace, Patpong Road, Don
                            Muang Airport, etc.) connect callers directly (no dialling) to the
                            tourist information office. The service, manned by English-
                            speaking staff, operates from 8.30am to 4.30pm.

Visa extensions   Requests for an extension to a visa can only be processed in
                            Bangkok. Applications should be made to:

                            Immigration Department
                            Soi Suan Phlu, Sathon Tai Road
                            Tel. 286 7003, 286 9230
                            Open: Mon.–Fri. 8.30am–noon

Getting around

There are a number of useful English language directories (also
Thai) giving up-to-date information about what's on and where
to go. Issued anything from weekly to bi-monthly by travel
agencies and independent publishers as well as by TAT, they
often include shopping tips in addition to addresses of restaurants, sports clubs and nightclubs, etc. Together with the section of street map ususally reproduced with them, these
directories can be very helpful when communicating with taxi
drivers, bus drivers or any passer-by.

English-Thai city and street maps of Bangkok, Pattaya, Kanchanaburi, Ayutthaya and other towns can be obtained from the
TAT offices in London, as well as in Bangkok (see Information).
Note that the maps are not always reliable as regards scale and
compass orientation.

The same is true of the colourful "Nancy Chandler's Map"
which includes detailed plans of such locations as the Chatuchak weekend market, Chinatown and the Sukhumvit district.
It also indicates which bus lines and "river taxis" boast
air-conditioning.

Interpreters and Secretarial Services

A number of Bangkok's international hotels (see Hotels) provide interpreting and secretarial services utilising all the latest
communications technology (telex, fax, BTX and word processing, etc.). A charge is made for the use of these services
which, as a rule, are available only to guests of the hotel.

Besides the hotels there are numerous private companies
offering a similar service, e.g.:

International Translations
22 Silom Road
Tel. 233 7714

Bangkok Business Service (office and courier services)
81 Sukhumvit Road Soi 2, 3rd floor Ploy Mitr Building
Tel. 251 0649, 251 9534

More addresses can be found in the Yellow Pages.

Language

See also Facts and Figures: Language

yes	krup (if you are man), ka (if you are a woman)
no	plao or mai chai
please	chui
thank you	korp koon krup or ka
you	koon, followed by krup or ka
hello	sa-wut-dee (at any time of the day)
sorry	mai pen lai krup/ka
Do you speak English?	koon poot pah-sah ung-grit bpen mai
I do not understand	mai khao jai
I do not speak Thai!	poot pah-sah thai mai phen!
How much is that?	ni rah-kha tao-rai?
It is too expensive	mai pairng mahk mahk!
The bill, please!	khop nang! check bin!
railway station	sa-tahn-nee rot fai
airport	sa-nahm bin
hotel	rohng rairm
Monday	wun jun
Tuesday	wun ung-kahn
Wednesday	wun poot
Thursday	wun pa-reu-hut
Friday	wun sook
Saturday	wun sao
Sunday	wun ah-tit
today	wun nee
yesterday	wahn nee
tomorrow	proong nee
0	soong
1	neung
2	sorng
3	sahm
4	see
5	hah
6	hok
7	jet
8	bpairt
9	gao
10	sip
11	sip-et
12	sip-sorng
13	sip-sahm
14	sip-see
15	sip-hah
16	sip-hok
17	sip-jet
18	sip-bpairt

19	sip-gao
20	yee-sip
21	yee-sip-et
22	yee-sip-sorng
23	yee-sip-sahm
30	sahm-sip
40	see-sip
50	hah-sip
100	neung roy
200	sorng roy
300	sahm roy
500	hah roy
1000	neung pun

Thai language courses

American University Alumni Association (AUA)
179 Ratchadamri Road, tel. 252 8170–3

Inlingua School of Languages
22 Phloenchit Road, tel. 254 7028

Nisa Thai Language School
27 Sathon Tai Road, tel. 286 9323

Lost Property

Thailand has no official lost property office. Any articles lost and subsequently handed in can be collected from the Tourist Assistance Service (see Practical Information, Emergencies). The level of honesty in Thailand is generally high – but as always of course there are exceptions.

Markets

Vegetable, fruit and flower markets (dta-laht sot) are held regularly all over Bangkok. Trading usually begins at 6am and ends in the late afternoon.

In addition to food, virtually any commodity or item it is possible to think of is traded in a market somewhere in the city, often in markets which specialise in a particular type of goods. One or two of the most intriguing speciality markets are described under the heading "Markets" in the Sights from A to Z section of this guide. (See also A to Z, Floating Markets. There are now hardly any floating markets left in or around Bangkok itself so to visit one involves an excursion further afield.)

Chatuchak weekend market

See A to Z

Massage

Traditional Thai massage has nothing whatsoever to do with sex or prostitution. The techniques practised are very much the same as those in common use for medical purposes in the West. For a small additional fee the masseur or masseuse (usually the same sex as the client) will make a home visit.

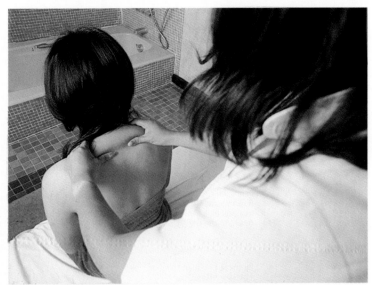

Massage medical style

"Massage for Tourists" on the other hand is prostitution masquerading (for legal reasons) under another name. It is mainly practised in the so-called Massage Parlours (see Nightlife) where regrettably, many young Thai girls and women are forced to work.

Anyone wanting a traditional Thai massage (a combination of European style and foot reflex zone massage) can hardly do better than to go to Wat Pho in Bangkok where, in a small inner courtyard to the right of the main entrance, expert massage is available from well-trained staff. A one-hour session generally costs between 150 and 200 baht. There can be few more refreshing ways of discovering an astonishing number of hitherto unsuspected muscles and bones!

Medical Assistance

Medical treatment

Bangkok (in preference to the rural areas of the country) is very much the place to work as far as Thai general practitioners and specialists in all branches of medicine are concerned. The Bangkok medical faculty has a particularly high reputation for training, many of its students having completed their studies or taken specialist courses in Europe or the United States. Doctors almost invariably speak English and sometimes other European languages as well.

General

As a result finding a suitable doctor is never a problem in the capital or one of the main centres of tourism. Tourists anyway will seldom need to go in search of a doctor themselves. In the case of illness or an emergency the hotel reception will always know of a doctor who can attend quickly and will visit patients in the hotel. A comprehensive list of recommended practitioners is available from the British Embassy in Bangkok (see Diplomatic Representation).

Payment

There is no social security agreement between the UK and Thailand providing for free access to medical services. Nor can the costs of treatment be reclaimed from the Department of Social Security on return to the UK. It is advisable therefore to arrange suitable medical insurance against these risks before leaving home. (Some private health insurance schemes already include cover world-wide – and therefore in Thailand – for up to three months from departure.)
Costs incurred through illness have to be settled immediately. Many hospitals in fact insist on payment of the full amount of the estimated bill on commencement of treatment.

In special circumstances the British Consulate (see Diplomatic Representation) may be able to assist in settling doctors' and hospital bills. Any money advanced will have to be repaid on return to the UK.

Hospitals

Bangkok Christian Hospital
124 Silom Road
Tel. 233 6981–89
24-hour out-patients department

Bangkok General Hospital
2 Soi Soonvijai 7 (Phetchaburi Road)
Tel. 318 0066–77, out-patients: 318 0066

Bangkok Mission Hospital
43 Phitsanulok Road (near Dusit Zoo)
Tel. 281 1422, 281 3020
24-hour out-patients department

Bangkok Nursing Home
9 Convent Road (near the German Embassy)
Tel. 233 2610–19, 233 4332
Good obstetrics department

Bumrungrad Medical Center
33 Soi Nana, Sukhumvit Road
Tel. 253 0250–69
24-hour out-patients department

Chulalongkorn University Hospital
Rama IV Road (near Dusit Thani Hotel)
Tel. 252 8131
Special burns unit

Ramathibodi University Hospital
Rama IV Road
Tel. 246 0024, 246 1102

Policlinic Münster
6/23 Soi Nana Nua, Sukhumvit
Tel. 253 5857

Police General Hospital
Ratchadamri Road,
Tel. 252 8111–20
24-hour out-patients department: tel. 252 2171

All branches of medicine from dentistry to surgery are represented in these hospitals and clinics. Out-patient facilities are provided too. Emergency services operate outside normal hours (the latter being Mon.–Fri. 8.30am–4.30pm, Sat. 9 a.m–3pm).

In addition to the usual hospitals most tourist resorts now have well-equipped medical centres. These are run by highly qualified staff and in many cases have a small infirmary attached. Ask at the hotel reception for the address of the nearest centre.

Medical centres

Serum for snake bites can be obtained from the Pasteur Saovapha Institute in Sala Daeng Road, Bangkok. At weekends and holidays when the Institute is closed serum is available from the Chulalongkorn Hospital (also in Sala Daeng Road). Anyone bitten by a snake in a rural area should tell someone on the spot what has happened and go at once to the nearest police station.

Snake bites

Private medical emergency services equipped with air ambulances and rescue helicopters are unknown in Thailand. Any emergency repatriation by air has therefore to be arranged through the UK. The British Embassy will assist in arranging the flight but cannot provide financial aid. It is best to take out adequate insurance to cover such an eventuality before leaving home.

Air ambulance

See Emergencies

Emergency doctor

See Chemists

Medicines

See entry

Drugs

See Travel Documents

Vaccination

See entry

Massage

Motoring

Thailand has no automobile clubs comparable to those found in western countries and there are no emergency telephones on Thai motorways or trunk roads. Drivers are consequently left to rely very much on their own resources and on such assistance as may be forthcoming from other road users. The best course of action for anyone whose vehicle breaks down on the road is to wave down another driver. Apart from being very helpful almost every Thai is of necessity something of a mechanic. It will not usually be long before someone stops, at least in daylight. If despite all efforts the fault cannot be remedied there and then, an offer to drive to the nearest garage is almost certain to be made.

Breakdowns

Anyone whose car breaks down on a long night drive however could be in for an unpleasant wait. Since robberies are not uncommon, particularly on the poorly lit motorways, Thais are often reluctant to stop when they see someone waving for help in the dark. In that case the only thing to be done is to wait for the Highway Patrol (dtum-roo-ut).

Motor repairs

When renting a car a comprehensive list of garages which can be relied upon to carry out repairs is usually provided. All the big car manufacturers, European included maintain service networks in Thailand and some even provide an emergency service. Most of the staff employed in these authorised repair workshops will be familiar with the English terms for the different auto accessories and spare parts.

Esso and Shell filling stations often have a workshop attached where minor repairs can be effected on the spot.

If repairs do prove necessary try to agree on the price in advance, keep an eye on the work as it is done, and insist on being given a written receipt and bill.

Some useful words for motorists

engine	yon
brakes	haarm lor/brayk
tyres	yahng
headlights	fai
cold water	nahm yen yon
oil	mun
tool	kry-ung
check	dtroo-ut, or check
change	bplee-un
not working	see-a

Filling stations

Fuel is readily available throughout Thailand. The major multinational oil companies (Shell, Esso, Texaco, Elf, etc.) provide a comprehensive network of filling stations covering the whole country. The pumps are always manned (by very obliging attendants), self-service being unknown. Signs on the pumps are usually in Thai so it is important to be able to explain what fuel or grade is required before filling up.

Thai words for fuel

diesel	num mun rot-dee-sen, or Sola
two-star petrol	tumma da
three-star petrol	priset or Special

Fuel is mainly sold by the litre, use of the gallon measure nowadays being rare. The indicators on the pumps display the amount to be paid in whole baht only.

Fuel prices

Diesel is state subsidised and very cheap (about 5 baht a litre). Two and three-star petrol (the octane ratings are the standard international ones) costs between 8 and 10 baht a litre.

Left-hand traffic

Traffic in Thailand travels on the left.

Rules of the road

The nearside lane (next to the pavement) is for buses only (though they do not always keep to it, especially when engaged in racing each other). Bus stops are generally found close to the little street markets where pavement vendors set out their stalls. The buses however seldom seem to halt at these official stops. Instead they pull up a bit before or beyond them, wherever the crowd happens to be biggest.

Traffic lights – often ignored – show red and green lights only. There are very few pedestrian crossings controlled by lights. Pavements are far from being a pedestrian preserve. Cyclists and motorcyclists not only use them as parking space for their bikes but frequently ride along them as well. In many of the narrow single-lane "sois" (alleyways between houses) there are no pavements at all.

When on foot Thais rarely seem to be in a hurry. Courtesy requires that those wishing to make haste do so bending forward slightly in a sort of perpetual bow. Walking in any case requires a fair amount of concentration. The pavements are very uneven and full of pot-holes and a good eye must be kept on the ground if hazards are to be successfully avoided.

Highways and major roads are usually in good condition, most being two-lane and surfaced with asphalt. There are a few four-lane expressways but only around Bangkok. Apart from one or two minor roads in the mountains or deep in the countryside all are passable even in the rainy season (June to September). | Highways

In Bangkok and also on trunk and other major roads signs are in both Thai and English. Mostly they are the familiar international signs and the few exceptions are easily understood. Speed limits are 60km per hour/37·5 mph in built-up areas and 100km per hour/62·5 mph on trunk roads. | Road signs

Newspapers and Periodicals

Three morning dailies, "The Bangkok Post", "The Nation" and the "Morning Post" are published in English, as is the evening paper "The Bangkok World". All three morning papers include information about what's on in and around Bangkok (cinemas, theatres, etc.) as well as radio and television schedules. | English language newspapers

British and other daily and weekly newspapers, periodicals and magazines are sold in drugstores in hotels and shopping arcades in Bangkok and Pattaya. They are fairly expensive however. UK newspapers are usually one or two days out of date by the time they come on sale but weekly magazines are generally available on the day of publication. | Foreign newspapers

Nightlife

Bangkok's nightlife is as rich and varied as anywhere in the world. The most notorious of the city's hot spots is Patpong Road (between Silom Road and Surawong Road). Here there is everything on which rests Bangkok's reputation as the sex capital of the tourist world. In many other parts of the city however a variety of other forms of nightclub entertainment will be found, most being of a rather more familiar and wholesome kind. | General

Generally speaking the establishments advertising themselves as "pubs", "bars", "cocktail lounges" or "nightclubs" are the ones which provide the sort of evening entertainment acceptable to the ordinary holidaymaker from the West. These nightspots are found mainly in the better class hotels and typically stay open until 1am. | Hotel bars

Night-clubs of the more traditional kind are not difficult to find. The clientele of these clubs is predominantly Thai and the | Traditional night-clubs

203

greater part of the club is usually kept in almost total darkness (waiters having to use torches). Young Thai girls, each wearing a numbered label, sit behind a glass or metal screen in a brightly-lit side room, waiting to be summoned as a dancing partner or to join a client at a table.

Coffee shops

The so-called coffee shops, found mostly in Phetchaburi Road but also in "tourist" and "economy" class hotels, are frequented mainly by holidaymakers from the West and by Japanese.

The more reputable of these coffee shops are normally well-lit. Food is served and there is dancing to "live" music (mainly of a Western variety). They are usually open until 2am and sometimes even later.

Massage parlours

Bangkok's notorious massage parlours are so numerous as to defy counting. Every week free newsheets appear aimed at tourists, choc-a-bloc with advertisements. The parlours are generally open from 10am to 11pm or midnight. Prices depend on the quality and reputation of the particular establishment.

Nobody should be under any illusions about the parlours – they have absolutely nothing to do with ordinary massage and are simply a front for prostitution (which is actually forbidden under Thai law). Potential clients should note that sexually transmitted diseases, including AIDS, are widespread in Thailand.

Sex shows

Strip clubs, sex shows and pornographic film shows abound, usually accommodated in back street premises. Many of them are simply a rip-off.

Taxi drivers are generally well informed about these venues (and of course expect to be tipped when dropping off their fare).

Opening Times

See Business Hours

Photography and Films

General

Thailand as a whole but Bangkok in particular offers amateur photographers a wealth of photogenic subjects. It is best to go already equipped with all the necessary camera supplies. Although films can be bought in Thailand they are expensive and there is often no way of telling how long they have been stored.

The optimum time of day for taking pictures is in the morning or afternoon (rather than the middle of the day when the sun is at its highest). A polarising filter is essential. Sea water and a salt-laden atmosphere are the worst enemies of any camera or lens, so take a supply of cleaning fluid and wipes from home. Always keep lenses covered when not in use.

Taboos

As a rule Thais enjoy having their photograph taken. If copies of the snaps are promised to the subject, the promise should unfailingly be kept. Otherwise there will be "loss of face", just about the worst thing that can happen to anyone as far as the Thais are concerned.

Visitors also need to recognise that certain photographic subjects are taboo (see Thai Society and the Visitor). Monks for example are often ill at ease in the presence of a camera and any form of religious observance should be treated with suitable respect. Thais generally do not take kindly to seeing the objects of their worship doubling as stage props on holiday snaps. Clambering about on figures of Buddha, or for that matter on temple statues of any kind, is strictly forbidden and likely to result in a heavy fine. Anyone who has the rare good fortune to meet the King and Queen, or to see them at some event, should bear in mind that no one is permitted to stand higher than the King. Intending photographers poised to take a shot from a good raised position will quickly be asked to get down – sometimes in none too gentle a tone. If infringing the rule cannot be avoided, e.g. by those on a balcony or roof of a house, a symbolic gesture should be made by kneeling.

There are film processing outlets all over Thailand which will develop ordinary film (but not transparencies) very quickly and at reasonable cost. The quality of the prints however is not always particularly good. If for some reason it is essential to have transparencies developed it can be done at the Kodak laboratories (situated outside Bangkok on the way to Don Muang Airport).

Developing films

The X-ray equipment used for checking hand luggage at Thai airports is of German manufacture and unlikely to damage films. Should there be any doubt (particularly in the case of highly sensitive films) it is advisable to insist on a hand search being carried out instead.

Airport baggage control

The following camera shops will undertake repairs:

Camera repairs

T.K. Fotoshop, 164 Sukhumvit Road (near Soi 8)
Apakom Shop, 44/7 Rama I Road
A.V. Camera, 310/2 Silom Road

Planetarium

For anyone with an interest in the starry heavens above Bangkok a visit to the planetarium is highly recommended:

Bangkok Planetarium
928 Sukhumvit Road
Open: Mon.–Sun. 10am–2.30am; admission fee.

Post

By south-east Asian standards the Thai postal services are efficient and reliable. Letters are dispatched quite quickly after posting, and if sent by airmail (par avion) usually take about six days to reach Europe (or the USA). Unless properly marked with an airmail sticker post will go by surface mail. In that case it can take up to three months to arrive.

General

Programme of Events

Main post office	Bangkok's main post office (Post and Telegraph Department) is located in New Road. There are branch offices at Don Muang Airport and in some of the big hotels. Letter boxes are red and have two openings, one for Bangkok addresses, the other for destinations outside the capital.
Post office opening hours	See Business Hours
Hotel services	The hotel reception is always happy to accept mail for dispatch.
Postal rates	At present postage is 8 baht for an air letter and 6·50 baht for a postcard. Registered letters cost an extra 10 baht (any important letters should always be sent by registered mail).
Poste restante	Mail forwarded to await collection (whether by visitors to the country or by Thais) is held for a maximum of three months at a special poste restante counter in the main post office. When claiming poste restante mail visitors are required to produce their passports.
Parcels and packets	Parcels and packets can be sent either by airmail (taking about a week) or by sea (taking up to three months). Any parcels dispatched abroad have to be made up in the presence of a customs official – go to the special Customs Window in the main post office. A packaging service selling all the necessary things for making up the parcel is available at the post office if required. Customs duty is not usually charged on gifts and personal items sent abroad.
Telephone	See Telephone and Telefax
Telefax	See Telephone and Telefax

Programme of Events

The monthly programme of films, concerts and theatre performances (sometimes including those at the National Theatre) is advertised in the various Cultural Institutes (see Information) and Embassies (see Diplomatic Representation). Advertisements are also carried in the daily papers (see Newspapers and Periodicals).

Radio and Television

General

Freedom of the Thai press and media is guaranteed under the democratic constitution of 1978. Even so Thai radio, television and daily papers tend to avoid being too critical in their coverage of the country's administration.

Four TV stations – one of them the official voice of the military – transmit nationwide. In addition there are several radio stations. Some programmes are broadcast in English. Daily papers carry previews of the day's programmes (see Newspapers and Periodicals).
Thai Travel, a tourist information programme, is broadcast every morning in English on VHF (6.30am; 97 MHz).

In many of the big hotels an information service is provided on the closed-circuit TV system installed in every room.

206

Restaurants

The best of food from almost any country in the world can be sampled in the restaurants of Bangkok. Hotel restaurants in particular are among the great number which, as well as serving oriental dishes, lay on a feast of international (e.g. French) cuisine. Many of these restaurants employ foreign staff (German or Swiss restaurant managers and chefs for example), the majority of whom do wonderful justice to the culinary traditions of their native land. Dutch restaurants incidentally are often listed as specialising in "Indonesian" cooking.

General

Amidst this mouth watering choice of international fare the local cuisine more than holds its own. Thai specialities are tastily prepared from the fresh produce of Bangkok's many markets and being only mildly hot are perfectly capable of being enjoyed by Western palates (see Food and Drink).

In popular tourist centres the menus are usually written in English as well as Thai. If not, the waiter may be able to translate the Thai names. Another solution is to order whatever the Thais at the next table happen to be eating!

Menus

As an alternative to a restaurant meal why not during the day at least follow the Thai example and eat at one of the city's innumerable street food stalls? This in fact is a pleasure not to be missed – many of the genuine local specialities cannot be sampled in any other way. Judged by Western standards some of the stalls may not seem particularly inviting and many tourists consequently pass them by, but the food will be found to be of impeccable quality and there is usually a choice of boiled, fried or braised dishes.

Street stalls

There are several hundred restaurants in Bangkok and the list which follows has been carefully compiled. Even so it is far from being exhaustive and is not intended to reflect badly on establishments not included. Two restaurants in particular are worth special mention. One goes under the somewhat startling name of "Cabbages & Condoms" and is owned by Mr Meechai, chairman of Thailand's recently instituted family planning initiative. The other is "Tum Nak Thai" which claims to be the largest restaurant in the world (seating 3000) and where the waiters are equipped with roller skates! Another experience not lightly to be forgone is enjoying a "Sundowner" on the terrace of the Oriental Hotel.

Baan Thai, Soi 32, Sukhumvit Road
Ban Nunthida, 110/26 Soi Santinives Ladprao
Bangkapi Terrace (in the Ambassador Hotel)
Cabbages & Condoms, 10 Sukhumvit Road, Soi 12
Lemongrass, Soi 24, Sukhumvit Road
Puang Kaew, 108 Sukhumvit 23
Sala Rim Nam, 531/1 Charoen Nakhon Road (opposite the Oriental Hotel)
Seefah Restaurant, 47/19–22 Ratchadamri Road
Silom Village, 286 Silom Road (Thai music and classical dancing)
Talad Nam, 209 Silom Road
Tum Nak Thai, 131 Ratchadapisek Road (open-air restaurant)
Whole Earth Café, 93/3 Soi Lang Suan (the Thai menu includes vegetarian dishes)

Thai cuisine

Restaurants

Seafood	Chinese Seafood, Wall Street Tower, Surawong Road Chom Talay (in the Central Plaza Hotel) Cosmopolitan, 10 Sukhumvit Soi 24 Lord Jim's (in the Oriental Hotel) Royal Seafood, 50 Soi Lang Suan, Phloenchit Savoey Seafood (in the Terrace River City Shopping Center) Seafood Bangpoo Restaurant, 199/5 Sukhumvit Road Seafood Restaurant, 1980 New Phetchaburi Road Seafood Market & Restaurant, 388 Sukhumvit (between Soi 16 and 18)
French cuisine	Thalay Thong (in the Siam Intercontinental Hotel) Floating Restaurant, Supakarn Shopping Complex Jazzy Queen and Oriental Queen (both in the Oriental Hotel) Salaloy Floating (in the Menam Hotel) Wah Fah, 671/3 Charan Sanitwong Road
Italian cuisine	Don Giovanni (in the Central Plaza Hotel) Il Colosseo, 578–580 Phloenchit Lumphini L'Opera Pizzeria, 55 Sukhumvit Road, Soi 39 Paesano, 97/7 Soi Ton Son, Phloenchit Road Pan Pan, 45 Soi Lang Suan, Phloenchit Ristorante Sorrento, 66 North Sathon Road Tratoria da Roberto, Patpong Soi 2
Chinese cuisine	Galaxy, 19 Rama IV Road Golden Gate 392/27–30 Siam Square 5 Jade Garden (in the Montien Hotel) May Flower (in the Dusit Thani Hotel; Cantonese food) New Great Shanghai, 648–52 Sukhumvit Road New Shangri-La Restaurant, 154/4–7 Silom Road
Japanese cuisine	Benkay (in the Royal Orchid Sheraton Hotel) Genji (in the Hilton International Hotel) Kobe Steak House, 460 Siam Square 4 Otafuku, 484 Siam Square 4 Shogun (in the Dusit Thani Hotel) Canton, 488/3–6 Henri Dunant Friendship Sukiyaki, 120/171 Ratchaprarop Sincere Sukiyaki, 392/34–38 Siam Square 7
Indian cuisine	Café India, 460/8 Surawong Road Himali Cha Cha, 1229/11 New Road
International cuisine	La Rotonde (in the Narai Hotel; revolving restaurant) Bolero, Lang Suan, Soi 2 Cosmopolitan, 4–10 Sukhumvit Road 24 Avenue One (in the Siam Intercontinental Hotel) Le Bistro, Soi Ruam Rudi La Brasserie (in the Regent Hotel) Le Chancelier, 70/1 Sukhumvit Road Le Vendôme (in the Ambassador Hotel) Metropolitan, 135/6 Gaysorn Road Orangery, 48/11 Soi Ruam Rudi, Phloenchit Road The Normandie (in the Oriental Hotel)
German cuisine	Bei Otto, 250 Sukhumvit Road, opposite Soi 17 Bier Kutsche, Sukhumvit Road, Soi 3 (beer garden) Bierstube, 569 Sukhumvit Road (between Soi 31 and 33) Haus Hamburg, 111 Sukhumvit Road Soi 15

Haus München, 4 Sukhumvit Road Soi 15
Ratsstube (in the Goethe Institute, 18/1 Soi Athakan Prasit
Road, Sathon Tai Road)
Singha Bierhouse, Sukhumvit 21, Soi Asoke
Wienerwald, 274/1 Sukhumvit Road
Zur Taverna, 1/11 Sukhumvit Soi 3

El Gordo's, Soi 8 Silom Road   Mexican cuisine
Tia Maria, 14/18 Patpong 1

Korea House, 2–4 Soi Tonson Phloenchit   Korean cuisine
Koreana, 488–50 Siam Square
Woo Gane, 5/9–10 Wireless Road

In restaurants serving Asian food customers are provided with
a "pah-yen" or "cool-cloth" both before and after their meal.
These wipes, often scented, come straight from the refrigerator
and are used to freshen face and hands.

Tips are only expected in the middling or top class restaurants.   Tipping
A tip should always be at least 10 baht – anything less might be
taken as an insult.

Over Christmas and the New Year a table at any of the restau-   Table reservations
rants in the international hotels has to be reserved. Reserva
tions are likewise necessary at Chinese restaurants over the
Chinese New Year.

Safety

Crime, theft and violence is no higher in Thailand than else-   General
where in the world. Indeed the country is widely regarded as
one of the safest for travelling in south-east Asia. Sensible
precautions need to be taken nevertheless – remember that
"opportunity makes the thief".

The Thais generally speaking are an honest people though as in
any country frequented by tourists there are always going to be
exceptions. Offences against visitors are nevertheless uncommon and can often be attributed to lack of proper care. It is as
well to bear in mind, for example, that a tourist can be carrying
more money than a simple hotel employee earns in a year.
Keep a careful watch on possessions, avoid any flaunting of
wealth, and deposit valuables in the hotel safe. Only carry as
much ready cash as is likely to be required.

Most hotels make no charge for the use of security boxes or   Safes and security boxes
room safes in which money and other valuables can be
securely stored. Since it is unlikely that the thief will be caught if
anything is stolen from a room, bulkier articles such as camera
cases should be deposited at the hotel reception.

Avoid taking valuables such as jewellery or large amounts of   Valuables
cash to the beach. Always hand the room key in at reception
when going out of the hotel.

It is a good idea to make duplicate photocopies of all travel   Travel documents
documents before leaving home. Having copies to hand can
make the replacement of any lost documents very much easier.

Shopping

Travellers' cheques	If money is carried in the form of travellers' cheques it is essential to keep the counterfoils safe, and separate from the cheques themselves. Only if the counterfoils can be produced is insurance cover against loss guaranteed.
Important telephone numbers	Make a note of any telephone numbers which might be needed in an emergency (e.g. credit card and travellers' cheque companies and the appropriate embassy).
Pickpockets	Over the last few years nimble-fingered pickpockets have regrettably made their presence felt in the popular tourist areas. The best protection is to carry cash and other valuables in special money belts or neck purses.
Extortionate bills	Anyone venturing into the Saturnalian world of Thailand's "classic" nightlife should anticipate the possibility of being ripped-off and having to contend with extortionate bills. One sensible precaution is to have nothing at all to do with touts.
Emergency telephone numbers	See Emergencies
Embassies	See Diplomatic Representation
Credit card companies	See Currency

Shopping

General

Those who think of Thailand only in terms of Thai silk will be surprised by the rich variety of merchandise available which catches the visitor's eye. Bangkok and indeed all the tourist centres (whether in the north or the south) are a real shopper's paradise. Not everything though is cheap. Imported goods such as optical and electronic equipment are heavily taxed and therefore expensive. And of course there is the familiar trash offered to tourists the world over.

The Thais are exceptionally skilled in all manner of crafts, their work generally being plain but occasionally very elaborate. The more traditional craftwork and folk products come mainly from northern Thailand (a mountain tribe called the Meo make lovely dolls and woven goods for example, which can also be purchased in Bangkok). In the south of the country tourists are most likely to be attracted by the articles fashioned from bronze, wood, ivory-like materials and "fish bone" (actually a yellow substance which is heated and then poured into a mould). The elaborately carved chess sets or hand-cast bronze cutlery can be very pleasing, but not everything is equally so.

Thai silk

Thailand has a long tradition of silk manufacture. It is only since Jim Thompson gave new impetus to the industry however that Thai silk has seen its world-wide reputation restored. It is somewhat less fine than the Chinese variety but has two overriding advantages being both stronger and more reasonably priced. Jim Thompson's Thai Silk Company has a shop at 9 Surawong Road. The Shinawatra shops in Bangkok (67 South Sathon Road and 390 Soi Sai Nam Thip, Rama IV) and Pattaya (Pattaya 3rd Road) can also be recommended. Every tailor's shop stocks Thai silk as well, and anyone who does not want a garment made-to-measure there and then (see Clothing) can buy material by the metre. Silks in pastel shades are usually the most popular since the patterns appeal more to Western tastes in fashion. The silks which include a small amount of man-made fibre have the extra advantage of being easy care.

Even apart from its silk Thailand is the best country in south-east Asia for textiles. Many of the goods are produced specific-ally for the tourist trade (warm sweaters for example are hardly designed for local wear given the temperatures that prevail). Imitations of well-known European and international makes of clothing can be particularly attractive, costing only a fraction of the price of the real thing. Be warned however that these cheap imitations are generally banned from Europe, the originals being protected by trade legislation. Customs checks at UK airports can result in bulging tourist suitcases suddenly becoming half empty!

Textiles

Patterned hand-woven and hand-knotted carpets of Thai silk make very attractive souvenirs from Thailand. The vendor will arrange transport by sea or air to the UK.

Carpets

Authentic Japanese watches of well-known brands are cheaper in Thailand than in Europe. There are reliable dealers from whom they can safely be purchased (who will provide for example all the necessary guarantee and service registration forms). But beware! There are also thousands of cheap imita-tions, even of famous Swiss makes, guaranteed only to stop working before the holiday's end! The manufacture of such imitations is banned in Thailand and from time to time Thai newspapers report a police raid on an illegal "factory". But even as the steam roller is about to crush the confiscated watches for the benefit of local press photographers, the coun-terfeiters will already be setting up shop in a new location and starting production again.

Japanese watches

As Asia's major producer of sapphires and the world's second largest producer of jewellery after Italy, Thailand is a shopper's dream in this respect too. The mines in the south of the country yield stones of excellent quality which are then incorporated into real masterpieces of classical jewellery-making in work-shops in Bangkok and elsewhere. Gems such as diamonds are also imported for cutting and setting and are then either sold in Thailand or exported all over the world. A visit to one of the stone-cutting workshops is virtually obligatory, especially on bus tours of the city. In anything from semi-darkness to a reassuring glare – depending on the size of the business – it is possible to look over the shoulders of the highly skilled Thai craftsmen and watch them as they work. Pieces of jewellery only just completed are displayed for purchase in an adjacent room. But a warning is again appropriate. Either the bus driver or the tour guide, sometimes even both, will be party to the arrangement and will receive their commission from the pro-ceeds of any sales. Recently also there have been an increasing number of complaints about unscrupulous traders offering the poorest quality or even worthless stones. The best advice is not to buy anything in a hurry and to take someone along if pos-sible who knows something about jewellery. Here as else-where, incidentally, it is taken for granted that buyers will haggle over the price.

Precious stones

Jewellery being hawked on the beach (or indeed anywhere else) should be treated with suspicion as a matter of course.

Hawkers

Shopping

The stones are almost certain to be worth less than the plated metal in which they are set!

Gold

Great care is needed too when buying gold. Thailand has its own system of measurement which differs from the internationally accepted carat scale. Most dealers will, if asked, specify the international standard gold content, and this information can (usually) be trusted. When it comes to the purchase of expensive items any reputable dealer will also provide a certificate guaranteeing the authenticity of the articles.

Crafts

Bronze tableware, ceramics and porcelain as well as typical Asian wooden lacquerware are cheap and make delightful souvenirs of a stay in Thailand. Although the felling of Thai teak has been prohibited since 1988 a wide variety of teakwood carvings are still on the market, the wood having been imported from Burma.

Ivory

Since the elephant became a protected species under the Washington agreement genuine ivory is as rare as it is expensive. With the import of ivory being banned by countries which are signatories to the agreement purchases should be confined to the quite authentic-looking imitation ivory craftwork (most so-called "ivory" work is far from genuine anyway).

Crocodile skin

The situation is much the same with regard to shoes, bags and other items made from snake or crocodile skin or certain animal pelts. Such articles can be legally imported only if they come from farms, so it is essential to check the certificate of origin before buying.

Herbs

The shops selling medicines and herbs on the New Phetchaburi Road are a Bangkok curiosity. The nature cure remedies available range from herb teas and various roots to dried snakes and sea-horses.

Antiques

See entry

TAT recommended shops

For the majority of tourists the best guarantee of value for money is to buy from shops recommended by TAT. The tourist authority keeps these establishments under constant scrutiny. Look out for the logo indicating TAT approval. If any problems are experienced contact the Tourist Assistance Center (see Emergencies; the Center takes telephone calls from 8am to midnight).

Shopping centres

As well as numerous markets (see entry) and shops Bangkok has a great number of good shopping centres with all the attendant advantages of finding "everything under one roof". Since even more shops tend to cluster around many of these centres (e.g. near the Siam Center) a huge shopping area is created. Here is a selection:

The Oriental Plaza, 30/1 Chartered Bank Lane (next to the Oriental Hotel)
Siam Center, 195 Rama I Road (next to the Siam Intercontinental Hotel)
Amarin Plaza, 496–502 Phloenchit Road
Riverside Shopping Center (near the Oriental Hotel).

Department stores

The general department stores which offer a great range of goods, albeit at fixed prices, can also be recommended. Addresses can be obtained from the hotel reception.

Thai Airways International has a duty-free shop at 485 Silom Road. Duty-free purchases are delivered direct to the airport and can be collected after passing through customs control. Having completed all the necessary immigration formalities it is also possible to buy duty-free goods in the departure hall at Don Muang Airport.

Duty-free shops

It is all too easy to forget that there are definite limits to the good will of airport ground staff responsible to the airline for checking in passenger baggage on the return flight home. Most airlines allow only 20 kg per passenger before imposing an additional charge (the exact allowance is printed on the airline ticket). Beyond this limit, sometimes more and sometimes less strictly applied, additional weight has to be paid for. This can work out very expensive because as a general rule every kilogram of excess baggage is charged at 1% of the first-class fare for the flight. Providing arrangements are made in good time however, heavy costs like these can be avoided. All the major airlines flying to Bangkok have air-freight services and will deliver baggage to a passenger's destination at the (considerably lower) standard air-freight rate. To make use of the service contact one of the airlines (see entry) and ask for the telephone number of their freight office.

Excess baggage

Sightseeing

The suggestions which follow are aimed at a first-time visitor to Thailand intent on making the most of a relatively short stay. Places features in the A to Z section of this guidebook are printed in **bold** type.

N.B.

Travellers on a flying visit very pressed for time can do no better than book a morning tour of the city, arrangements for which can be made in any hotel. This will give the newcomer a good initial picture of the city overall, as well as of the most important sights. The tours generally take in the **Grand Palace**, the "Golden Buddha" in **Wat Traimit**, Wat Sutat together with Sao Chingcha Square and the Giant Swing, a typical Thai market (see Markets) and some of the city's historic streets. A visit to a diamond cutting workshop or drapers shop is also usually included, giving at least the opportunity to buy something.

Flying visits

With an afternoon free as well there is the choice of a walk though the bustling city streets, a visit to the famous snake farm at the **Pasteur Institute**, or a visit to **Jim Thompson's House**.

To round off the day an evening's entertainment beckons, perhaps a typical Thai meal to be followed by a display of classical Thai dancing.

For anyone with more time at their disposal there is the lure of a richly rewarding walk through Old Bangkok, some of the ancient boundary of which is still partly visible in the shape of the city wall. No fewer than seven of Bangkok's most beautiful temples lie on the suggested route. Equally well worth seeing however are the streets of Old Bangkok, full of the hustle and bustle of typically Asian city life.

A city walk

The walk begins at the Golden Mountain (see **Wat Sakhet**) where the climb up to the imposing chedi is well worth the effort for the magnificent view it gives of Bangkok and Thonburi (on the opposite bank of the Chaophraya/Menam). From there cross Phanfa Lilaat bridge, built during the reign of Rama V (it once spanned a now no longer visible moat) and proceed along Ratchadamnoen Klang Road to the Democracy Monument which commemorates the introduction in 1932 of Thailand's first democratic constitution.

A good ten minutes' walk further along Ratchadamnoen Klang Road lies King's Square (see **Sanaam Luang**), formerly the site of a big weekend market before it moved to the north of the city (see **Chatuchak weekend market**). The square is mainly used for a variety of leisure activities. Fortune-tellers, palmists, lottery ticket sellers and antiquarian book and junk dealers also set up their stalls there.

On the north-west side of Sanaam Luang are the buildings of the **National Museum** for which at least half a day needs to be reserved. Next to it stands Thamasat University.

A visit to **Lak Muang** where in popular belief dwell the real but unseen guardians of Bangkok, is almost obligatory. Day in and day out supplicants come in their thousands to the shrine (opposite the Defence Ministry buildings) seeking the spirits' blessing for earthly ventures great or small.
Diagonally opposite is the entrance to the **Grand Palace**, the biggest and at the same time most interesting of Bangkok's temple complexes (Wat Phra Kaeo). Set aside at least two hours for visiting it.

Leaving the Grand Palace follow the outer wall on the east side to **Wat Po**, traditionally regarded as Bangkok's first "university". The buildings on the other side of Sanam Chai Road are the headquarters of Thailand's armed forces. Go past them and then up Rachini Road to Saranlom Palace, now a public park. Adjacent to it on its northern side the unremarkable looking Wat Rajapardit has some lovely painted panels but is closed more often than not. Directly across from the palace however is another beautiful temple, Wat Rat-bo-bitr. It is a skilful blend of elements drawn from both Thai and Western architecture and is well worth a visit.

Walking up Fuang Nakhon Road, a typical Old Bangkok street on the far side of Wat Rat-bo-bitr, be sure to take a look into the little shops before turning right along Bamrung Muang Road to **Wat Suthat** on Sao Chingcha (Giant Swing) Square. The painted wall panels in the wiharn were restored in superb colours at great expense a few years ago.

Continue a short distance along Bamrung Muang Road and then left into Maha Chai Road for a quick look at Wat Thepthidaram (built under Rama III and dedicated to the popular poet Sunthorn Phu). From there we return to the start of the walk.

Boat trips

Another half day should be reserved for a boat trip on the Chaophraya/Menam and the klongs. Among the sights are the stilt dwellings along the waterways of Thonburi, at one time the Venice of south-east Asia. There are in addition a great number of temples to see situated outside Old Bangkok, in particular **Wat Arun**, the "Temple of the Dawn", from where there is another delightful view of Bangkok. The best place for hiring a boat is at the pier close by the Oriental Hotel (ask for "Taa Orientään").

The third day of sightseeing should be devoted to the environs of Bangkok, ideally setting out really early for Damnoen Saduak (see **Floating Markets**). Day trips there are usually combined with a visit to **Nakhon Pathom** the cradle of Thai Buddhism. On the way back there is an opportunity to discover a little more about the Thai way of life and national culture, facets of which are put on entertaining show at the **Rose Garden**.

Further afield

Sport

With the exception of European-style winter sports virtually every form of modern sport can be enjoyed in and around Bangkok. Apart from the Royal Sports Club which is members only, the clubs, grounds and courts are open to everyone – including visitors – for a modest fee. The necessary sports gear can also generally be hired. Many of the hotels have an arrangement with nearby golf courses and tennis clubs and a number even boast such facilities in their own grounds. In Pattaya the facilities for windsurfing and paragliding get better every year.
Thailand has already been host to the ASEAN Games on three occasions (the last being in 1978) and has been sending teams to the Olympic Games since 1952.

General

The most popular sport of all is soccer. Every young Thai's dream is to get a chance to play in Europe and the streets of Bangkok are deserted when there is international football on television. Girls as well as boys know the names of all the famous players.

Soccer

Some hotels in Bangkok and Pattaya have laid their own running tracks. Lumphini Park (see entry) is also suitable for a lengthy jog.

Jogging

Thailand's second most popular sport is horse racing – though its popularity has rather more to do with gambling than with an interest in the sport itself. Race meetings are held regularly at the Royal Bangkok Sports Club (on Saturdays) and the Royal Turf Club (on Sundays).

Horse racing

Thai boxing is more a martial art than a sport. A ritual ceremony (the ram muay or "boxing dance") precedes each bout, after which the combatants do battle with fists, elbows, feet and knees over five three minute rounds. To be successful a Thai boxer needs not only exceptional strength and fitness but also tremendous concentration. Each fight takes place to a frenetic accompaniment of Thai music, goading the boxers into ever greater efforts and the audience into ever increasing excitement. Thai boxing is held regularly in the Lumphini Stadium (Tues., Fri. and Sat. beginning at about 6pm) and in the Ratchadamnoen Stadium (Mon., Wed., Thur. and Sun. also from 6pm). Tickets should be obtained in advance from Lumphini Stadium, Rama IV Road, tel. 252 8765, and Ratchadamnoen Stadium, Ratchadamnoen Nok Avenue, tel. 281 8546.

Thai boxing

Sword fighting is one of the traditional Thai martial arts and often forms part of the supporting programme at performances of classical dance. Like Thai boxing it demands extreme

Sword fighting

concentration and a high degree of physical fitness. Each contestant wields two swords so the sparks really fly!

Cock and fish fighting

The venues of cock and fish fights are not easily discovered during a short stay in Thailand (though they can occasionally be seen in Sanaam Luang in front of the Grand Palace). Exhibition fights are put on for tourists at the Rose Garden.

Kite fighting

Kite fights, also held in Sanaam Luang during the windy months from February to April, are one of the most fascinating of all Thai spectacles. Unlike the contests fought out between the equally colourful kites of neighbouring Chinese and Muslim countries, Thai kite fighting is an aerial version of the battle of the sexes. Chula, the male kite, is as big as a man and not unlike a fighter aircraft in shape, with a wing-span of over 1m/3¼ft. These kites are masterpieces of craftsmanship – and very costly masterpieces too. The frames are of three-year old, well seasoned and carefully stripped, bamboo, this being required by the rules of kite fighting.

Takraw

"Takraw" (pronounced "daggro", with an open "o" as in "law"), played with a canework ball 12cm/4¾ in. in diameter, is also very popular in Thailand. The aim, using every part of the body, not just the hands, is to keep the ball in the air and either get it through a 2.75m/9ft high hoop into the opponents' basket or – another version of the game - over a 4.52m/14¾ft net into the opponents' half of the pitch. By mutual agreement among the Asian countries this latter is the version used in the annual ASEAN Games. The most popular form of the game in Thailand however is yet another version involving a circle of six to eight players, equally spaced out, sometimes with and sometimes without a basket suspended in their midst. Points are scored depending on how long the ball stays in the air, how much the players contort themselves, how high they head the ball, and how many different parts of the body and types of jump they use to propel it. A "catch-throw" scores particularly highly, the ball being kicked through a loop formed by the player's arms (in front of the body or behind the back) while jumping into the air! Should the ball touch arm or hand the player is just as "dead" as if it lands on the ground. The game lasts 40 minutes without a break.

It costs very little to buy a ball and try a "blinkblenk" or "solo". Nine different exercises in ball control, throwing it around the body or rolling it off various parts of the body, are the absolute minimum expected of anybody! Performing a 10–12 minute "blinkblenk" would be qualification enough for a Western circus and is considered fairly good even by Thai standards.

Golf

In recent years Thailand has developed into something of a Mecca for golfers with numerous new courses being created throughout the country. Several are within easy reach of Bangkok and many make their facilities available to visitors. Apart from those in and around Bangkok (e.g. Ekachai, 81 Petchakasem Samut Sakhorn; 18 holes) there are some very attractively laid out courses near Hua Hin and Bang Saen, in the Kao Yai National Park, and at Pattaya. The Siam Intercontinental Hotel has a driving range. The clubs listed below are open to non-members on payment of the usual green fees. All are 18-hole courses unless otherwise stated.

Army Golf Course, Ram-intra Road, tel. 521 1530
Bang Phra Golf Course, Chonburi, tel. 240 9170–2

Krungthep Sports Golf Course, Hua Mak, tel. 374 6064
Navatanee Golf Course, Patanasamakki Road, tel. 374 7077
Navy Club Golf Course, Bang-na, tel. 393 1652. 9 holes
Railway Training Centre Golf Course, Phahon Yothin Road, tel. 271 0130
Rose Garden Golf Course with a hotel, (32km west of Bangkok), reservations tel. 253 2276 and 253 0295–7
Royal Bangkok Sports Club, Henri Dunant Road, tel. 251 0181–6
Royal Dusit Golf Course, Phitsanulok Road, tel. 281 1330–1
Royal Thai Air Force Golf Club, Don Muang Airport, Tel 523 6103 (this must surely be one of the strangest golf courses in the world, being laid out between the airport's two main runways. Ear muffs are recommended!)
Siam Country Club: tel. (038) 428 002; reservations in Bangkok: tel. 215 3334
Sattahip Navy Golf Club: tel. 601 185, ext. 2600

TAT's London office has brochures listing other golf courses. There are specialist tour operators in the UK who organise golf holidays in Thailand.

Stations

None of Bangkok's four railway stations are for city traffic as such. Hua Lumpong, the Thai state railways' (SRT) main-line station, occupies a very central position between the New and Old Towns. From here passengers embark on journeys to all corners of the country and to Malaysia. Trains to Kanachanaburi and the "Bridge on the River Kwai" depart from the station in Thonburi. Thai railways have virtually completed a changeover to diesel – even in south-east Asia the romantic age of steam is at an end.

Railway stations

Bangkok has three bus stations, the northern terminal (Neu-a), the eastern terminal (Ekamai) and the southern terminal (Dai), from which regular services run to all parts of the country. In addition to the ordinary buses modern air-conditioned coaches are currently being brought into service. The majority of lines north (e.g. to Chiang Mai) and south (e.g. to Pattaya) run hourly except between midnight and 5am. There are direct connections three times daily (9am, 11am and 8pm) between Don Muang Airport and Pattaya. Most of the express buses (rot-may dew-en) are fully air-conditioned. The ordinary long-distance buses (rot-may tama-daa) on the other hand only have air-conditioning by the driver's seat if at all and then just the front part of the bus stays pleasantly cool. The ordinary long-distance buses are also much slower, making more frequent stops

Buses

Information about fares and departure times for the air-conditioned lines can be obtained from the three terminals.

South Bus Station (Dai), Charan Sanitwong Road, tel. 411 4978–9
East Bus Station (Ekamai), Sukhumvit Road, tel. 391 3310
North and North-East Bus Station (Neu-a), Phahon Yothin Road, tel. 279 4484–7

Taxis

See Transport

Telephone and Telefax

Telephone

Thailand's telecommunication systems are currently being brought up to international standards, a process which should be completed before very long. In the meantime however telephone lines particularly in the capital are overloaded, telephone numbers change frequently and at short notice, and directories, if available at all, are usually out of date (the English language directories found in hotels are generally the most reliable). Virtually all the operators manning telephone enquiries (dial 9) speak only Thai.

Charges

Local calls cost 1 baht but hotels usually add a heavy surcharge. International calls to Europe via satellite are rather expensive, a three-minute call (the minimum) costing about 250 baht. It pays therefore to set a time limit when booking the call.

Reversed charge calls are no longer possible, the caller always being required to pay.

Telefax

Telefax services are widely available in Thailand in the sense that even moderately-sized hotels are equipped with a fax machine. Guests of the hotel can normally make use of these facilities (though there will be a charge).

Thai Society and the Visitor

General

Despite an ever-increasing exposure to the ways of the West Thai society still manages to preserve its own distinctive codes of behaviour. The Thai people for example conduct themselves with exceptional politeness, patience and tolerance. They also attach much importance to hospitality, a fact greatly in evidence in their dealings with the "farung" (or foreigner).
That said, visitors also need to observe some basic "do's" and "don'ts" if they are to avoid giving offence, however unintentionally.
Adults and children alike are naturally curious, and questions about a person's age, partner, children, occupation, etc. are considered a sign of genuine concern and indeed good breeding. A woman though may be asked whether she is travelling alone (kon dee'o) as a prelude to making advances (or even as a preface to an attempted handbag snatch). An appropriate response to "kon dee'o" might be "mai chai" (not really), or "bai pop sah-mee" (I am just on the way to meet my husband). Unwanted questions about age can be deflected with "mai bork" (I'm not saying) or "mai sahp" (I don't know), but by far the easiest solution is to say "mai kao jai" (I don't understand). Above all else however never stop smiling, and the more negative the answer the friendlier the smile should be.

Politeness

The Thai notion of politeness is not such as to require a seat on the bus or boat to be given up to the elderly, mothers with babies, or pregnant women etc. (though seats are sometimes offered to monks and the back seats in buses are usually reserved for them). A European who gets up can expect to be acknowledged with nothing more than a very fleeting, sympathetic smile.

Of all Thai habits however, the one that Westerners tend to find most disconcerting is having their conversation totally ignored – during a meal for instance. Even if all the Thais present speak the relevant foreign language they will only take notice of topics which interest them. It is quite normal to have them interrupt and start up a conversation among themselves in Thai, even when they are in the position of guests. Also, if a Thai married couple are invited out, the wife may well send her apologies, pleading a headache or other engagement. The husband is then likely to arrive accompanied by two or three friends instead!

It is not uncommon for Western visitors to be shown special hospitality in the form of an invitation to visit a Thai home. Thais seldom entertain just a single guest however, usually inviting several at once to make up as interesting a gathering as possible.

Invitations

Dress is unlikely to be prescribed (unless for an official occasion). Nevertheless great care should be taken to arrive suitably attired (never in black because of the association with death). Something more than shorts and a T-shirt is almost certain to be required.

Nine different spirits watch over a Thai home, living both in the garden and in the house itself. There is one in particular, the threshold spirit, which the unwary visitor is liable to offend. If the door has a threshold be sure to step over it rather than on it! Shoes must also be removed before entering. Small gifts will be expected by the hosts – flowers are normally correct for the lady of the house while children love receiving little toys. Baby clothes should never be taken to expectant mothers – they are thought to bring bad luck.

The three most important social taboos for foreigners are: never touch another person's head; never point your feet at anyone; and never publically make bodily contact with a member of the opposite sex.

Social taboos

Thais regard the head, the highest part of the body, as sacred, the locus of a person's spiritual being and humanity. No one's head should ever therefore be touched. Even a pat on the head for a child, however well intentioned, will give offence. Passing something over a person's shoulder is equally taboo since their head runs the risk of being touched in the process. Respect for the head also requires that looking down on someone be avoided, especially elders or superiors. This creates difficulties for Europeans who, being for the most part taller than Thais, cannot always help looking down on them. A token gesture e.g. bending over somewhat, or sitting when the other is standing (though never the reverse), is then appropriate. This taboo is the reason why processions or parades are never watched from upper floor windows or balconies. If the King (above whom no one is permitted to stand) were present for example, taking up such a viewpoint would amount to sacrilege.

Since the feet are the lowest part of the body they are regarded as unworthy, offensive and unclean, the very opposite of the respect afforded to the head. Consequently it is considered rude to point a foot towards another person. The Western habit of crossing legs should therefore be avoided (unless out of sight under the table). Feet being unclean (even when spotless), shoes are deemed even more so, and so are always removed before entering a temple or private home.

To avoid bodily contact, especially between the sexes, the Thai form of greeting, the "wai", should be used. This involves pressing the palms together in a prayer-like gesture – not to be confused though with any form of prayer. Bringing the hands up to the level of the forehead (or higher) denotes particularly deep respect, as would be shown to a monk for example. When greeting one's peers or strangers the hands should be level with the chin or nose, and a warm smile is appropriate too. Adults responding to a "wai" from a child ordinarily do so with a "wai" at chest level, though nowadays a nod of the head sometimes takes its place. Greetings apart, the main thing to remember is that a man and a woman never display their affection in front of others (even their own children). Only since the 1973 revolution has it become acceptable for a young couple to hold hands in public. On the other hand it is not at all uncommon to see people of the same sex linking arms or embracing in the street – even uniformed officers.

Religious taboos

In cosmopolitan Bangkok (as opposed to the provinces) a great deal is capable of being forgiven or at least made light of. This only applies however to any infringements of social taboos. Religious taboos in contrast are enshrined in law, and any transgressions are liable to meet with severe punishment in the form of a stiff fine or at worst even imprisonment.

According to article 206 of the penal code it is unlawful to commit, with regard to "any object or place of religious worship of any community, any act by any means whatever in a manner likely to insult the religion concerned".

This means, for example, that Buddhist statues should not be touched or even pointed at with hand or foot (let alone climbed upon). Nor should holiday snaps be posed for in front of statues of Buddha (or in front of pictures of the Royal Family).

These laws apply not only to Buddhism (the religion of the vast majority of Thais) but also to the other faiths represented in the kingdom. Thus to disturb people at their devotions is equally illegal whether in a Buddhist or Hindu temple, a church or a mosque.

There are some basic rules to observe when visiting places of worship or the Grand Palace (see entry):

In general dress neatly. Do not go shirtless or wear shorts, mini skirts or other unsuitable attire. At Wat Phra Kaeo shoes must be removed before entering the inner "bot" (or temple). Visiting a mosque women should wear a long skirt or slacks, with a long-sleeved blouse buttoned to the neck. Men should wear a hat and women a scarf over their heads. Everyone should remove their shoes before entering. If an act of worship is in progress, leave at once.

Buddhist monks are forbidden to touch or be touched by a woman or to accept anything direct from a woman's hand. If a woman wants to give anything to a monk or novice, she must first pass it to a layman or place it on a piece of cloth (sometimes a handkerchief) which the monk sets down before him.

Royalty

The Thais have a particularly deep devotion to their Royal Family, based on long tradition. Visitors too should accord them the utmost respect, including in conversation. Stand to attention at once when the King's picture is shown in cinemas or whenever the national anthem is played.

Seemingly trivial things can sometimes offend Thai sensibilities in this respect. For example, baht notes, which bear the King's portrait, should never be crumpled up, and certainly not thrown away. Mistreatment of Thai banknotes has led to several unpleasant incidents in recent years involving Western tourists.

Theatre

See Folklore

Time

Bangkok is seven hours ahead of British time (GMT + 7), or six hours ahead when British Summer Time is in force.

Time difference

The lunar calendar was still in use in Thailand until the turn of the century and the dates of traditional and religious festivals continue to be set by it. For all other purposes the Western calendar is now followed. Monday is also regarded as the first day of the week, appearing as such on bus, train and airline timetables.

Lunar calendar

One important difference all too easy to overlook is in the way the years are reckoned. The year in which Buddha entered Nirvana (543 B.C.) is the Buddhist year 1. So A.D. 1991 corresponds to 2534 on the Buddhist reckoning.

The Buddhist year

Thais divide the day into four six hour periods, each marked with a special term. For visitors this can be a rich source of confusion, best avoided by insisting on exact times being given using the twenty-four hour clock.

In Thai "chao" refers to any time between 6 and 11am while "tee-ung wun" is midday. 1pm is "bai mohng" and 2pm "bai sorng mohng". In the cool of the evening "yen" together with a number gives the hour after 6pm. After 10pm however the word "keun" is used, midnight being logically enough "tee-ung keun". Once the clock has struck for the beginning of the new day the cycle starts afresh with "dtee" before the number – all of which may or may not be easy to follow!

Times of the day

Toilets

To ask the whereabouts of the toilet say "horng nahm yoo tee nai", "horng nahm", literally "water room", being the Thai for toilet. (In the simpler sorts of hotel as well as in private homes it can also mean the bathroom.) Instead of "tee nai" (i.e. "where?") an enquiring gesture might do the trick.

If all else fails, saying "soo-um" may well save the day. If the toilets are not clearly marked ask for "chai" (men) or "ying" (ladies).

Tourist Information

United Kingdom	Tourism Authority of Thailand 9 Stafford Street, London W1 3FE; tel. (071) 499 7679
In the United States (East Coast)	Tourism Authority of Thailand 5 World Trade Center, Suite 2449 New York, N.Y. 10048; tel. (212) 432 0433
West Coast	Tourism Authority of Thailand 3440 Wilshire Boulevard, Suite 1101 Los Angeles, CAL 90010; tel. (213) 382 2353–6
In Canada	85 Range Road Suite 7004 Ottawa, Ontario K1N 8J6; tel. (237) 1517, (237) 0476
Australia and New Zealand	Tourism Authority of Thailand 12th Floor, Royal Exchange Building 56 Pitt Street Sydney 2000; tel. (02) 277 549, (02) 277 540

In Thailand

The Tourism Authority of Thailand (TAT) operates an information service from offices in Bangkok, at the international airports, and in the main resorts. As well as supplying useful
brochures, etc. (either free or for a nominal charge) TAT offices
will also try to help resolve any specific problems tourists may
encounter.

Tourism Authority of Thailand
4 Ratchadamnoen Nok Avenue, Bangkok
Tel. 282 1143–7
Open: Mon.–Fri. 8.30am–4.30pm, Sat. 8.30am–noon

Don Muang International Airport
Tel. 281 5051, 281 0372

382/1 Chaihat Road
South Pattaya
Tel. 428 750 and 429 113
Open: Mon.–Fri. 8am–4.30pm

Yellow telephones

Telephones installed in conspicuous yellow kiosks at sites frequented by tourists (e.g. the Grand Palace, Patpong Road, Don
Muang Airport, etc.) connect callers directly (no dialling) to the
tourist information office. The service, manned by English-
speaking staff, operates from 8.30am to 4.30pm.

Visa extensions

Requests for an extension to a visa can only be processed in
Bangkok. Applications should be made to:

Immigration Department
Soi Suan Phlu, Sathon Tai Road
Tel. 286 7003, 286 9230
Open: Mon.–Fri. 8.30am–noon

Getting about

There are a number of useful English language directories (also
Thai) giving up-to-date information about what's on and where

to go. Issued anything from weekly to bi-monthly by travel agencies and independent publishers as well as by TAT, they often include shopping tips in addition to addresses of restaurants, sports clubs and nightclubs, etc. Together with the section of street map usually reproduced with them, these directories can be very helpful when communicating with taxi drivers, bus drivers or any passer-by.

English-Thai city and street maps of Bangkok, Pattaya, Kanchanaburi, Ayutthaya and other towns can be obtained from the TAT offices in London, as well as in Bangkok (see Information and Tourist Information). Note that the maps are not always reliable as regards scale and compass orientation.

The same is true of the colourful "Nancy Chandler's Map" which includes detailed plans of such locations as the Chatuchak weekend market, Chinatown and the Sukhumvit district. It also indicates which bus lines and "river taxis" boast air-conditioning.

Transport

According to official statistics there are almost 16,000 taxis in Bangkok (not counting drivers who are simply earning a bit extra on the side). Many taxis have at least moderately efficient air-conditioning, which partly compensates for their otherwise general lack of comfort. They have meters but these are seldom used. The vast majority (99%) of taxis, incidentally, run on environmentally friendly liquid gas. There are no taxi ranks; instead people phone and ask to be picked up from wherever they are. Bangkok is divided into four zones for this purpose. The appropriate number to call can be found under "Taxi Services" in the Yellow Pages or elicited from the nearest restaurant or hotel.

Taxis

In the street follow everyone else's lead and simply hail a taxi from the curb – at least half a dozen will usually pull up. Taking advantage of the competition to bargain over the fare can result in a cheap ride. If the price demanded seems too high and there is no particular hurry, simply hail another cab. Be sure however to chose one that is insured – look for the disc on the windscreen marked with the current year (the Buddhist year, remember, e.g. 1991 + 543 = 2534!)

The majority of hotels have their own limousine service. The cars operate from the front of the hotel and can be hired by anyone. Limousines are expensive but they are well cared for, air-conditioned and are certain to be insured. The fares are fixed and bargaining is possible only for longer excursions. Thai Airways International runs its own taxi service catering for transfers to and from the airport (see Getting to Bangkok). Reservations and bookings can be made at the airline's offices, at Don Muang Airport, or in any hotel.

Limousines

The so-called "pickups" operate mainly in resorts such as Pattaya, though they are also found in the north of the country. They are shared taxis which usually make regular runs along a particular route, taking anyone who catches the driver's attention in time. Fares can be extremely cheap. On request pickups will deliver holidaymakers right to their hotel (but agree on a price first!).

Shared taxis (pickups)

Transport

Tuk-tuks or samlors

A ride in one of the innumerable three-wheeled samlors, also known as tuk-tuks, costs about half as much as a taxi and is infinitely more interesting. Since bicycle rickshaws were abolished in the city samlors have come to dominate Bangkok's streets. No matter how impossible it may seem to get through the traffic, the fearless tuk-tuk driver will always find a way (though the well-being of his passengers may not always appear paramount in the process). Tuk-tuks with their noisy two-stroke engines not only transport tourists on their sightseeing but children to school and trades people to market. In the evenings whole families drive out in them. A tuk-tuk ride in Bangkok is a never-to-be-forgotten experience and one that should definitely not be missed.

Motorcycle taxis

The chaos on Bangkok's roads is the chief reason for this enterprising innovation – the motorcycle taxi. They beat limousines and even tuk-tuks hands down for sheer speed of journey, being able to wind their way quickly through the traffic. They are recognised by the numbers on the motorcyclists' vests.

River boats

Boat traffic on the Chaophraya/Menam is as important today as it always has been, especially as a link between the "new" capital Bangkok and the one-time capital Thonburi on the opposite bank. Thousands of people ranging from school children to market traders use water transport every day. Altogether there are sixteen piers or landing places in Bangkok. The word for them is "taa", followed by the particular location (e.g. "Taa Orientään", Oriental Hotel Pier). Make sure the boatman knows your destination, they only stop on request. The boats run from 6am to 6pm.

River taxis

River taxis can be hired by the hour, the best place being the pier beside the Oriental Hotel. A speedboat trip (two or three hours) through Thonburi's ancient klongs is particularly recommended.

Buses

Travelling on Bangkok's buses is rather more fun than might appear. Just get on any bus and wait to see where it ends up. The ride will prove a real experience. It will also prove very cheap, usually only one baht, often collected by a conductor hanging precariously from the door. To return to the starting point simply cross the road to the bus stop opposite – but remember to take note of the route number.

There are basically two types of buses, the ordinary ones which have to cope with transporting hundreds of thousands of people every day, and the somewhat more comfortable and hence more expensive air-conditioned ones. These latter charge 5 baht for the first 8km and 2 baht for every 4km thereafter. Buses run continuously during the morning and evening rush hours, otherwise every 10 minutes throughout the day.

No. 1 Happyland – Bangkapi – Ramkhamhaeng University – Sukhumvit Road – East Bus Station – Siam Square – Hualampong Railway Station – Pak Khlong Market.

No. 2 Happyland – Bangkapi – Lardphrao – Central Plaza – North Bus Station – Victory Monument – Siam Square – Lumphini Park – Silom Road.

No. 3 Rangsit – North Bus Station – Victory Monument – Ratchadamnoen Stadium – Democracy Monument – Sanaam Luang – Pinklao.

Hanging on for dear life during the rush-hour

No. 4 Rangsit – Airport – Pratunam – Erawan Hotel – Lumphini Park – Silom Road – Bangruk – Krungthep Bridge – Suanthonburirom.

No. 5 Pak Kret – Bang Lampoo – Sanaam Luang – Wongwien Yai – Phra Pradang.

No. 6 Pak Kret – Bang Lampoo – Sanaam Luang – Wongwien Yai – Phra Pradang.

No. 7 Samrong – Bang Na – Rama IV Road – Hualampong Railway Station – Sanaam Luang – Pinklao Bridge – South Bus Station – Phetchakasem Road – Poo Market

No. 8 Paknam – Samrong – Bang Na – Sukhumvit Road – East Bus Station – National Stadium – Katsatsuk Bridge – Tharatchawaradit.

No. 9 Nonthaburi – Kaset – North Bus Station – Victory Monument – Ratchadamnoen – Sanaam Luang – South Bus Station – Setthakit Village.

No. 10 Ransit – Airport – North Bus Station – Victory Monument – Phra Mongkut Hospital – Grungthon Bridge – South Bus Station – Wongwien Yai – Bang Phra Kaew.

No. 11 Paknam – Bang Na – East Bus Station – Erawan Hotel – Phetchaburi Road – Phanea Bridge – Pinklao Bridge.

No. 12 Chatuchak Park (weekend market) – North Bus Station – Laksi – Bangkapi – Ramkhamhaeng University – Phetchaburi Road – Pratunam – Sanaam Luang – Pak Klong Market.

No. 13 North Bus Station – Victory Monument – Pratunam – Sukhumvit Road – East Bus Station – Poo Jow.

No. 14 Siam Park – Bangkapi – Ramkhamhaeng University – Phetchaburi Road – Din Daeng Road – Victory Monument – National Stadium – Democracy Monument – Pinklao Bridge – South Bus Station – Bangkok Noi.

No. 29 Rangsit – Airport – North Bus Station – Victory Monument – Siam Square – Hualampong Railway Station.

No. 44 Happyland – Bangkapi – North Bus Station – Rama IV Road – Democracy Monument – Sanaam Luang – Wat Pho.

No. 126 Samrong – East Bus Station – Phetchaburi Road – Bangkapi – Kaset – Nonthaburi.

N.B. The bus routes change quite frequently.

Travel Agencies

General

Bangkok and Pattaya together boast 300 travel agencies. Be sure to deal with one of the more reliable ones, choosing for example from among those recommended by TAT (look for the blue sign in the window or on the door). As well as arranging trips for tourists travelling independently or in groups, the majority of travel agents also perform other services such as confirming airline tickets.

In Bangkok

Arlymear Travel
CCT Building, 6th Floor, 109 Surawong Road
(opposite Montien Hotel), tel. 236 0103

Arosa Travel Service
699 Silom Road
Tel. 233 4526

Dee Jai Tours Co Ltd
119 Mahesak Road
Tel. 235 9896

Diethelm Travel & Co Ltd.
140/1 Wireless Road (Kian Gwan Building 11)
Tel. 255 9150, 255 9160, 255 9170
Open: daily 9am–noon and 2–5pm; after hours telephone service.
Bangkok's oldest travel agency. It is Swiss run and offers a comprehensive range of tours lasting from one to several days not only in Thailand but throughout south-east Asia (including Malaysia, Singapore, Burma, Hongkong, Cambodia, Laos, etc.)

King's International Travel
121 Soi 7 Sukhumvit Road
Tel. 255 4676

Medee Tour
11/4 Sukhumvit Road, Soi 1
Tel. 252 2096

Sawadee Travel Ltd
21/6–7 Sukhumvit Road, Soi 23
Tel. 258 4366

World Travel Service
1053 Charoen Krung Road
Tel. 233 5900–9
Many branches in Bangkok and Pattaya

KN Travel   In Pattaya
597/2 South Pattaya Road
Tel. 429 134 and 429 143

Travel Documents

All visitors to Thailand must have a passport issued by a coun-   Passports
try with which Thailand has diplomatic relations. The passport
should be valid for three months beyond the intended departure date.

No visa is required for a stay of up to 15 days provided the   Visas
visitor holds a confirmed return or onward air, sea or rail ticket.
In such cases an extension of stay is only granted in exceptional
circumstances. Applications should be made to the immigration department in Bangkok (see below, Immigration Office; an
additional fee is payable).
Even if intending to stay no more than 15 days, all of them in
Thailand, it is still a good idea to obtain a "Tourist Visa for
Multiple Journeys" before leaving home. Changes in the regulations governing entry may occur at any time, and illness or
accident may prolong a visit unexpectedly. Tourists travelling
overland e.g. on the Singapore Express (Bangkok to Kuala
Lumpur, Penang or Singapore) should remember that they still
require a visa.

Visas can be obtained from Thai embassies and consulates
(see Diplomatic Representation). Lacking access to a Thai
embassy or consulate anyone requiring a visa for a stay in
excess of 15 days should write directly to the Immigration
Division, Soi Suan Phlu, Bangkok 10120, Thailand (see below,
Immigration Office).
Applications for a visa should be made at least two weeks prior
to the date of travel. Two completed application forms are
required together with three photographs, the applicant's
passport, and the fee. Tourist visas are valid for 60 days. For
stays of more than 60 days application should be made for a
90-day "Non Immigrant Visa".
Delayed aircraft, ships or trains are not a reason for granting an
automatic extension to anyone travelling without a visa. It is
always advisable to check the passport date of arrival stamp
and if any unforeseen delay occurs caused e.g. by illness,
report immediately to the authorities (Airport, Port Authority,
Immigration Division).

It is a good idea to make immediate duplicate photocopies of all   Some advice
important travel documents, including visa and entry forms

and passport pages containing personal details, place of issue, and expiry date. Always keep the photocopies separate from the originals. In the event of the originals being lost, having the copies to hand will almost certainly speed the process of replacing them while abroad.

Tax Clearance Certificate

Anyone who spends more than 90 days in Thailand in any 12 month period (several shorter stays are added together) is required to certify that no employment has been entered into during the stay. A so-called Tax Clearance Certificate to this effect must be submitted to the Immigration Department at least 15 days before departure. Further information and forms can be obtained from the Revenue Department in Bangkok.

Vaccinations

A vaccination certificate is not required in the case of visitors travelling direct to Thailand from North America or Western Europe. Anyone who has stopped over in an infection area (India, Sri Lanka, Nepal, Burma, etc.) should enquire in advance at a Thai consulate (see Diplomatic Representation) as to the regulations currently in force. It is likely that a smallpox vaccination certificate (not more than three years old) will be required even though the World Health Organisation has declared the world free of smallpox. Those making trips outside the normal tourist areas (e.g. round Thailand tours) or during the rainy season are advised to have themselves vaccinated against cholera and to carry malaria prevention tablets. Anyone leaving Thailand for one of the above-mentioned countries can arrange vaccination at Bangkok airport. Although considerably cheaper than in the West this may of course leave the tourist feeling off colour for a time.

When to Go

Climate

See Facts and Figures: General

High season

The best months for Europeans and others from temperate climes are from November to mid February when temperatures are at their coolest and the humidity is relatively low (65%–70%). This being the peak tourist season however, prices are at their highest. For Thais on the other hand, the high season – and the only time they go to the beaches – is from March to the end of May when the children are on holiday. From a European point of view Bangkok becomes unbearably hot at this time of year, with up to 95% humidity and temperatures of over 95°F/35°C. All the same these months are made very interesting by the great number of local festivals.

Mid season

Mid season (from mid August to late October) can be thoroughly recommended. Although flooding has to be contended with in towns and on smaller cross-country roads, the countryside is greener, more lush and more in bloom than at any other time. Unlike a visit in the peak season, advance booking is also unnecessary, accommodation being available everywhere at moderate prices. The oppressive humidity is at an end and in central Thailand at least (i.e. in and around Bangkok) it rains only once a day for about 30 to 50 minutes, usually in the late afternoon.

Young People's Accommodation

Collins International House (YMCA), 27 Sathon Tai Road, tel. 287 2727, 287 1900, ext. 2321; (suitable also for families)

YWCA, 13 Sathon Tai Road

Scout Hostel, Physical Education Department, Rama I Road

Student Christian Center, 382/2 Phaya Thai Road

Bangkok Christian Guest House, 123 Sala Daeng Road, Soi 2

Patumwan Youth Hostel, Triem Udom School, Patumwan (Information obtainable from the Thai Youth Hostel Association, The Bangkok Planetarium, Sukhumvit Road, tel. 391 0544.)

Each hostel has a reasonably priced self-service cafeteria serving simple food. Alcohol is generally prohibited and some of the hostels are locked at night.

Anyone unable to find a bed in a hostel or who would prefer a little more personal freedom should enquire about guest houses (see Hotels).

Avoid accommodation in the more squalid localities. Such places are kept under surveillance by the Drug Squad and not infrequently raided.

Useful Telephone Numbers at a Glance

Airlines
Air Canada   234 5593
Air New Zealand   233 5900–9
British Airways   252 9871–9
QANTAS   233 8701
  234 4951
Thai Airways Co. Ltd.   282 7151–9
  2882 7640
Thai Airways International   234 3100–9
  233 3810
TWA   233 7290–1
  233 1412

Car Rental
Avis   253 6251
Hertz   251 7575

Embassies
Australia   287 2680
Canada   234 1561–8
New Zealand   251 8165
United Kingdom   253 0191–9
United States of America   252 5040–9

Emergency calls
Crime Suppression Division   221 9111 or 221 5151
General emergency   191
Doctor or ambulance   252 2171–5
Fire brigade   1199 or 246 0199
Highway patrol   281 5051 or 1955

Hospital
Bangkok Christian Hospital   233 6981–9

Institute
British Council, 428 Soi 2 Siam Square   252 6136

Tourist Information in Bangkok
Tourism Authority of Thailand   282 1143–7
Don Muang Internationlal Airport   531 0022–59

Tourism Authority of Thailand
in Australia and New Zealand (02) 277 549
in the United Kingdom   (071) 499 7679
  (071) 499 7670

In North America
New York   (212) 4320 433
Los Angeles   (213) 3822 353–6

Index

Index